Citizenship and Service

Citizenship and Service

The Politics of Civic National Service in Israel

ETTA BICK

Published by State University of New York Press, Albany

© 2020 State University of New York

All rights reserved

No part of this book may be used or reproduced in any manner whatsoever without written permission. No part of this book may be stored in a retrieval system or transmitted in any form or by any means including electronic, electrostatic, magnetic tape, mechanical, photocopying, recording, or otherwise without the prior permission in writing of the publisher.

For information, contact State University of New York Press, Albany, NY
www.sunypress.edu

Library of Congress Cataloging-in-Publication Data

Name: Bick, Etta, author.
Title: Citizenship and service : the politics of civic national service in Israel / Etta Bick.
Description: Albany : State University of New York Press, [2020] | Includes bibliographical references and index.
Identifiers: ISBN 9781438480954 (hardcover : alk. paper) | ISBN 9781438480947 (pbk. : alk. paper) | ISBN 9781438480961 (ebook)
Further information is available at the Library of Congress.

10 9 8 7 6 5 4 3 2 1

Contents

Acknowledgments — vii

Introduction — 1

1 Alternative Ethea of Citizenship: Republican, Liberal, and Communitarian — 11

2 Religious Girls and Civic National Service, 1951–1953: An Initiative That Failed — 37

3 Republicanism and Volunteerism: Civic National Service for Religious Girls, 1970–2018 — 55

4 Fighting to Serve: Youth Excused from Service — 73

5 The Haredim: Will a Communitarian Approach Bring Them to Serve? — 89

6 From National Service to Community Volunteering: Israel's Arab Citizens and the Controversy over Civic National Service — 121

Conclusion: Four Tribes: Is a Communitarian Model the Answer? — 159

Notes — 173

Bibliography — 211

Index — 223

Acknowledgments

The idea for this book took form almost ten years ago when I realized that there were no academic studies of civic national service in Israel and the politics surrounding the program. There were several studies written by educators and social workers on the impact of service on the youth that serve or on the recipients of their services, but there were no studies that asked the hard political questions that seemed to beg for answers. For example, when civic national service was instituted in Israel, why did it remain voluntary and the exclusive domain of religious Zionist girls? Why weren't all Israeli youth who were exempted or excused from military service required to do civic national service, for example, the ultra-orthodox Haredim? Israeli Arabs? Youth excused from service by the Israel Defense Forces (IDF)? And why were they not able to volunteer? Were there initiatives to extend national service to all? And what happened to them? It was these questions that set me off on a journey to explore the politics of civic national service in Israel. It led me to explore the meaning of citizenship, and of rights and obligations, in democracies in general and in Israel in particular, and to focus on national service, as an expression of civic obligation. This book is the result.

For the past 25 years I have been privileged to teach Political Science at Ariel University, a growing, vibrant academic institution in Israel. I have seen the school grow from a small local college to a highly respected research institution. I would like to thank my colleagues in the Department of Middle East Studies and Political Science, Ronen Cohen, Eyal Lewin, Bosmat Yefet, and Chen Friedberg for their warm friendship and encouragement while I researched, wrote, and prepared this manuscript for publication.

I would also like to thank my research assistants over the years who contributed to the research on this book, Nirit Ofir, Boris Smetanin, Aryeh Toren, Michael Polevoy, and Daniel Wachtel.

My thanks to the editors at the State of New York University Press for their work to improve this book, and to Mr. Rafael Chaiken, acquisitions editor, for his support throughout this project and for his helpful suggestions during the manuscript revision process.

Many thanks to Sar Shalom Gerbi, former director general of the Authority for National-Civic Service, and to Reuven Pinsky, the present director general of the ANCS, who permitted me access to its staff and to internal statistical data. Staff members and supervisors Malkiel Dahan, Avinoam Meir, Zenav Abu Said, and Amir Abu Issa were extremely helpful in providing information for this research. I thank them for giving me their time and their insights on civic national service, particularly in the Haredi and Arab sectors.

I would also like to thank the Israel State Archives for giving me access to documents and files in the reading room and online.

I would like to thank Taylor and Francis for granting me permission to reuse some of the discussion of civic national service from my article "Equality, Orthodoxy and Politics: The Conflict over National Service in Israel," *Israel Affairs* 19, no. 3 (July 2013): 525–505, in chapters 2 and 3; Oxford University Press for permitting me to use part of the contents of my article "The Tal Law: A Missed Opportunity for 'Bridging Social Capital' in Israel," *Journal of Church and State* 52 (February 2010): 298–322, in chapter 5; and to Sage Journals for allowing reuse of part of my article "Institutional Layering, Displacement, and Policy Change: The Evolution of Civic Service in Israel," *Public Policy and Administration* 31, no. 4 (October 2016): 342–360, doi:10.1177/0952076715624272, in chapter 6.

On a more personal note, I would like to thank my husband Ezra, who has always encouraged me in my research pursuits and who, with his sharp intellect, broad interests, and humor, continues to enrich our life together. Finally, I would like to thank our dear children Atira, Rahelle, Moshe, Batsheva, and Shraga, who have watched this project grow and develop and have supported me throughout with their love.

Introduction

We will call for civil disobedience. Start building more prisons since all our youth will prefer prison rather than to serve in civic service.

—MK Chanin Zouabi, February 18, 2013

If Jews serve, Bedouin serve, and Druze serve, there is no reason that Moslems who are Israeli citizens do not serve. In the end, we all live in this country.

—Hussein Abu Bakr, 19, a national service volunteer in the police department, Zichron Yaakov, *Ynet*, February 25, 2013

Former MK Chanin Zouabi and Hussein Abu Bakr represent two sides in the contentious debate taking place within the Arab sector in Israel regarding civic national service. Zouabi represents the position of the Arab leadership, which opposes civic service for Arab youth and has branded those who volunteer "traitors" or "lepers." Civic service, it contends, is a government ruse to conscript Arabs into the Israeli military. On the other side is Hussein Abu Bakr, one of a small but growing number of youth who have chosen to volunteer for civic service in order to contribute to their communities and to advance their own personal development.

A similar debate has been taking place within the ultra-orthodox (Haredi) sector in Israel regarding military and civic national service. There, too, are those among the rabbinical leadership that have threatened to fill the prisons if the government implements legislation to draft yeshiva students to service, military or civic. They insist that the deferment policy that began under David Ben-Gurion in the first years of the state must continue unchanged, the fact that the number of deferments has reached a staggering 60,000 notwithstanding. Ultra-orthodox yeshiva students are usually married with families. They study until age 40 and beyond and, as yeshiva students, avoid conscription. Most live in poverty on meager stipends and government subsidies. In effect, neither the Arabs nor the Haredim have served in the military over the years and until recently were not eligible to serve in civic national service. Both groups live in mostly segregated communities, maintain separate educational systems, and participate at much lower levels than average in the workforce. Both reject the nationalist Zionist ethos upon which the state was founded, albeit for different reasons, and do not see special virtue in service to the state.

Presumably the option of civic service as an alternative to military service would have sidestepped the ideological difficulties that service in the military presents for Israeli Arabs and would have been welcomed. In civic service, they would not be expected to raise arms against fellow Arabs in the West Bank and Gaza or on Israel's borders. Service could be done in their own communities in the areas of health, welfare, education, and social services, which would benefit greatly from volunteers. For the ultra-orthodox, too, civic service would be a benefit to the community. Military service was discouraged, if not forbidden, in part because of its secular, mixed-gender environment. Civic service however could be performed within the community and in placements that are appropriate to a restrictive religious lifestyle. Upon completion of service, volunteers would receive the same rights and benefits as those who serve in non-combat assignments in the military. However, we shall see that both the Arab political leadership and many Haredi rabbis oppose civic service and actively discourage volunteering.

National service in Israel has been traditionally defined as service in the military. The National Defense Law, enacted in 1949, established a "citizen army" to which all able-bodied men and women were drafted to serve. In addition, males were required to serve in the reserves until age 54.[1] (Today the age ceiling has been dropped to age 40.) The IDF (Israel Defense Force) was assigned civic tasks as well. Soldiers were assigned to jobs in education, welfare, and immigrant absorption. Military service was a rite of passage into Israeli society for young men and women and for new immigrants. It was integrative and inclusive for those who shared the Zionist ethos. Conversely, for the non-Zionist Haredim who deferred service and for Israeli Arabs who were exempted from military service, failing to serve was clearly a barrier to integration into Israeli society and the economy.[2]

In Israel today, many youth do not to serve in the military for a number of reasons. Statistics published by the IDF in 2018 indicate that approximately 50 percent of youth at conscription age were deferred, excused, or exempted from military service.[3] This new reality where half of the youth serve and half do not has generated protests by those who serve against the government's conscription policy, which they view as highly inequitable and unfair.

In the past, this gross disparity between those who serve and those who do not had been compensated by ideology, a commitment to Zionist ideals, and pride in service. In the first decades after the establishment of the state, secular Israelis and religious Zionists shared a strong republican ethos that lauded and extolled military service and contribution to the state. These values were promoted in the curriculum of secular and state religious schools, in the media, and by Zionist youth movements. Israelis being "a nation at arms" regarded service in the IDF, its "citizen army," as an essential component of good citizenship.

Studies of those early years describe how military service contributed to social integration, creating "social capital" among those who served.[4] Service created social bonds between soldiers, veterans and immigrants, Ashkenazi and Sephardic, and provided those who served with a network of contacts that was then helpful in finding a job. An applicant's service record was often a trump card in employment. By the same token, those who were excluded from service, particularly the Haredim and the Arabs, remained outside.

Religious girls were also excluded from service, although they shared the Zionist republican ethos. The 1949 defense law exempted religious girls from service in the military if they so requested. This provision was passed at the insistence of the religious and Haredi parties. However, rather than exempt them entirely, the Knesset later passed a national civic service law in August 1953 requiring religious girls to give two years of alternative civic national service. This was the first attempt to legislate a civic alternative to military service and as we shall see it did not succeed. It ignited the first impassioned battle over civic national service, between the secular Israeli government and the Haredi and religious parties who used their pivotal position as partners in government coalitions to ensure that the law would not be implemented. And when a voluntary national service program was established in 1971, it remained limited to religious Zionist girls and closed to youth from other sectors excused or exempted from service.

We shall see that the debate over who should serve and in which framework, civic or military, mandatory for all or voluntary for some, has engaged Israeli policymakers since the state's inception. It has been framed differently during various periods in Israel's history, reflecting the ethos prevailing at the time. In the early years of the state, a nationalist republican ethos that extolled service prevailed. However, in the 1990s there was a gradual shift in ethos toward liberalism, particularly among second- and third-generation middle-class secular Israelis, who placed greater emphasis on personal advancement and individual development, rights, and equality rather than obligation to the collective. The socialist founding fathers were replaced by leaders who encouraged neoliberal economics and free enterprise and a more activist High Court of Justice became the protector and promoter of individual rights and equality.

This change in discourse from "we" to "me" impacted the younger generation's view of service as well. We shall see that this change in ethos encouraged challenges to the long established deferment/exemption policies of the IDF. It raised questions of fairness in service, asking, "If we serve, why don't they?" This question was directed primarily at the thousands of Haredi men who failed to serve but was also applied to Israel's Arab citizens. For many second- and third-generation Israelis, military service was a "burden" rather than a privilege and as such needed to be borne equally by all. Civic national service became a possible alternative. If some Haredim and Arabs were not suited to military service, should they not serve in civic national service instead? Should civic national service remain the exclusive domain of religious girls?

This transition from broadly accepted republican values toward greater individualism and citizen equality would find expression in the High Court of Justice's intervention to expand civic national service to populations other than religious girls, for example, the physically impaired, and in petitions to the Court by reservists and others challenging the legality of the government's deferment policy. The deferment policy that was ironclad in political agreements between secular parties and the Haredi parties for almost 50 years now came under the scrutiny of the Court, which held equal application of the law as its standard. The amended Defense Service Law, in its various versions, which included provisions for civic national service as well, failed to meet its standard of equality and was struck down by the Court. This set the stage for renewed and repeated battles with the Haredim over a new service law.

While the overwhelming majority of Jewish citizens support the idea that all citizens should be obliged to give some form of service to the state, both the Arab leadership and the Haredim have rejected initiatives to require their communities to serve. Arab leaders point to the governments' inveterate policy of discrimination against Arab citizens and submit that equal rights must precede citizen obligation.[5] The Haredim, who numbered 1,000,000 in 2017, also reject service.[6] They give unreserved support to the policy of long-term deferments for yeshiva students and consider their dedication to Torah study as their unique contribution to the spiritual well-being of the nation.

The evolving process of citizenship, identity, and national integration in Israel is the subtheme of this book. We will explore this subject through the circumscribed study of national civic service policy in Israel as it has evolved from the early years of the state until today. Our analysis will consider the prevailing ethos within which policymaking took place and how it influenced policy choice. We will show that neither a republican nor a liberal ethos of citizenship succeeded in integrating Israel's minorities into Israeli society, nor did they allow for a practicable service policy. We will suggest that a shift toward a more communitarian ethos of citizenship, which recognizes difference and appreciates the ties of citizens to their communities, will achieve greater participation in service and better integration of minorities. Rather than ignore the minorities and relegate them to the status of outsiders, as was the case during the republican era, or compel them to "share the burden" in service, as was the intent during the neoliberal period, a communitarian approach will encourage policymakers to construct a service program that includes minorities while at the same time respecting difference. Neither community should be required to abandon its identity nor to adopt the Zionist narrative in the interest of republican orthodoxy, nor should it be forced to serve against its will in the name of equality; at the same time neither community should be excluded from the opportunity to serve and to gain the commensurate benefits that service provides. A civic national service policy that gives cognizance to community difference will contribute to the integration of these minorities into Israeli society.

There are signs that indicate that the seeds of change toward communitarianism are taking root, albeit slowly. Among the first to recognize this process was Israel's president, Reuven Rivlin, who in a groundbreaking speech at the Herzliya Conference in 2015 said that the time has come for

Israelis to recognize that there is a new order. There is no longer a ruling majority of secular Zionist Jews but rather an Israel with "four principal tribes," secular Zionists, religious Zionists, Arabs, and the Haredim, "with at least four different competing narratives about who we are and what we want to be." Rivlin called on Israelis "to abandon the accepted view of a majority and minorities, and move to a new concept of partnership between the various population sectors."[7] Although he did not utilize the term communitarian, the President was in effect calling for the adoption of a communitarian ethos of citizenship which would recognize Israel's different communities and at the same time unite them in partnership.

As we explore the politics of civic national service, we will follow the shift in ethea that has taken place in Israel. We will seek to understand why civic national service has been such a controversial issue and why it is still a contentious subject in some sectors today. We will study legislative proposals to establish a national civic service program and seek to explain why they were rejected by Israel's government, despite its need for volunteers. We will ask why the civic service program established in 1971 remained restricted to religious girls for almost 30 years and not extended to other populations, not even to those excused by the IDF because of a physical ailment. We will take note of the difficulties and challenges facing policymakers when instituting civic national service in the Arab and Haredi communities, particularly in light of the opposition of their respective leaders. And we shall see that despite this opposition a growing number of Arab youth are participating in civic national service and, in the Haredi sector, there is a small number that serve in the military and in civic service in programs specifically designed to meet their needs.

In chapter 1 we will present three ethea of citizenship, republican, liberal, and communitarian, as they have evolved in Western political thought, and we will show how each has found expression in Israeli politics during different periods in the country's history. We will see how the republican ethos was an important component of Israeli citizenship, which motivated and united Israeli Zionists, religious and secular, during the critical years of nation-building but excluded the Haredim and the Arabs who did not share this ethos. We will trace developments in Israel in the mid-1980s and 1990s that encouraged a more liberal ethos of citizenship supported by a High Court that promoted liberal values and principles. We will suggest that a communitarian ethos may be more appropriate to Israel because it would recognize and respect difference and at the same time be integrative and inclusive. Voluntary programs of civic service designed specifically to accommodate the needs and cultures of different communities could be an expression of this innovative model of citizenship.

In chapter 2 we will explore the concept of *mamlachtiyut* (statism) as presented by Ben-Gurion, Israel's first prime minister, and how this concept found expression in service in the IDF during the critical years of nation-building. We will describe the first initiative by Israel's government under the leadership of Ben-Gurion to institute national civic service for religious girls who were exempted by law from service in the IDF. This initiative, while ostensibly representing lofty republican ideals, became embroiled in the religion-state politics of those early years. We will seek to understand the motives of Israeli leaders in proposing a national civic service law and why it was so vehemently opposed by the Haredi and religious parties. Even more curious, after the law was passed in 1953, we will ask why it was not implemented.

In chapter 3 we will describe developments that led to the establishment of a civic national service program for religious girls and the political circumstances surrounding it. We will seek to understand why the civic service program that was adopted was restricted to religious girls alone and why it was left voluntary. We will show how this program became the flagstaff of religious Zionist girls and their commitment to the republican ethos, and we will take note of the competition this program now faces from new and attractive programs introduced by the IDF in order to attract religious girls to military service.

In chapter 4 we will show how civic national service was expanded to include youth excused from service by the IDF, youth with special needs, those at risk, and youth from disadvantaged backgrounds. We will see that the quest of these youth to serve was essentially an expression of their commitment to republican ideals, but the decision to open up civic national service to include them was based on the liberal ethos of the 1990s that put special emphasis on equality and individual rights as interpreted by the High Court of Justice. Offering these youth with special needs the option of serving in civic national service was a significant step toward their greater inclusion in Israeli society.

In chapter 5 we will focus on the ultra-orthodox, the Haredim, who maintain a relatively segregated existence outside the Israeli mainstream. During the republican period, the government permitted a limited number of Haredi yeshiva students to defer military service in order to study Torah. The number of deferments rose significantly after the Likud party came to power, and eliminated the ceiling placed on the number of deferments. The political influence of the Haredi parties increased significantly during this period. We will see that as the number of deferments increased, they caused greater resentment among those who serve, particularly in light of the shift in ethos taking place in Israel from republican to liberal. We will see how the High Court responded to the petitions of the reservists against the existent deferment policy and to the resultant conscription legislation passed by the Knesset. This legislation also extended the option of civic national service to the Haredim. We will assess the legislative efforts to find a solution to the need for an equitable policy of service that would be acceptable to the Haredim and would meet the equity standard of the High Court. Finally, we will question whether the civic service program as implemented today is a missed opportunity to improve conditions in the Haredi community and to integrate Haredim into Israeli society.

In chapter 6 we will turn our attention to the Arab community in Israel and examine its attitude toward civic national service. While there were many proposals raised in the Knesset regarding civic service in the Arab sector over the years, the issue remained mainly academic until 2007, since until that time civic national service was essentially restricted to Jewish youth. We will review the many proposals both by government committees and by members of Knesset to introduce civic national service in the Arab sector and we will explain why they were not adopted. The establishment of a separate track for Arab volunteers in the Administration for National-Civic Service (ANCS) in 2007 unleashed a vigorous and ongoing debate within the Arab community over civic national service, with the Arab leadership taking a clear stand against service. We shall see that although the number of Arab youth volunteering for civic service increases each year, it is still only a minority. We will suggest that a communitarian approach to service will develop more participative citizens, improve education and social services in the Arab communities, and encourage greater integration of Arabs into Israeli society.

In our concluding chapter we will assess the changes that have taken place in civic service policy in Israel over the decades, and we will explore whether adopting a more communitarian approach to service is likely to bring together Israel's separate and diverse communities. Clearly military service will have first priority in Israel so long as its security needs remain great. Mandatory conscription of Israel's Arabs to military service would be met with stiff opposition and even civil disobedience, as would mass conscription by force of yeshiva students. However, this does not mean that these communities should not be offered other opportunities to contribute to their communities and to Israeli society at large. Civic national service is one such opportunity. It will benefit the volunteers who serve, their communities, and ultimately, strengthen the nation as well.

1

Alternative Ethea of Citizenship

Republican, Liberal, and Communitarian

Civic national service is a form of contribution by a nation's youth to the state and to society. Youth volunteers give of their time and labor without payment or remuneration to make the society in which they live a better place. While most Western states today do not require their youth to perform military or civic service, they do encourage volunteering in either a military or civic context. The volunteer army serves the national defense, and many states have chosen to have smaller, more professional armed forces rather than general mandatory conscription. The alternative to military service is civilian or civic national service. Civic service programs provide public goods and services that may not be available in sufficient quantity or quality due to market and government failure. They fill the gaps and provide services that could not be otherwise provided due to government budgetary constraints.

The civic importance of volunteering should not be underestimated. Studies have shown that in addition to the social and economic benefits that society gains from the contribution of volunteers in areas ranging from health education and welfare to policing, firefighting, and protection of the environment, there is also a civic engagement benefit that accrues from service.[1] Volunteers are more likely to become more politically aware and socially concerned. They are often involved in projects in their communities throughout their lives, as well as being more politically active. In other words, volunteering in civic service has a positive impact on the nature and quality of citizenship. Moreover, it also contributes to greater social integration, creating bridging social capital particularly in situations where the volunteers and the service recipients come from different ethnic groups and communities.[2]

The nature of citizenship and the relationship between the state and the individual citizen have engaged the thought of political philosophers from Aristotle to Marshall and contemporary theorists such as Rawls, Petit, Walzer, and Sandal. Citizenship over the centuries has taken a variety of forms in different geographies and epochs. The expectations of citizens from their state have changed over time and place as have the benefits and obligations expected of citizens.

In the context of political life within the setting of the state, the most basic distinction in citizenship is between citizenship granted to an individual and citizenship granted to a group. The question of citizens' rights, individual or group, and the related discussion of citizen obligations relevant to our analysis of civic service in Israel will be addressed using three theoretical models of citizenship, republican, liberal, and communitarian. In order to understand the evolution of civic service policy as a component of citizenship, our discussion will focus on these models and how they have described state-citizen relations during different periods in Israel's history.

Classic Republicanism

We will begin our discussion of citizenship with classic republicanism, an idea that dates back to ancient Greece and to the writings of Aristotle. Aristotle regarded man as a political being who is dependent on his fellow man to establish a framework of good government in order to protect his freedom. Government is established by the community and binds the members to each other in the creation of a common political system. Fundamental to Aristotle's thought is the state, whose purpose it is to advance the common good of its citizens. Likewise, it is the responsibility of the citizens to be active participants in the state's defense and in its civic life in order to protect and advance the common good for all. And the rule of law is of utmost importance in the republican state because only under a system of law and its strict enforcement can the individual be truly free, protected from unfettered domination by others.[3]

In order for men to legislate the laws that serve the common good and that will be truly enforced, they must be educated as to their importance. The ideal citizen, according to Aristotle, is one who participates in the collective deliberations about how best to achieve the common good, serves in public office, and defends the polis from its enemies. For a republican citizen, seeking the common good was clearly a higher order than seeking one's own self-interest.[4]

Aristotle describes the common good as a goal that is greater than just mere survival or living together. It is to live well. The purpose of setting up a political community is to be virtuous and to share in virtuous activity with other citizens; its ultimate goal is to attain the good life for its members.[5] For that reason the ideal ruler aims at the good of his citizens. But in order to guarantee that rulers advance the good of the citizens rather than selfish self-seeking interests, it is imperative that citizens participate in political discussions and have access to political office. It is important here to note that in Aristotle's concept of the common good, slaves and resident foreigners were excluded.[6]

Similar republican ideas found expression in the writings of Cicero, the great theoretical proponent of republicanism during the Roman republic. Cicero's writings centered on the Roman republic and its political and moral traditions; their clear purpose was to support and celebrate the republican ideal and Cicero's own political beliefs and actions.[7] Cicero described himself as being completely devoted to *res publica*, to public life. As did Aristotle before him, he too prescribed the ideal of civic virtue, which placed the welfare of the political community above the interests of the individual. "Some are called to put their lives at risk, others their glory and the goodwill of their fellow-citizens. We must be more eager to risk our own than the common welfare and readier to fight when honor and glory, than when other advantages are at stake."[8] The duty of the citizen is to protect the community and to promote the common good, themes that we find in republican thinkers throughout the centuries.

In the 16th century, in *The Discourses* Machiavelli too expounds on the importance of citizen involvement in defending the republic against corrupt leaders who put their own interests ahead of that of the republic. In order to combat corruption, the republic must develop citizens who have virtue and are educated to obey the law, to serve in the military, and to promote the common good. Machiavelli designates an important role for those who "neither arrogantly dominate nor humbly serve"; and prescribes that those who promote their own self-interest against the interest of the republic, that is, those who are corrupt, should be severely punished.[9]

Later thinkers, notably Jean-Jacques Rousseau and James Madison in the 18th century developed the idea of republican responsibility within the framework of the sovereignty of the people. Rousseau recognized that while people must be free to rule themselves and are not bound to the authority of kings, they are dependent on each other collectively to create good government and to establish the rule of law. Freedom, according to Rousseau, means to live according to a law that one makes for oneself. The question is how to form "an association which will defend the person and the goods of each member with the collective force of all, and under which each individual, while uniting himself with others, remains as free as before."[10] Rousseau places the political responsibility on the citizens to act to advance the common good and to root out corruption. In a collective where citizens rule themselves, they must consider the common good or the "general will" when making political decisions in order to preclude corruption. Rousseau admits that the "general will" will be hard to ascertain. "One has to know it and above all clearly to distinguish it from the particular will beginning with one's self; a distinction it is always very difficult to draw and on which only the most sublime virtue can shed adequate light." Citizens too must be disposed to embrace the general will, "for when the people is seduced by private interests . . . the public deliberation will be one thing and the general will another thing entirely."[11]

James Madison, the architect of the American constitution and the first experiment in modern republican government, defended republicanism in *The Federalist Papers*. For Madison, as for Rousseau, good government meant seeking the common good; however he also feared the formation of factions that would subvert the common good to their own self-interest. Madison believed in setting up institutional checks and balances to prevent selfish interests from misusing democracy against the general will. He advocated granting citizens the right to choose their representatives and at the same time limited the effect of this choice through a system of checks and balances that would prevent mob rule. According to Madison, representative democracy needed to be controlled through a system of checks and balances, federalism, separation of powers, and bicameralism in order to prevent its corruption by selfish passions and interests.[12] In its ideal state, representative government should give decision-making power to those who are public spirited, who will act in the public good, which Madison recognized may not always be the case. He therefore placed great importance on educating the citizenry in civic virtue. He writes, "To suppose that any form of government will secure liberty or happiness without any virtue in the people is a chimerical idea."[13]

Republican theorists in the 20th century also linked concepts of self-government and political and civil rights with civil virtue. In his discourse on citizenship, Marshall critiques contemporary Western democracies for moving away from citizen obligations in their emphasis on citizen rights. Citizenship, he argued, requires achieving a balance between rights and obligations. Political and social rights need to be accompanied by citizen duties, that is, civic obligations that include paying taxes; serving in the armed forces; educating one's children to be loyal, committed, and productive members of society; and "promoting the general welfare of his or her community."[14] Marshall writes:

> If citizenship is invoked in the defense of rights, the corresponding duties of citizenship cannot be ignored. Those do not require a man to sacrifice his individual liberty or to submit without question to every demand made by government. But they do require that his acts should be inspired by a lively sense of responsibility towards the welfare of the community.[15]

Similarly, Janowitz in his discussion of citizenship cites Marshall's synthesis of rights and obligations and suggests that in order to create the moral framework by means of which social democracy can be pursued, it is necessary to clarify citizen duties and obligations. Clearly, writes Janowitz, "a democratic polity rests as much on the implementation of citizen obligation as it does on the exercise of civil and political rights."[16]

This integration of citizen rights and obligations forms the essence of republican thought throughout the centuries. And intrinsic to republican thought is the need to establish political institutions that will protect the rule of law and guard against arbitrary unaccountable political power.[17] Strong emphasis is placed on the importance of good government as practiced by these institutions and on the need for a separation of powers in multiple institutions so that none is so powerful that it can take control and take away the people's freedom. For all republicans, from Aristotle to Marshall, the citizens' active involvement is necessary to keep government institutions attentive to people's needs and to promote the common good.[18]

Common too to all republicans is the belief that there is something enriching about public life. Political participation draws people out of themselves, gives expression to their talents and capabilities, and it unites them in a political community, a base of shared solidarity.[19] It develops within them "civil virtue," which is the "ethical" aspect of citizenship. Like in ancient Athens, in republican thought not only is the citizen entitled to participate in public affairs, he is also expected to do so. There are standards of good citizenship that include fulfilling obligations to the community, which may range from voting and participation in local government, to performing jury duty, or serving in the armed forces or in civic service. The republican model builds a sense of community and therefore, almost by definition, this means that a republican cannot be a true cosmopolitan. He is anchored to the republic in which he is a citizen.[20]

Liberal Citizenship

The liberal idea of citizenship has a different emphasis. It gives primacy to human freedom. This fundamental right to freedom is axiomatic in liberal thought; the onus to justify restricting such freedom is on those who would seek to limit it. That means in effect that political authority and restrictive laws must be justified, especially if coercion is applied.[21] Social contract theory as developed by early English theorist John Locke is often seen as the precursor of liberal thought because of his foundational postulate that human beings began life in a state of nature in which they were free and equal. For this reason, to accept restrictions on this freedom can only be justified if they protect human beings them from harm.[22] This "harm" principle became the basis of liberal thought that maintained that the first objective of the state is to protect the rights and liberties of individual citizens. The state does this by setting up and enforcing the rule of law that protects individual liberties and prevents any individual or group from impairing the rights of others. As part of its designation as the protector of individual rights, it is the responsibility of the state to defend those rights against aggressors from within or from without. John Stuart Mill writes, "The only purpose for which power can be rightfully exercised over any member of a civilized society, against his will, is to prevent harm to others. His own good, either physical or moral, is not a sufficient warrant."[23]

According to liberal theory, individuals are rational beings and sovereign over their lives; as such they must be free to pursue their advantage, interests, and conceptions of the good. In the 18th century, philosopher

Immanuel Kant set three preconditions for liberalism to prevail in human society. First, the freedom of each person must be assured because he or she is a human being and as such conceives of happiness in his or her own way. To interfere with another's freedom is, in a sense, to coerce him or her to accept another's definition of happiness, which is unacceptable. Second, each person as a subject in a society must be equal to other members, hence equality before the law is essential; third, each member of society as a citizen of a state should be granted the right to participate in the making of the laws and to be bound by them.[24] For liberals, liberty and equality before the law are the two fundamental values that must be protected for all people in general, and for citizens of a state in particular. It is therefore incumbent on the state to maintain a standing military, a police force, and other law enforcement agencies in order to protect the lives, property, and well-being of its citizens and to defend their rights and liberty. And, in return for this protection, citizens are obliged to obey the law, pay taxes, and serve in the military if called.

The liberal ethos places the individual in the center and protects his freedom to live as he so chooses. It prioritizes his right to choose his own ideal of the good life, within such constraints as respect and consideration for the rights of others.

Freedom of speech and thought was fundamental to 19th-century liberal thought. Mill defines essential liberties as including liberties of conscience and expression, of tastes and pursuits, and of association.[25] He writes, "If all mankind minus one, were of one opinion, and only one person were of contrary opinion, mankind would be no more justified in silencing that one person, than if he had the power, would be justified in silencing mankind."[26] He was particularly concerned lest democracies in the name of the "common good" degenerate into tyrannies of majorities.[27]

An essential condition for human normative competence was having a quality education. Mill thought that it was justified for the state to require parents to educate their children or to tax them in order to provide education in their stead.[28] Values such as tolerance, and respect for the other's way of life and ideas, were to be inculcated by the education system, as well as encouraging achievement and teaching independence and critical thinking.[29]

In later understandings of liberal democracy it became incumbent upon the government to also supply other basic necessities needed for a person to be free, that is, a minimum income, housing, and other essentials. True liberalism according to John Rawls is a society where equal liberties are guaranteed and where there is also basic distributive justice, that is, those with comparable talent and motivation face more or less commensurate chances for personal benefit and development, including the least advantaged.[30] In the liberal tradition, Rawls too postulates that human beings are rational beings and have the same basic interest. If they were to be placed in what he calls "the original position," a condition under which they would be positioned behind a "veil of ignorance" not knowing their position in society, wealth, status, or abilities, and not knowing the type of society that they would belong to, its climate, economy, or political environment, all men and woman would make the same choices. According to Rawls, all people as rational beings who are concerned to advance their interests and not knowing what their real conditions are would agree to a social contract in which there would be an equal distribution of liberties and social goods. The parties to the contract would determine through reason two fundamental laws that he calls the "Two Principles of Justice." The first would give each individual the most extensive basic liberties possible without infringing on the liberties of others, and the second would ensure that each individual would have an equal opportunity to achieve his or her social and economic goals. Any inequalities that would arise would be corrected by society by providing a minimum of primary goods for the least advantaged.[31]

Liberal theorists in the last two centuries have critiqued the republican model for being discriminatory against minorities and anemic on equality and equal rights. Dagger writes that according to the republican model of citizenship, "To be a citizen . . . is to be a partner in a common enterprise, and people will be likely to put the common interest ahead of their own—to act as true citizens—only when they feel themselves to be part of such an enterprise."[32] Minorities who face discrimination and exclusion often do not identify with the "common interest" but rather with a different interest. The downside of republican theory is that by definition it excludes those who do not share the same ethos or who are prevented from sharing in it. Republican citizenship almost by definition denies the differences between groups included in the polity in its effort to establish one "civic public" but by the same token excludes those groups that do not share in the national ethos. As Iris Marion Young writes:

> This ideal of the civic public . . . excludes women and other groups defined as different, because its rational and universal status derives only from its opposition to affectivity, particu-

larity. . . . In so far as he is a citizen, every man leaves behind his particularity and difference, to adopt a universal standpoint identical for all citizens, the standpoint of the common good or general will. In practice republican politicians enforced homogeneity by excluding from citizenship all those defined as different.[33]

Historically, the shared common values that became the basis of republican citizenship in the Euro-American tradition served to justify the hegemony of a particular group, usually that of white, affluent males, and to exclude those who were not part of that group. Women and minorities were conveniently excluded, debarred from both the rights and responsibilities incumbent on citizens. The republican discourse may strengthen the attachment of core citizens to the collective while at the same time discriminates against those it excludes.[34]

Communitarian Citizenship

Communitarian theorists challenge the liberal model of citizenship while sharing its concern for citizen rights. They present two basic arguments; the first questions the basic premise of liberal thought and the second its prescription for the good society. The first argument disputes the foundational liberal premise that human beings as rational individuals choose their values and lifestyle freely. Michael Sandel in *Liberalism and the Limits of Justice*, Alasdair McIntyre in *After Virtue*, and Michael Walzer in *Spheres of Justice* all take issue with this premise. In contrast to Rawls, they maintain that there are social attachments in human society that determine the self and, as a result, individuals are constituted by the community to which they belong.[35] In that sense the image of an independent free individual, what Sandel calls "the unencumbered self," is ontologically false.[36] People are the product of community norms and values that they internalize in the framework of family, schools, and the community.

Sandel writes:

> To say that the members of society are bound by a sense of community is . . . that they conceive their identity—the subject and not just the object of their feelings and aspirations—as defined to some extent by the community of which they are

part. For them, community describes not just what they have as fellow citizens but what they are, not a relationship they choose (as in voluntaristic associations) but an attachment they discover, not merely an attribute but a constituent of their identity.[37]

A community has two main characteristics: it is a web of affect-laden relations among a group of individuals that often crisscross and reinforce one another and has a commitment to a set of shared values, norms, and meanings, a shared history and identity—in short, a shared culture.[38] Persons are embedded in communities and communities are not just aggregates of individuals acting as free agents but are collectives that have their own identities and can act together as a unit. Belonging to a community is not necessarily voluntary and social attachments are not necessarily chosen.[39] In short, an individual is a product of the community that he shapes, and he is also shaped by it.[40]

The second communitarian argument is directed at liberals who do not ascribe value to the community as such. The normative and prescriptive discourses of communitarians assign intrinsic value to the community itself and to the individuals' relations with other members of the community. Communitarians maintain that it is natural to have obligations to the community such as obligatory participation in the community's defense, because the individual is constituted by his relations with the community and feels therefore an obligation and interest in sustaining it. Charles Taylor explains:

> The free individual of the West is only what he is by virtue of the whole society and civilization which brought him to be and which nourishes him; . . . this creates a significant obligation to belong for whoever would affirm the value of this freedom. . . . since the free individual can only maintain his identity within a society/culture of a certain kind, he has to be concerned about the shape of this society/culture as a whole.[41]

He concludes that the self whose identity is formed and enriched by his membership in society "has an obligation to complete, restore, or sustain the society within which this identity is possible."[42]

As in republican thought, an important theme of communitarianism is citizen participation and responsibility. Active political participation is itself of value, an activity that is devalued and regarded as an instrumental good by liberal thinkers. However, rather than concentrating on citizen obligation to the nation, communitarians see a two-tier edifice, the lower level being obligation and service to one's community, and the second level, the improvement of the general society, state, or nation.

Mary Ann Glendon describes modern liberal societies as overly "rights centered," a development that has steered them away from solving problems collectively and has led them to rely on national governments to correct inequities and to protect individual rights. This "rights centered" view, she argues, should give way to "duty centeredness," with an emphasis on the duties and responsibilities of citizens to each other and to the community, together with a concern for individual rights.[43] Similarly, Sandel writes that liberalism is the politics of rights while communitarianism is the "politics of the common good."[44]

Rather than placing the emphasis on the individual who has defensive rights against society and who acts instrumentally to promote his own self-interest when interacting with the other, communitarian thinkers value community itself and its traditions and give importance to a variety of intermediary institutions such as families, voluntary organizations, religious institutions, corporations, and occupational groups with whom and through which individuals interact. In these institutions individuals enter into relationships with one another that are governed by a variety of shared norms and practices.[45]

One of the central criticisms by communitarians of the modern market-based neoliberal society at the end of the 20th century was that it has lost a sense of social solidarity. It is for this reason, they argue, there must be a new balance between rights and responsibilities and a reintroduction of such values as civic pride, social obligation, solidarity, and tradition instead of the individual and his rights being the primary focus.

Political communitarians give a prominent place to community activism, emphasizing the role of the local community in solving problems of crime, housing, and social welfare.[46] Community involvement has a number of political and democratic benefits. It creates "civic bonds," providing people with relationships and roles outside the family in addition to market relations. It creates an additional level of commitment and membership, loyalties and obligations that enrich relations within the local community and spin off to relations that transcend the local environment. The involvement in community action brings politics down to the individual and connects him to the political structure. Citizens learn how decisions are made that impact their daily lives, and they are the ones who will know best what problems beset their community.[47]

This empowerment of the citizen begins on the local level, but communitarians anticipate that its effect will radiate to wider circles and will impact relations between the citizen and the government on the national level as well. For this reason, communitarian theorists view community action as both an instrumental value and as an absolute good. It is a preventive of oppressive state power and at the same time an empowerment of the citizen.[48] They recognize that it is not always easy to find the proper balance between individual rights and social responsibilities. It is therefore to be expected that as new issues arise there will be public debate over the contribution required of the citizen.

Communitarian ideas found expression in the New Labor platform in Great Britain in the 1990s under the leadership of Tony Blair, who chose the term "The Third Way" (rather than the more cumbersome term "communitarianism") to put forth ideas of social solidarity and community. As Blair explained:

> The basic principle is solidarity that people can achieve much more by acting together than by acting alone. I think that all this is best represented by the idea of community, in which each person has the rights and duties which go with community. . . . Rights are not enough. You can't build a society that isn't based on duty and responsibility.[49]

In a later speech to the Labor Party Conference in Blackpool in 1998 then–prime minister Tony Blair said:

> It is that same spirit of determination and the power of community that should be the country's guide. . . . The challenge we face has to be met by us together. One nation. One community . . . the belief that the best route to individual advancement and happiness lies in a thriving society of others. . . . "It's up to me" is being replaced with "it's up to us." The crude individualism of the '80s is the mood no longer. The spirit of the times is community.[50]

Critics of communitarianism express concern that also in a society of communities those who are seen as different, for example, immigrants or members of racial or ethnic groups, may be excluded and may find that there is hostility toward them, as we have seen under republicanism. Moreover, communities may be quite intolerant and even hostile toward each other. Identification with a community may deteriorate into intertribal or intercommunity warfare and lead to the breakup of states because of demands for autonomy or independence. They too may be intolerant of individuals who are different, who do not conform to community standards.[51]

Communitarian theorist Amitai Etzioni admits that overidentification with the community could indeed present a danger to the nation. However, the way to forestall such centrifugal developments is to develop those social processes that foster "layered loyalties" in members of different communities. If "layered loyalties," or in the terminology of Robert Putnam, bridging social capital,[52] are fostered, members would see themselves as belonging to more than one community, that is, to the larger nation-state as well as to the smaller community. The nation, Etzioni writes, is actually a "community of communities" and loyalties can be multiple.[53]

National Service as a Communitarian Project

Communitarians as do republicans view service to the state or to the nation as an integral part of citizenship, which should involve both rights and obligations. However, their point of reference is different. The community is the intermediate link between the citizen and the state and service therefore need not be only in the armed forces but also in civic national service in the community. Barber, for example, recommends instituting mandatory civic service programs in the United States for all youth that would be community based. National service, he wrote, is "an indispensable prerequisite of citizenship and thus a condition for democracy's preservation."[54]

Etzioni too included a program of national service in his communitarian agenda. He wrote, "A year of national service could be the capstone of a student's educational experiences. . . . It is a major way to build up the moral tenor and sense of social responsibility among the young." Service is of value both as a public policy and as a program of character-building. Aside from giving "legitimate and meaningful work" to youth who might be otherwise unemployed, it would develop the character of those who serve and enhance the individual's self-respect, sense of worth, and outlook on the future.[55]

Finally, a year of national service could serve as an important community builder because it would act as a "grand sociological mixer. . . . Service, especially if it was designed to enable people from different geographical and sociological backgrounds to work and live together . . . would allow people to come together constructively while working together at a common task."[56] Moreover, after service, the volunteers will be more mature and skilled when entering university or vocational training, and as a result will be more successful in their studies.[57]

Clearly influenced by communitarian thought, US presidents George H. W. Bush, Bill Clinton, George W. Bush, and Barack Obama promoted the expansion of civic service programs in the United States. In 1990 President George H. W. Bush established the Commission on National and Community Service to study the possible expansion of civic service in the United States and on the basis of its recommendations signed into law the National and Community Service Act, which created a federal agency (the Corporation for National and Community Service) devoted to national and community service. In Bill Clinton's first inaugural address in 1993 he called on the youth of America to give a "season of service" and less than a year after taking office established the AmeriCorps National Service Program, which expanded volunteer programs in the United States and increased significantly the number of youth engaged in civic service.[58] George W. Bush too gave strong public support for civic national service programs.

In his State of the Union address in 2002, coming only months after the tragic events of September 11, George Bush called on every American to give 4,000 hours, or two years of service. He pledged to double the number of slots allotted to the Peace Corps and to authorize a 50 percent increase in the number of volunteers in AmeriCorps. Similar promises were made by President Barack Obama, who reauthorized and expanded the national service programs administered by the Federal Corporation for National and Community Service. Congress however was less than supportive. The Republican congress in 2011–2013 voted to cut funding for community volunteers. In 2014 there were many more applications to AmeriCorps than assignments available.[59]

As a result, the total number of participants in national service programs remained small, only 77,000 volunteers in 2017.[60] In 2019 President Donald Trump proposed shutting down the Corporation for National and Community Service in 2020 and canceling its funding.[61]

Republicanism in the Israeli Context: The Mapai Period

Israel's founders were dedicated advocates of republicanism during the pre-state period and in the decades following the establishment of the state. The Socialist Labor movement that dominated the pre-state and early independence period was a "republican virtue enterprise" that utilized its youth movement, schools, trade unions, and militia to inculcate republican values in its members. As Gershon Shafir and Yoav Peled write, "The civic virtue . . . was a composite of two virtuous qualities corresponding to the two bases of legitimation invoked by the Zionist settlers: Jewish historical rights in Palestine and the redemptive activity of the pioneers, consisting of physical labor, agricultural settlement and military service."[62]

In the pre-state period, when the state was more a dream than a reality, Ben-Gurion underscored the importance of setting up national institutions that would represent the general will of the Jewish nation and that would be accepted and supported by all members of the Knesset Yisrael, a body that represented all the Jews living in Palestine, with the exception of some ultra-orthodox sects. All members of the polity were to be given political rights as free and equal citizens to elect their representatives, in order to establish a democratic base of republican government. Intrinsic to the Zionist concept of republicanism was a politically involved citizenry that was mindful of its rights and of its obligations to the collective.

Knesset Yisrael had many affiliate political and social organizations and political participation in civil society was encouraged. Zionist leaders on the left and right of the political spectrum, such as David Ben-Gurion and Ze'ev Jabotinsky, commanded sacrifice from their supporters and commitment to the nation. Evidence of the Jewish public's support of republican values in the pre-state period was their mass participation in elections to select the leaders of the pre-state political institutions and their voluntary compliance with their decisions.[63] Ben-Eliezer describes the pre-state community as a "community of civic republican virtue" in which the democratic element was eclipsed by an emphasis on rights and duties, voluntarism and mobilization, commitment and indoctrination.[64]

In the early years of the state David Ben-Gurion, Israel's first prime minister, published an essay in which he outlined his theory of mamlachtiyut, which in effect mirrors classic republicanism without his having labeled it as such. He wrote:

> A state cannot exist without government, coercion, and majority rule (if it is not a totalitarian country ruled by an autocrat). But a state cannot exist only by the use of force by the government, coercion and majority rule. Its vitality, power and integrity are derived from the general will of the nation, from its shared historical needs, from mutual obligation, and inner responsibility that prevails over conflict and rivalries.[65]

Mamlachtiyut was not just a theory describing the central importance of stable sovereign political institutions, which was itself a revolutionary idea in the context of the Jewish experience in the Diaspora, but was also the consciousness or awareness of sovereignty and its appreciation in the minds of citizens.[66] At least in theory, loyalty to the state and its institutions was to take precedence over allegiance to political parties.

Ben-Gurion conceptualized three levels of citizenship. On the most basic level, he wrote, were the political rights of citizens, granted to all those born in the land of Israel, whether Arab or Jew, and granted to Jews from the Diaspora upon immigration to Israel. All would be granted equal political rights as citizens of the state. This minimalist definition of citizenship was to be applied equally to Arabs residing in Israel upon independence and would be denied to Jews who chose to live outside the state, regardless of the intensity of their emotional ties to Israel and their political and economic efforts on its behalf.

The second level of citizenship was that of the citizen who is connected to the Jewish nation, to the land, to its history, and to others in the community. It was important to create a new citizen who would be bonded to his fellow citizens irrespective of his country of origin. He would identify with the land of Israel, its history and its future. This was no small challenge given the multitude of Jews who had assembled in Israel with the establishment of the state from countries across the globe, with different languages and cultures. The goal was to forge a new Israeli identity, rooted in the land. This would be done via the state-run education system, instruction in the Hebrew language, and universal army service. The latter was more than just a means to achieve security, it was to be the facilitator of political and cultural socialization. Service in the armed forces, according to Ben-Gurion, "would create a 'melting pot' of youth, who would begin service bearing diverse cultures but would complete their service as 'Israelis,' inspired by love for their country and for its citizens."[67]

Most relevant for our discussion of republicanism in the Israeli context is Ben-Gurion's third level of citizenship. For Ben-Gurion, the highest form of citizenship is that of the "pioneer," he or she who is not only law abiding and loyal to the state but one who actively contributes to the state and fulfills his or her duties beyond what is required. The ideal pioneer "citizen" gives of him- or herself to achieve the national objectives of the state, as determined by the government. The state, and only the state, could create the framework for altruism and service that would give citizens the opportunity to be "citizen pioneers."[68]

One important mode through which the citizen-pioneer ideal was to be achieved was in universal service in the military, by both men and women. The armed forces in Israel were assigned nation-building tasks in immigrant absorption and education that encompassed more than just national defense. From the start, the army was given a dual mission: military and civic. In fact in the first draft of the Defense Service Law proposed by the government, all conscripts were to spend one year working in agriculture in new settlements and one year in military training and defense assignments.[69]

Opposition MKs from the right end of the political spectrum also supported the call for citizen participation in the state-building endeavor. Menachem Begin, leader of the Herut party and later to become the prime minister of Israel, eulogized Ze'ev Jabotinsky, the founder and ideological leader of the Herut movement in 1944:

> He [Jabotinsky] educated and formed a generation of Hebrew fighters. . . . He knew not how to surrender but knew love, bravery, sacrifice and suffering. Jabotinsky represents not only classic Zionist thought but also the ideas of militarism and Hebrew revolt without which there can be no achievement and no redemption for our people. . . . Jabotinsky raised a generation that gave of itself in order to fulfill the vision.[70]

Confronted with the challenge of absorbing tens of thousands of Jewish immigrants from different countries and cultures, Israel's leaders utilized the republican ethos to enlist the Jewish population to support the state and to contribute to its economy. Israeli leaders, bolstered by a supportive media, instructed Jewish youth in the Zionist ethos, enlisted them in national endeavors, and instilled in them a sense of national purpose that gave inspiration and support in the face of adversity. The fallen in Israel's wars were the heroes who gave their lives so that a Jewish state could be established and sustained.

The Zionist republican ethos deemphasized the parochial identities of the immigrants and created in their stead a new "citizen pioneer," an "Israeli" who sacrificed for the nation. This shared republican ethos created bonding social capital among those who served the nation. At the same time it excluded the Haredim (ultra-orthodox), who rejected the Zionist ethos, and Israeli Arabs, who regarded the Zionist endeavor as a foreign occupation, a colonial enterprise.

Sociologist Yagil Levy described Israeli society in the first decades of the state as one that extolled service in the military and sacrifice. He wrote:

> Due to the republican ethos that defined Israeli society's devotion to the military effort as a supreme social value, military service became a decisive standard by which rights were awarded to individuals and groups who were portrayed as acting in the service of the state. Secular, male Ashkenazi warriors identified with the glorification of the military and succeeded in translating their dominance in the military into what was regarded as legitimate social dominance.[71]

There was often a smooth transmission into politics by retired military generals who had stature in the eyes of the public because of their service. Parties on both sides of the political spectrum sought to improve their electability by adding a high-ranking former officer in the military high up on their candidate list.

The socialist philosophy of the Mapai (Labor) party, which was the dominant party in Israeli politics until 1977, had profound influence on Israel's social and economic system in the direction of social equality. From the start, there was almost universal health care, free public education, national social insurance, public housing construction, and progressive taxes on earnings. These policies ensured a minimum standard of living for most citizens and a relatively narrow income gap between rich and poor. The Histadrut labor union, an affiliate of Mapai, was the largest union in the country with 1,600,000 members in the 1980s.[72] The Histadrut was also the largest employer in the country, owning much of Israel's industry. There was a mixed economy, which allowed for free enterprise and private ownership to coexist with state-owned enterprises in key sections of the economy, particularly in public utilities and defense. Other key manufacturing and industrial companies were owned by the Histadrut. Israel's policy of import substitution in its first three decades protected local industries, limited competition from foreign producers, and maintained the value of its currency. Government expenditures in 1970 were 65 percent of the GNP.[73]

The republican ethos remained strong and was reinforced even more by the victory of the Israeli army in the 1967 war and the resultant expansion of Israel's borders. During this period nationalism was at its height, reinforcing an even greater commitment to the republican ethos. As we will see in chapter 3, it is during this period that religious Zionist girls who had been exempted from military service for religious reasons initiated a program of voluntary civic national service in order to serve the country as did their brothers.

The near defeat and trauma of the Yom Kippur in October 1973 had a negative impact on the national morale and on the economy, which set off a gradual change in the national ethos. The war had caused serious losses in human life, over 2,000 dead, and nearly 6,000 wounded, and thousands of others were conscripted to the reserves for many weeks. The Arab states' oil boycott caused oil prices to reach unprecedented highs, causing a severe deficit in the country's balance of payments and high inflation.[74] While the Labor party won the election immediately after the war, many in the electorate had reached the conclusion that the time had come to change the political elites and give the country a new direction.

The Rise of Liberalism: The Likud, Individualism, and Free Market Capitalism

The upset elections in Israel in 1977 marked the transition from the old Mapai socialist leadership that had endorsed pioneering republican values and a collectivist state-dominated economic policy to the Likud, a coalition of parties that were nationalist in their politics but liberal in their economic orientation. The Likud supported the expansion of free enterprise, the growth of a competitive market economy, and the privatization of government corporations. At the same time, it shared the Zionist goals of its predecessor and was even more nationalist in its policies; for example, the Likud expanded the previous government's selective settlement policy in the territories occupied by Israel in the 1967 war to areas throughout the territories. It initialized a process of privatization of state-owned enterprises, took steps to limit the power of the Histadrut labor union, and initiated the sale of its holdings. This process was accelerated in the mid-1980s, after Israel's economy went into a tailspin and experienced a severe financial crisis. The National Unity government (Labor-Likud) formed under the premiership of Shimon Peres in 1984 adopted an Emergency Stabilization Plan to reduce triple-digit inflation and a budget deficit of 17.3 percent.[75] As part of its reform package, the government further reduced state intervention in the economy, liberalized capital markets, and opened up the economy to international trade.

The socialist infrastructure that had characterized the first decades of the state, notably the Histadrut trade union and its extensive manufacturing empire, lost its position of dominance. Israel's largest industrial conglomerate, Koor Industries, owned by the Histadrut, which had accounted for a large percentage of manufacturing in Israel, filed for bankruptcy in 1988, and many of its industries were sold off and privatized. Similarly, HaSneh, the giant Histadrut insurance company, folded in 1992. Oddly enough, however, it was Haim Ramon and Amir Peretz from within the Labor party itself who took steps to further enervate the Histadrut. They succeeded in passing a law that severed the Gordian knot that had conditioned health coverage by the Clallit health insurer with membership in the Histadrut. As a result, Histadrut membership plummeted within a decade, from 1,800,000 in 1994 to 560,000 in 2001.[76] The Histadrut giant that had been the bastion of socialist hegemony in Israel's economy for many decades and the mainstay of the Labor party lost its position of influence as free market reforms were instituted and neoliberal economics took hold.

In the 1990s there emerged a business community made up of professional executives motivated by profit and committed to the expansion of trade. Koor Industries, which had been reorganized under different management, adopted an export business strategy that was profit oriented and competitive. This swing toward globalization and the expansion of international trade influenced the business community to support various peace initiatives in the 1990s in order to make Israel a more attractive venue for investment. Tired of wars and understanding that armed conflicts are bad for business, Israel's economic elites welcomed a peace process with Israel's Arab neighbors and with the Palestinians.[77] And Israel's middle and upper middle classes began to adopt a more liberal ethos in their attitudes toward citizenship and toward their responsibility to the collective.

As a result of the change in the political leadership from Labor to Likud and the free market neoliberal policies that were adopted in the mid-1980s, there occurred a shift in values between the founders' generation and their children and grandchildren. There was a clear change in the way the public viewed sacrifice for the nation versus that of promoting one's own personal goals and interests. Longitudinal surveys conducted by Asher Arian, Nir Atmor, and Yael Hadar found a significant shift in what Israelis (Jews) thought about self-interest or serving the interest of the country. When asked in 1981 whether in their opinion most Jewish Israelis preferred their own self-interest to the interest of the country as a whole, 64 percent thought that the public gave preference to the interests of the country over their self-interest, 25 percent said both private and national interests, and only 6 percent thought that people gave preference to their own self-interest. By 1996, however, these numbers had shifted significantly. Only 35 percent thought that the public preferred the country's interest, 59 percent thought they preferred their private interests and the country's interests equally, and 7 percent said the public would prefer their own individual interests.[78] Clearly, Israelis themselves intuited that there was a significant decline in the public's support for the republican ethos when compared to the first decades of the state. This may also be a reflection of what they read in the media with the decline and demise of ideologically oriented party newspapers.[79]

Survey results in 2007 showed an even greater decline in republican values, at least from the perspective of what Israelis thought their fellow citizens believed. Only 27 percent thought that people preferred the country's interest over their own personal interests, 37 percent thought that the public gave equal importance to their own interests and to those of the country, and a whopping 36 percent believed that Israelis gave more importance to their own individual interests than to that of the country.[80]

Israel's legal system also went through changes reflecting the shift in ethos. In 1992 the Knesset passed the first constitutional law that pertained to human rights and freedom, the Basic Law: Human Dignity and Liberty, which guaranteed basic freedoms and rights to citizens. On the basis of its own interpretation of this law, the High Court in the late 1990s assumed the authority to review the constitutionality of laws passed by the Knesset if petitioned, and to annul them if they were found in conflict with a Basic Law. This power of judicial review together with a more activist High Court provided an address for appeals from groups and movements in civic society who wished to challenge government policy.

The New Liberalism and the Demand for Equality in Service

This shift from a republican ethos to a more liberal, individualistic, and self-interested ethos found expression in attitudes toward military service as well. By the mid-1980s glorification of sacrifice through service declined among the Ashkenazi elites as they adopted a more liberal individualistic ethos. While in the first decades the military elite had been mainly from the Ashkenazi middle classes and from the kibbutzim, in the 1980s their ranks had expanded to include Mizrahim[81] and national religious officers. While Mizrahim, national religious youth, and new immigrants were still chiefly motivated by republican values, it was less true among sons of the secular Ashkenazi elites. More of them were enrolled in university studies than ever before and were more career oriented and materialistic than their parents' generation. They were more motivated to achieve personal success and less inspired to sacrifice for the well-being of the country. Some sought assignments in "safer" types of service or in advanced technology units rather than in combat, and a small but growing number sought to avoid service entirely.

Sociologist Yagil Levy suggests that there were several factors that explain this shift in attitude toward military service. The first was the market economy. As mentioned earlier, the cultural and economic globalization of Israeli society in the 1980s and 1990s transformed Israel into a market society. Globalization, Levy writes, "strengthened the ethos of the market economy with its characteristic liberal discourse, which challenged the previous collectivist commitments and symbols."[82] Values such as individualism, competition, achievement, and privatization replaced the previous values of sacrifice and contribution, comradery, and patriotic nationalism. Military forays and a burdensome defense budget were seen as hindering growth and prosperity. Moreover, the call up to reserve duty disrupted the efficient management of businesses and impacted the studies and family life of the reservists.

The second factor was the change in the criteria that determined social standing in Israel. The priorities and values of the market economy also impacted social status. While an individual's contribution to the state through military service was still considered of value, it was no longer the main criterion for social recognition. Achievement in business and personal wealth, or being a stage or television celebrity, became alternative measures of success that gained increasing social approval.

A third factor that explains the shift in attitudes toward service was resentment against those who do not serve. There was growing anger about the tens of thousands of deferments given to yeshiva students each year. These young men sat and studied Torah while their secular counterparts had to postpone academic studies until completing service. This was particularly jarring given the greater political influence and visibility of the Haredi (ultra-orthodox) parties. After the Likud came to power in 1977, they became essential players in forming and maintaining the government coalition. Their pivotal role as powerbrokers enabled them to advance legislation that gave increased government payments to large families and subsidies and draft deferments to yeshiva students. Particularly vexing was a change in policy in the early 1990s that eliminated military service as a prerequisite for employment in the public sector and as a criterion for increased child allowances. This caused additional resentment among secular Israelis who saw their years in the army as now being without recompense.[83]

Reservists were further riled by the unequal call up to reserve duty that continued even after completion of military service. They were still expected to disrupt their lives and jobs to serve in the reserves until age 50 while the Haredi did no service at all.[84] Second- and third-generation Israelis held growing resentment, asking, "If I have to serve, why shouldn't they?," rather than taking pride in the "privilege to serve the country," the republican catchphrase of their parents' generation. These sentiments were shared by several secular parties in the Knesset in the 1990s, who proposed legislation to end yeshiva students' deferments and exemptions and to make service mandatory for all citizens.[85]

This movement away from the republican ethos also found expression in the kind of demands put forward by some upper middle class recruits as to their placements in the military. Levy wrote of the "sayeret or nayeret" (an elite unit or a desk job) ultimatum that had become more common at the conscription office. While the conscripts' wish to excel was seemingly admirable, their motivation to serve in an elite unit was in fact based on personal ambition and self-fulfillment rather than the good of the country. If a recruit failed to be accepted to one of the prestigious elite squads, he would ask for a noncombat desk assignment rather than be placed in an ordinary combat unit.[86]

Another indication of a decline in republican values was the increased number of recruits from urban upper-middle-class families that sought exemptions from military service or an early discharge because of psychological incompatibility. While the number of those who dodge the draft in Israel is still relatively negligible, those seeking medical discharges has increased.[87] This suggests a weakening of the social stigma traditionally associated with failure to serve, an act that was viewed as totally unacceptable during the republican era.

It is important here to note that at the same time that the secular Ashkenazi upper-middle-class elites were shifting their ethos from republican to liberal, the mantle of republican citizenship was being claimed by the religious Zionists, many of whom identified with Gush Emunim, a religious Zionist settlement movement that was founded in 1974 and was particularly active in the 1980s and 1990s. Gush Emunim activists were at the forefront of settlement activity in the territories administered by Israel after the 1967 war and were part of a new younger leadership that came to dominate the National Religious Party (NRP).[88] Religious Zionists, often the graduates of pre-army seminaries and yeshivas, stepped into the breach with republican and religious nationalistic fervor and determination, much to the unease of the former elites. Highly motivated to serve, they began entering the officer ranks of the IDF and high-level positions in government service. Together with the sons of immigrants from the former Soviet Union and Mizrahim from poor urban neighborhoods and towns on the periphery, they formed a new elite of service.[89]

Conclusion

In this chapter we presented three models of citizenship that will serve as the basis of our analysis of the politics of civic national service in Israel. Each model reflects an ethos of citizenship that gives central importance to some values over others. The republican model emphasizes the obligation of the citizen to contribute to the well-being of the state and to take on responsibilities in order to achieve a better society. The liberal model underscores the rights of the individual and his personal well-being and sees as a caveat equality of rights and opportunities. The third, the communitarian model, places an emphasis on the rights and obligations of the citizen as did the republican theory but views the citizen as an integral part of a community that molds his or her identity, inculcates values, and gives a feeling of belonging. As a member of a community a citizen is obliged to contribute to its welfare and, by doing so, the community and the greater society will thrive.

In the second half of this chapter we saw how republicanism was put into practice in Israel in the early years of the state by Prime Minister Ben-Gurion and the Mapai party. And we saw how this dominant ethos gradually gave way to a more liberal ethos, a free market economy, civic equality, and individualism in the 1990s.

In the next chapter we will examine the efforts by the Mapai government under the leadership of David Ben-Gurion to introduce an alternative civic service program for girls who for religious reasons requested not to serve in the IDF. This initiative we will see reflected the republican Zionist ethos that prevailed in the early years of the state. We will seek to understand what motivated Israel's leaders to initiate this policy and why it aroused the vehement opposition of the religious and Haredi parties. Even more curious, we will seek to understand why, after the law was passed by the Knesset, it was never implemented by any Israeli government.

2

Religious Girls and Civic National Service, 1951–1953

An Initiative That Failed

In theory, the establishment of a national civic service program in the first decades of the state should have been welcomed by all sections of Israeli society. As an alternative to military service, it would have enabled those who for whatever reason could not serve in the military to be able to serve in a civic capacity. At a time where republican values formed the national ethos and the challenges facing the country were great, it was practically a given that all youth should be called upon to serve. The civic national service option should have been particularly attractive to women from orthodox or traditional religious backgrounds whose upbringing and family values precluded them from serving in the military. There was no dispute that the needs of the country were great, that civic service was both necessary and beneficial, and that its contribution to nation-building could be significant.

Yet in Israel during the first decades of the state, the issue of civic national service was the subject of political conflict and confrontation. Ministers resigned from the government and mass demonstrations against the government were held in Israel and in the Diaspora over this issue. Despite the opposition, legislation authorizing mandatory civic service for religious girls was passed by a large majority in the Knesset and then never implemented.

Why was the establishment of a national civic service program so controversial? What does it tell us about the kulturkampf that raged at the time between religious and secular in Israel and how it was mediated?

Religious Girls and the Defense Service Law, 1949

Israel was established in May 1948, only three years after the end of World War II and the loss of 6,000,000 Jews in the Holocaust. At the time of independence Israel's small Jewish population numbered only about 650,000. It had to contend with daunting concurrent challenges of nation-building, defense, the establishment of state institutions and the absorption of mass immigrations, the survivors of the Holocaust, and Jewish refugees from Middle Eastern countries and North Africa who fled persecution in the aftermath of the war over Palestine. Most immigrants arrived in Israel without means, spoke a multitude of languages, and came from diverse cultures.[1] In addition, the government had to establish its authority over large concentrations of hostile local Arabs, who were shell-shocked by the victory of the Jews over the Arab armies and were only just beginning to comprehend their new situation: they now would be a minority in a Jewish state.

Not surprisingly, defense concerns naturally took precedence over other issues. The Defense Service Law was among the first pieces of legislation passed by the Knesset in 1949. It established mandatory military service for both men and women. The army was assigned a double task: military and civilian. This would prove significant to our understanding of the politics of civic national service in Israel since many "civic" assignments were in fact filled by soldiers in the IDF. In the first draft of the law all conscripts were required to work one year in agriculture as part of their military service in addition to their defense assignments.[2] While this requirement was rescinded in the later version of the law, it does reflect the ideal of the "pioneer soldier" as extolled by Israel's first prime minister, David Ben-Gurion, who both works the land and defends it.

In Ben-Gurion's view, army service would inculcate the republican ethos among Israeli youth. It would also be an educational and integrative process for new immigrants and veteran Israelis. Service in the IDF would "create a unified society, a 'melting pot' of youth, who would begin their service bearing diverse cultures but complete their service as 'Israelis,' inspired by love of country and its citizens."[3] Army service was more than just a means to achieve security; it was to be the facilitator of political and cultural socialization and education:

> The Defense Law. . . . is intended to imbue our army with two characteristics that are essential to our defense: military fitness and pioneering capability. The army will not fulfill its mission

if . . . military service will not be directed toward raising the physical, cultural and moral level of the youth. Our defense and our nation-building needs will not be met if the army does not become the breeding ground of a pioneering soldier youth, healthy in body and spirit, that takes initiative, is brave, alert, . . . and conscientious.[4]

Women were to be an integral part of nation-building. Clearly influenced by the role of women as pioneers in the kibbutz movement and as fighters in the Haganah in the pre-state period, Ben-Gurion instituted mandatory conscription of women. During the Knesset debate, he stated his view categorically:

We will not build our future in accordance with our Diaspora past or how we lived thousands of years ago. We cannot have a future if women do not play a responsible and active role in all areas of life. . . . Without the participation of women, we will not build [the country], we will not make the desert bloom nor will we have security.[5]

The defense law exempted married women and women with children from service. It also exempted women whose religious beliefs or conscience prevented them from serving. This provision was a concession made to the Religious Front, a short-lived coalition of four religious parties who were partners in the government coalition: the Zionist orthodox Mizrachi and the Hapoel Hamizrachi parties,[6] and the Haredi (ultra-orthodox) Agudat Yisrael[7] and Poalei Agudat Yisrael[8] parties. All four parties opposed military service for women.

There was a religious basis to their stand. Orthodox rabbis with few exceptions had ruled unequivocally that women were forbidden by the Halakha (Jewish law) to serve in the military. This ruling was based on several Halakhic considerations. The first and most basic was a biblical injunction that prohibits women from wearing male attire (or for that matter a man to wear female attire). In the eyes of the Halakha a firearm constitutes "male attire" and was thus forbidden.[9] While this argument refers to the letter of the law, there were several rabbis who permitted women to carry a weapon for self-defense under certain circumstances.[10]

The rabbis, however, had a more compelling argument against service. They objected to having women serve in the male-dominated, "licentious" environment that prevailed in the armed forces, where they feared the modesty of young women, both religious and secular, would be compromised. In the debate in the Knesset regarding the law, the MKs from the Haredi parties alluded to alleged improprieties in relations between male commanders and female recruits that were prevalent in the IDF, provoking an indignant denial from representatives of the secular parties. Women did not belong in military camps living alongside men, the ultra-orthodox MKs argued. Rather they should serve the nation in their role as wives and mothers, raise families, and remain at home under the jurisdiction of their parents until they marry.[11]

Rabbi Pesach Frank, chief rabbi of Jerusalem, and one of the leaders of the struggle against the conscription of women, articulated concisely the rabbis' perspective, "It is not a matter of permissible or forbidden, based on an intricate Halakhic debate. When I see the results of what happens to girls in the army, it is clear that it is like '*arayot*' (engaging in forbidden sexual relations)!"[12] Rabbinical opposition was not limited to the ultra-orthodox. The Chief Rabbinate, which was closely aligned with the religious Zionist Mizrachi and Hapoel Hamizrachi parties, also ruled categorically against women serving in the military.[13]

Rather than have a head-on confrontation with the religious parties in his coalition, Prime Minister Ben-Gurion included section 11d in the Defense Service Law, which gave religious women the option of an exemption from the draft if they chose not to serve. He was unwilling to compromise on the general conscription of women. This willingness to meet the religious parties partway followed a pattern of religious-secular relations that predated the state.[14]

Already then ultra-orthodox girls were exempted from the draft. During the War of Independence, the Hazon Ish (Rabbi Avraham Yeshayahu Karelitz), considered to be the most esteemed ultra-orthodox rabbi of his time, had sent Rabbi Y. Levin of the Agudat Yisrael party to Ben-Gurion to plea for an exemption for orthodox girls from military service. Ben-Gurion agreed to excuse any girl who would bring a letter from a religious party attesting to her religiosity.[15] It was not surprising, therefore, that in 1949, when he proposed the Defense Service Law, he automatically included a provision that exempted girls whose orthodox upbringing prevented them from serving. The ultra-orthodox MKs, however, were not placated by the exemption provision and they argued in the Knesset against the general conscription of women. In his response, Ben-Gurion scoffed at what he considered their "insular antiquated position." The ultra-orthodox, he said, were preoccupied with "imaginary dangers" to their daughters, while he was concerned with the real dangers facing the country, the problem of national security. He taunted them, citing biblical texts to show that their understanding of Jewish law was in error and contrary to the literal text.[16]

In general, Ben-Gurion had mixed feelings toward the religious parties. Not unlike many socialists at that time, he was convinced that in the modern world, religion and religiosity were going to disappear. Given that belief, he did not view them as serious competitors for the minds and hearts of the people. He was therefore amenable to making limited concessions to them as the "remnants" of Eastern European Jewry and Judaism as it had been practiced before the Holocaust.[17] The world of Torah scholarship had suffered irreparable destruction in the Holocaust. Thousands of rabbis and scholars had been put to death, their yeshivas destroyed. For this reason, in his capacity as minister of defense, Ben-Gurion agreed to grant deferments from military service to 400 yeshiva students engaged in full-time Torah study. He also thought it vital to avoid a culture war between religious and secular given the daunting challenges, domestic and external, facing the country.[18]

A second consideration not to force the issue with the religious parties was the support of Jews in the Diaspora, which Ben-Gurion wanted to maintain. The charitable contributions of Jews abroad were vital to the state's economy and so was their political support. The religious parties, religious Zionist and Haredi, had many loyal supporters in the United States and in Western Europe who would not support the forced conscription of religious girls.[19]

A third consideration was the need to have a smooth absorption of new immigrants from North Africa and the Middle East. Israel was then in the midst of absorbing tens of thousands of immigrants, many of whom were religious from Yemen and other countries, and were very traditional in their view of the role of women. Ben-Gurion recognized that at this juncture government policy must respect these values and not force conscription, particularly if the country could manage without the service of all young women.[20]

The Religious Front understood that it was critical for the security of the country to pass the Defense Service Law and for that reason it did not resign from the government or vote against the law despite its opposition to the conscription of women. The Hapoel Hamizrachi religious party however was troubled by the carte blanche exemption from military service granted to religious girls and was discomfited to be aligned with the non-Zionist Haredim on this issue. MK Moshe Unna (Hapoel

Hamizrachi) expressed unease with the wording of the exemption. While he agreed that religious women who found military service to be in conflict with their beliefs and lifestyle should be exempted from service, he argued that the exemption should be on a case by case basis based on the "conscience clause" and not by establishing a "class of exempted." Clearly reflecting the republican ethos that prevailed within the religious Zionist parties, Unna said, "We don't want the public to think that the religious woman does not fulfill her obligations to the state." For this reason, the Hapoel Hamizrachi began discussions of a civic alternative to military service for religious girls at the party's general assembly in 1949, the first discussions of this issue. It also decided to encourage religious girls to serve in the Nahal Hadati, a special military unit established for orthodox soldiers that combined military service with pioneering, setting up new religious agricultural settlements on the periphery.[21]

Civic Service for Women: A Republican Obligation or a Political Resource?

Civic service as an alternative for religious girls exempted from the IDF first appeared in legislation proposed by Ben-Gurion in 1951. Israel's second government had ended in February 1951, less than four months after it was established, with the resignation of the prime minister. Previously, Ben-Gurion had lost a vote of confidence in the Knesset on his government's education policy in the immigrant camps. The Religious Front, which had been a member of the government coalition, had voted against the government in protest against the Mapai party's "anti-religious policies" in the camps.[22] Ben-Gurion resigned and called new elections but continued to head the transition government until late July. Furious at the Religious Front for its act of rebellion, Ben-Gurion brought before the Knesset a series of amendments to the 1949 Defense Service Law, two of which were specifically designed to arouse the ire of the religious parties.

The first amendment would tighten the procedures regulating the exemption process for religious girls. If until then religious girls were exempted from military service almost automatically on the basis of their affirmation that they were religious, they would now be required to appear before a committee and would be questioned as to the extent of their observance. The second amendment was more far-reaching. Religious women exempted from the army would now be required to do 24 months of civic national service in the areas of health, education, immigration absorption, and defense, within the framework of the IDF. And at the start of their service they would be required to do basic training to learn methods of self-defense.

The ultra-orthodox parties rejected the proposal out of hand and threatened to organize an all-out fight against it. The Hapoel Hamizrachi party, which in principle was in favor of an alternative civic service, also was opposed because civic service would be consigned to the authority of the IDF, making it another form of "military service," which was prohibited by the Chief Rabbinate. Moreover, the law did not assure a religious environment for those who served. Intent on punishing the religious parties, Ben-Gurion brought the proposal to the Knesset without engaging in any preliminary consultations with them. In effect he utilized it to gain political capital with secular voters who would support his tough "republican" stance against the religious parties.[23]

Elections for the second Knesset were held in July 1951. Disagreements over civic national service succeeded in dismantling the Religious Front. The Hapoel Hamizrachi party pulled out of the front over civic national service and because it could not accept the authoritative role of the Council of Torah Sages in the decisions of Agudat Yisrael.[24]

The new government formed by Ben-Gurion in October 1951 was comprised of Mapai and the four religious parties. As part of the coalition agreement, Ben-Gurion agreed to pass religious legislation that would extend the authority of the rabbinical courts over matters of marriage and divorce for all Jewish citizens, a status that they had enjoyed during the Mandate period. He also agreed to establish two separate streams of state education, religious and nonreligious, and he reached a special agreement with Rabbi Yitzchak Meir Levin, leader of the Agudat Yisrael party, that discussion of the national service proposal would be postponed for one year.[25] However, already in August 1952 Ben-Gurion began work on the civic national service law initiative. He set up a committee headed by MK Zerach Warhaftig (Hapoel Hamizrachi) composed of three MKs from Mapai, two from Hapoel Hamizrachi, and one from the Mizrachi to determine the guidelines of national service for religious women.

The Council of Torah Sages of Agudat Yisrael reacted sharply to the Ben-Gurion initiative. It directed the Haredi parties to resign from the government immediately if it did not terminate all discussion of national service for orthodox girls. When Ben-Gurion rejected the ultimatum,

Rabbi Levin resigned from the government, and the Agudat Yisrael and Poalei Agudat Yisrael parties left the coalition.[26]

The issue of national service incited a strong reaction in the Haredi community. The Council of Torah Sages issued an unequivocal ruling prohibiting any and all forms of national service for religious women. It established a Public Committee to Stop the National Service Decree to spearhead the campaign in Israel and in the Diaspora. This "decree," as it was labeled by the Haredim, was seen as a dangerous precedent. It was the first time the government had proposed legislation that would compel the ultra-orthodox to violate their rabbis' rulings. The Haredim were convinced that this move was another step in the campaign by the socialist, secular leaders of Mapai to destroy traditional Judaism, first with a multipronged assault against Jewish education in the immigrant camps and next with national service, a law that threatened the modesty of Jewish women and attacked the sanctity of the family.[27]

An editorial that appeared in the Agudat Yisrael newspaper *Digleinu* expresses the outrage felt by the Haredim and their strong determination to fight the law. The call for suicide was not intended to be taken literally but rather to express how serious the threat was in their eyes:

> It is doubtful if there was ever a ruling that compares to this ruling by the Sages, . . . which has called on girls not only to choose to suffer in jail [rather than serve], but even to choose mass suicide. . . . Our Sages regard the girls who will be drafted to national service as "captives" [According to rabbinical law, women who are taken captives by the Gentiles are considered victims of rape unless they or others testify otherwise, because of the assumed licentious behavior of their captors.] and that is why they publicized their ruling. . . . Throughout thousands of years of exile we have been tested and tried by the Gentiles and were found without fault. Now we have reached the last link in the chain of trials, a trial at the hand of our brothers who are [emotionally] disturbed. We will overcome this too, for their sake and for ours.[28]

The protests against the law spread throughout communities in the Diaspora as well. Orthodox rabbis in the Diaspora contacted the Prime Minister's Office to express their "grave concern and distress" over the proposal. The Rabbinical Council of America, a centrist orthodox rabbinical forum, sent a strong letter to Prime Minister Ben-Gurion urging him to cancel the law, reminding him of their congregations' staunch support for Israel and of their "large contributions" in the past to the United Jewish Appeal and to the Bonds for Israel campaign.[29]

The Poalei Agudat Yisrael party, while aligned with the Agudat Yisrael party, differed from it somewhat in that it shared the pioneering republican ethos of the Zionist parties. Its leadership, while accepting the authority of the Council of Torah Sages, was uncomfortable with its hardline position against any and all national service. In an effort to defuse the crisis, MK Binyamin Mintz reached a compromise with Pinchas Lavon (Mapai) Minister without Portfolio that he thought would be acceptable to the religious parties. Civic national service would be detached completely from the IDF in deference to the rabbis' ruling against army service for women and would not include any military training. The program would be administered by a civilian government office, not the Ministry of Defense. The girls would serve in education, health, and agriculture and in government offices and would have the option of living at home, except those serving in agriculture who would be sent to religious settlements. Married women would be exempt from all service as before.[30] When the compromise was brought to Ben-Gurion, he rejected it out of hand. He seemed to be determined to continue on a collision course with the Haredim and religious Zionist parties.

A new version of the law was brought before the Knesset for first reading on July 22, 1953, by Labor Minister Golda Meyerson (Meir). The new proposal required all religious girls exempted from service on religious grounds (paragraph 11[d] of the Defense Service Law, 1949) to give two years of mandatory service in agriculture, health, social welfare, education, or in auxiliary jobs in national defense. It specified that religious girls would be assured "a religious way of life" during their service. This phrase was left intentionally vague and open to interpretation. It also included a provision that the most insular ultra-orthodox girls could ask to be exempted entirely from service. A committee would be established to consider special requests from those who for reasons of family, education, economics, or "distinct family lifestyle" wished to be excused. The proposal also included sanctions against girls who failed to report to national service or who violated the terms of their service. They would face up to one year in prison.[31]

Supporters of the law argued that service was a republican obligation for all Israeli youth, men and women, religious and secular. All should contribute to the national endeavor without exception. The proposed legislation would redress the inequity between secular young women who served two years in the IDF and religious women who were excused from service but then went out to work in a secular environment or studied in university.

The exemption clause failed to placate the ultra-orthodox. They distrusted the government and saw the law even with the exemptions as but the first step in the government's plan to conscript orthodox girls to the IDF. The Council of Torah Sages warned that the government was planning to forcibly remove religious girls from their homes and from their parents' jurisdiction and place them under the authority of the state, a move that was clearly forbidden under Jewish law. Civic national service would expose the girls to the same immorality and threats to their modesty that are found in army service. Under these circumstances, a religious Jew must choose "to be killed rather than to transgress."[32] This extreme "directive" reflects the gravity of the matter in the eyes of the rabbis.

The Haredim held impassioned demonstrations against the law. Notable among them was a demonstration of several thousand Haredi women and girls who marched to the Knesset under the banner "we will protect our daughters' honor." The demonstration was dispersed by the police, who sprayed the women with water hoses. The women then regrouped outside the prime minister's residence where the police used batons to disperse them. Several women were arrested, inflaming the ultra-orthodox street further.[33] The leading Sephardic rabbis in Israel joined the protest as did rabbis in the Diaspora. The participation of Sephardic rabbis was particularly significant since many of the girls who sought exemptions from IDF service came from traditional Sephardic homes.[34]

As a last attempt at compromise, MK Binyamin Mintz (Poalei Agudat Yisrael) proposed that national service be made voluntary. This he thought would reduce the opposition to the law and yet would provide a republican alternative for those religious girls wishing to serve, particularly from the religious Zionist sector. Ben-Gurion however rejected the suggestion out of hand. He also refused to postpone the vote in the interest of finding a compromise.

Ultra-orthodox rabbis, among them the renowned Hazon Ish, pressured the Mizrachi and the Hapoel Hamizrachi parties to resign from the government. The Hazon Ish, who usually shied away from politics, had thrown his full weight behind the fight to stop the law. He sent letters to the Mizrachi and Hapoel Hamizrachi MKs telling them that they were required according to the Halakha to vote against the law.[35] On the day the law came before the Knesset for a second reading, he sent a letter to Minister of Religions Haim-Moshe Shapira (Hapoel Hamizrachi) ordering the religious parties to abstain on the vote regardless of the political consequences. He rejected the concerns raised by the Hapoel Hamizrachi that a vote against the law may jeopardize passage of the Rabbinical Courts Law (marriage and divorce), saying that this argument "was comparable to a situation where a man is ordered to kill one of his sons and is threatened that if he does not do so his other sons will be killed; [naturally] he is forbidden to kill his son." The Rabbinical Courts Law, he warned, could not be a recompense for a law that will endanger the welfare of Jewish girls.[36]

The religious Zionist parties were pulled in two directions. On the one hand, they shared the republican ethos of service to the country. Service to the state was a value taught to both girls and boys in their youth movement, Bnei Akiva and religious Zionist girls were admittedly less insular and more modern than Haredi girls. Most went out to work or studied in university after high school in a mixed environment. It was hard to justify why they could work outside the home for a salary and yet service was forbidden. Another consideration was the political consequences of a vote against the law or of abstaining. It was likely that they would then have to resign from the government, thus jeopardizing the marriage and divorce legislation they had worked on.

If they voted for the law, they would be acting in defiance of the chief rabbis, whose authority in the Jewish state they were trying to strengthen. The chief rabbis had ruled in 1951 that the conscription of women to any military framework was forbidden according to the Halakha and were now under heavy pressure from the Hazon Ish and Rabbinical Torah Council of Agudat Yisrael to issue a clear ruling against the proposed civic national service law. In fact, Haredi protestors demonstrated daily outside Chief Rabbi Isaac Herzog's house to pressure him to issue the ruling.[37] The religious Zionist MKs were also reluctant to defy the ruling of the Hazon Ish, who was revered by many of their constituents.

The Mizrachi and the Hapoel Hamizrachi parties announced that they would follow the directive of the Chief Rabbinate in the hope that they would succeed in convincing the chief rabbis to permit them to vote for the law. But in order to do this they needed more time. They appealed to Ben-Gurion to postpone the vote until after the holiday recess so they could continue discussions with the chief rabbis. The prime minister refused, for reasons that will soon become clear.

The national civic service law was brought to the Knesset for second and third readings and passed by a vote of 57 to 15. The Mizrachi and Hapoel Hamizrachi parties voted for the law. The chief rabbis had carefully refrained from instructing them how to vote, but had advised obliquely "not to cause the dissolution of the coalition by their vote."[38] This gave the MKs leeway to vote for the law without having to defy the rabbis. The rabbis had been concerned as well that agreements reached with the secular Mapai party on legislation important to Jewish observance would be canceled if the religious parties abstained or voted against the law. This was not a simple decision for the chief rabbis considering the barrage of pressure placed upon them by the Hazon Ish and others. In the end, Ben-Gurion succeeded in passing the national service law over the protests of the ultra-orthodox and forged a serious divide among the religious parties.

Determined Republicanism or Shrewd Party Politics?

The national service law was steamrolled through the Knesset without compromise or concessions, and yet it was never implemented during the 24 years of Mapai party rule. Why was Prime Minister Ben-Gurion so intent on passing the national service law without delay and why did he reject all compromise proposals? He had already taken his revenge on the ultra-orthodox and religious parties by proposing the bill. What interest did he have in provoking the ultra-orthodox parties further and inciting demonstrations against the law at home and abroad? Was the republican principle of national service such a cardinal issue that no compromise would be allowed? Alternatively, were the country's problems so acute that a national service program had to be established regardless of the political fallout? If that were the case, we would have expected the law to have been implemented immediately. Funds would have been allocated, the infrastructure for recruitment and placement set up, and the program begun.[39]

It seems that for Ben-Gurion the national service law was a means to achieve an unrelated political end. He sought a balance between accommodation and confrontation in relations with the religious and secular sectors in order to advance his policy. On the very same night that he forced the national service legislation through the Knesset against the wishes of the religious parties, the government passed historic far-reaching religious legislation in the area of personal status opposed by many in the secular camp. It passed the Rabbinical Courts Law (marriage and divorce), which gave the Chief Rabbinate a monopoly over marriage and divorce for all Jews living in Israel, religious and secular. The passage of this law meant in effect that there would not be civil marriage or divorce in Israel, a situation that still exists today. It would also disallow intermarriage and would not recognize marriages performed by rabbis belonging to any stream of Judaism other than Orthodox. Secular courts would not have the authority to dissolve marriages and in cases where a husband would refuse to grant a religious divorce to his wife, the woman would be unable to remarry.[40] The secular antireligious Mapam party, the Israel Communist party, and the Progressive Party, as well as many members of Ben-Gurion's own Mapai party, strongly opposed the law, seeing it as a serious infringement on civil rights. Ben-Gurion used the civic national service law as a foil against his secular critics on the left.

The Rabbinical Courts Law became part of a package deal with the national service law. Ben-Gurion required all members of the coalition to support both laws, which were passed consecutively on the same night. In an unprecedented move, the Knesset Committee on Procedures stipulated that both laws would be voted on in one session. The session began at 8:40 p.m. with the second and third readings of the national service law. The debate on the Rabbinical Courts Law (marriage and divorce) began at 10:45 p.m. and continued into the wee hours of the morning, despite requests by opposition MKs to continue the deliberations the next day. The session ended at 3:00 a.m. with the passage of the law.

If the religious parties had not agreed to support the civic national service law, the prime minister would have allowed the Mapai MKs freedom of conscience on the Rabbinical Courts Law, a move that would have prevented it from passing. By standing firm in the face of the Haredi protests against the national service law, Ben-Gurion was able to demonstrate to the antireligious wing in his own party and to its socialist rival, Mapam, that he was not conceding to pressure from the religious parties. Ben-Gurion had needed the civic service law to counterbalance the concessions he was making on marriage and divorce. The demonstrations of the Haredim outside the Knesset played right into the hands of the prime minister.

Opposition MK Moshe Sneh commented astutely, "Mapai made a coalition deal with the Hapoel Hamizrachi. Give me [national] service for girls and I'll give you marriage and divorce, and the exchange had to be done in one night, since no one in the coalition believes the other until the morrow."[41]

Implementation: "The Devil Is in the Details"

In a consociational democracy a compromise between the majority and a minority is likely to be achieved at the implementation stage of a law when the discussions center on the details rather than principle.[42] This was the case in Israel after the national service law was passed. At the close of the Knesset debate Labor Minister Golda Meyerson (Meir) gave oral assurances to the religious parties that the ministry would be forthcoming regarding requiring placements away from home, army uniforms, and work in agriculture.[43]

In October 1953, an exhausted Ben-Gurion announced his resignation and was replaced by Moshe Sharett, also a supporter of national service for religious girls.[44] After he took office, there was an exchange of letters with Chief Rabbi Isaac Herzog in which the chief rabbi asked that the civic service law be suspended. Herzog expressed his deep anguish over the law, which he said was causing a rupture with religious Jews in Israel and in the Diaspora. Sharett refused to suspend the law but assured the rabbi that the greatest sensitivity and consideration would be given to the religious needs of orthodox girls in the law's implementation, and those with a "strict religious lifestyle" would be excused. The girls would be allowed to choose their service assignments and only girls who specifically request to serve in agriculture would be assigned away from their homes, and then only to religious settlements; no one would be obliged to serve away from home against her will. It is important to note that the assurances given by Sharett in February 1954 followed almost exactly the compromise proposals suggested by the religious representatives before the second reading that had been categorically rejected presumably on Ben-Gurion's instructions.[45] Sharett asked the rabbi to use his influence with the Haredim to calm tensions at home and abroad and to end their protests.[46]

Sharett assigned the task of implementing the law to Minister of Labor Golda Meyerson (Meir). Ministry officials started a round of discussions with representatives of the Hapoel Hamizrachi party, which quickly reached a dead-end. Ministry officials proposed guidelines that contradicted the promises made by Sharett to Herzog. The representatives were particularly concerned that the guidelines did not stipulate that the supervisors of the girls must be orthodox or that religious representatives sit on the service exemption committee. They tried to convince the minister to appoint an orthodox woman to head the national service program, but they failed.[47] They also questioned the supposed "religious environment" promised to the girls. Who would be authorized to determine if the environment were sufficiently "religious" and the food really kosher? The guidelines proposed by the ministry also reneged on the assurances given by the minister that the girls could live at home if they wished. Instead the proposed guidelines stipulated that girls could live at home "if their placement assignment permitted it" and, if not, they would be assigned accommodations away from home "in a suitable religious environment."[48]

The religious Zionist parties were concerned that service away from home would weaken the girls' commitment to orthodoxy and lead them to become secular. This was an important consideration for many in the religious community. As a minority within a hegemonic society that was secular and often antireligious, sustaining religious observance was often a challenge, particularly while serving in the IDF and in other secular environments.[49]

Labor Ministry officials complained to the minister that the national service law would be emptied of all content if the demands of the religious parties were to be met. If, for example, assignments in agriculture were to be left to choice alone, they would be eliminated entirely since few girls would choose them voluntarily. Work in agriculture was particularly suitable for girls from the transit camps, they said, "since they are not suited for any other form of service" (*sic*).[50] Moreover, national service would not alleviate the shortage of teachers and social workers in the peripheral areas, in development towns, and border villages if the girls were to be permitted to live at home. The girls most suited to fill these assignments lived in the big cities and if they remained at home this would not meet the needs on the periphery. Moreover, in the health field, the girls who served as nurses would have to do night shifts and stay overnight in hospitals, not at home.[51] Labor Minister Golda Meyerson (Meir) warned Sharett (March 1954) that if he continued to make promises to the religious parties regarding the guidelines, the law in effect would prove worthless.[52]

When Mapai leaders weighed the potential contribution of national service with all its conditions and limitations against the political fallout that it was causing at home and abroad, it became clear that it was politically expedient to let the subject rest. There were only 1,300 religious girls exempted from service in 1954, 600 of them with less than an elementary school education. The latter would have been rejected by the IDF anyway as unsuitable for service.[53]

The law became a dead letter. Failing to reach an agreement with the representatives of the Hapoel Hamizrachi, Sharett and Meyerson decided to let the matter rest. Labor Ministry officials never completed the guidelines. There was an understanding reached between Mapai and the religious parties to let the subject die. Former Minister of Religions Zerach Warhaftig took some credit for this, writing in his memoirs that the law was not implemented due to the Mizrachi and Hapoel Hamizrachi ministers' vigorous opposition.[54] The ultra-orthodox also claimed credit for the law's demise. When the Mapam party reopened the subject of mandatory national service in 1978 and the Labor Party pressed for its immediate implementation, MK Menachem Porush of Agudat Yisrael reacted angrily, charging Labor with violating the long-standing "agreement" it had with the Agudat Yisrael party not to implement the law.[55]

As we wrote at the start of this chapter, the dominant ethos of citizenship in the 1950s and 1960s was republican, which emphasized service, sacrifice, and nation-building. Tens of thousands of immigrants arrived in Israel from Eastern Europe, the Middle East, and North Africa requiring shelter, food, and basic services. With no alternative program of civic national service, the IDF became the sole national organization capable of meeting the challenge. The IDF engineering corps constructed immigrant camps. Soldier-teachers were assigned to schools, assisted in providing health services and welfare, and strengthened agricultural settlements on Israel's borders. This extension of the IDF into civilian tasks was part and parcel of Ben-Gurion's republican vision of the "pioneer-soldier."[56] A small minority of religious girls, mainly from the religious kibbutz movement, served in the IDF in religious Nahal units and in regular units despite the ruling of the rabbis. With national service effectively buried by the politicians, most religious girls did not serve at all.

Conclusion

As we have seen, the Mapai government in 1954 failed to institute a program of civic national service for religious girls exempted from the military despite its republican declarations that all youth should serve. Although it passed a law requiring religious girls to serve two years in civic national service, the government failed to implement it. Although Prime Minister Ben-Gurion was a strong supporter of republican values and had declared on many occasions that all youth should serve, he also used civic national service as a political means to punish the religious parties for voting against the government. For that reason, he was loath to accept a compromise worked out between MKs Pinchas Lavon and Binyamin Mintz that would have made the civic national service law acceptable to the religious Zionist sector. He later used the law as an inducement to his secular and antireligious supporters to help him push through the Rabbinical Courts Law (marriage and divorce), which they opposed. He used it to prove that he was tough and uncompromising in his relations with the religious parties and did not capitulate to their pressure.

The real casualty of these political maneuverings was the civic national service program itself that, as a result, remained dormant for decades. Had the government been willing to institute a voluntary program, as proposed by MK Binyamin Mintz, it would have been enthusiastically embraced by religious Zionist girls who wanted to serve and shared the republican ethos. They could have contributed to social and educational services at a time when their service was most needed. With the law postponed indefinitely, they were in effect excluded from service, although they shared the republican ethos. They remained spectators while others served.

In the next chapter we will discuss how the voluntary civic service program for religious girls did in fact come into being and where it stands today. We will see that all the years Mapai ruled the government (until 1977) it did not implement the 1953 civic service law but did give tentative approval to a voluntary program of service initiated by religious girls and the religious Zionist parties themselves.

3

Republicanism and Volunteerism

Civic National Service for Religious Girls, 1970–2018

As we saw in chapter 2, the civic national service law was passed in the Knesset in August 1953, but remained a dead letter, with no government interest in it. This state of affairs continued without change until 1970. After the 1967 war, Israel faced serious shortages in manpower, particularly in the areas of health and education. One thousand teachers were needed on the periphery, as were nurses. The IDF had increased defense responsibilities with the occupation of the West Bank, Gaza, Sinai, and the Golan Heights and it too faced a severe shortage of manpower. It began to assign women to noncombat jobs that had previously been filled by men. It also lowered its conscription standards in order to recruit conscripts from a low social and educational stratum rejected previously from service. With this lower admission standard, the IDF reported that it had inducted 2,000 more conscripts into the IDF in 1970 than in 1969.[1]

There were 7,500 girls exempted from service for religious reasons in 1970. The IDF, in that year, tightened the procedure for granting religious exemptions after it was reported that an increasing number of girls were falsely claiming to be religious in order to avoid service. Until then, girls who asked for an exemption had been required to appear before a committee and were questioned as to the extent of their religious observance. Under the new policy, the committee sent observers to check up on the girls at their schools and places of work to verify if they were truly observant. This increased scrutiny showed recognizable results. The number of girls inducted to the IDF rose significantly, from 7,750 in 1967 to 12,000 in 1971.² This however was still less than half the number of girls at the age of conscription.³

Most religious Zionist girls in the 1960s did not serve in the army, with the notable exception of girls from the religious kibbutz movement. Many studied in the university and teacher seminaries after completing high school or went out to work. According to one newspaper report, there were 3,800 girls exempted from service for religious reasons studying in universities and colleges in 1970, among them 1,800 in completely secular programs.⁴ Clearly they were not being kept "sheltered" in an insular religious environment, but had no "religiously acceptable" alternative to service in the IDF.

This anomaly became even more jarring after the 1967 war. Soldiers returned from the front with stories of sacrifice and bravery. The country was filled with a patriotic nationalist spirit and faced new challenges of settlement and national renewal. Religious Zionist girls were also swept up in the new wave of patriotism, yet were assigned no role in the new national endeavor. They shared the republican ethos prevalent in the country, yet few served in the IDF.⁵ This inconsistency between patriotism and nonservice became less and less justifiable from the perspective of the girls themselves, particularly in light of the growing social welfare crisis in the development towns and the extreme shortages of manpower in health and education.

The Civic National Service Initiative, 1970

The initiative to resurrect national service came mainly from the grass roots, from the girls themselves and their teachers.⁶ Their motivation was clearly republican, patriotic, and nationalistic. The girls sought a way to serve the country without defying the rabbis. The seeds were sown on a visit to Jerusalem by a group of high school girls from Ulpanat Rav Baharan in Kfar Pines in 1970 where they met with Avraham Hoffman, the spokesman of the Welfare Ministry from the National Religious Party (NRP), formerly the Mizrachi and Hapoel Hamizrachi parties.⁷ Hoffman presented the dire situation facing the country because of the severe shortages in social workers and youth counselors. The girls asked whether volunteers would help alleviate the problem, and Hoffman responded in the affirmative. He asked them if they were willing to take up the challenge.⁸ This set off a grassroots initiative led by their principal, Rabbi Avraham

Baharan, who organized a program of voluntary service for his graduates with the assistance and encouragement of officials at the Welfare Ministry. Forty girls signed up from the *ulpana* (religious private school) in Kfar Pines as the first volunteers. They were sent to development towns and villages in the north to teach and tutor in the local schools and to assist the short-staffed social workers. The girls were housed together in a dormitory in Hazor Haglili under the strict supervision of an orthodox counselor and were provided with living expenses and a small monthly allowance.[9]

The program was deemed a success by the girls and by the participating local councils and brought in its wake an increased demand for volunteers. In the second year of the program additional development towns were designated to receive volunteers, and five more "dormitories" for volunteers were established in Tiberias, Beit Shean, Kiryat Shemona, and Maalot in the north and Netivot in the south. Three more religious high schools joined as centers for recruitment. Rabbi Tzefania Drori, the chief rabbi of Kiryat Shemona, strongly supported the program and assisted it from the start. Several hundred girls applied to do service the second year. Funds for the program were allotted through the Ministry of Welfare, whose minister, Yosef Burg, was from the NRP.[10]

It is important here to note that the initiative in 1970 came from a narrow stratum within the religious community and at its inception was not broadly welcomed. Ultra-orthodox (Haredi) girls were forbidden by their rabbis to serve and were also not interested in service to the "Zionist" state, so they were not potential participants. Many girls from traditional Sephardic homes who had studied in state religious schools sought exemptions because their fathers or brothers who served in the army determined that the IDF was "no place for their sisters." These girls were often less ideologically committed to serving the country than the girls from the ulpanot; few had belonged to a religious Zionist youth movement. Many welcomed the exemption from the IDF because it allowed them to "get on with their lives," to work, study, or marry. Their decision not to serve was also in compliance with the ruling of Sephardic rabbis, among them Rabbi Ovadia Yosef, the future leader of the Shas party, who ruled that girls were prohibited from doing national service, even if it were to be voluntary and under religious supervision.[11]

The Hapoel Hamizrachi faction of the National Religious Party strongly welcomed the new initiative since it had been on record since 1953 in support of civic national service. The Kibbutz Hadati, the religious Zionist kibbutz movement within the Hapoel Hamizrachi, had required its girls to serve in the IDF from the start, preferably in the Nahal Hadati, against the directives of the Chief Rabbinate against military service. The kibbutz movement's support for military and civic service was based on its republican understanding of citizenship and its egalitarian perspective on the role of women.

The national service initiative gained the enthusiastic support of the Young Guard of the National Religious Party, which became actively involved in designing the program and negotiating its terms with the Ministry of Welfare,[12] and of the National Religious Zionist Women's Organization, later to be known as Emunah. The national convention of the women's organization passed a resolution in June 1971 in support of national service.

Some rabbis affiliated with the NRP were concerned that the program may not be suitable for girls from homes where the commitment to the observance of Halakha was weak.[13] The Chever Harabanim, the rabbinical organization affiliated with the NRP, issued a statement saying it would support service only if it were to remain voluntary and administered by a religious nonprofit organization. It opposed having civic national service under the aegis of a government agency because it feared that the program would begin as voluntary and then the government would take steps to implement the National Service Law of 1953 that would require all religious girls to serve.[14]

The grassroots initiative of national service proved to be popular among religious girls and in the National Religious Party but needed government recognition and support if it were to take off. Discussion of national service was placed on the government agenda in May 1971 by Moshe Kol, minister of tourism (Independent Liberal Party), Victor Shemtov, the minister of health (Mapam), and Yigal Alon, the minister of education (Labor). The Health Ministry faced a serious shortage of nurses and the Education Ministry was short 1,000 teachers and teacher aides in the north and south of the country. The ministers asked that in light of these shortages in manpower, the government implement the 1953 national service law forthwith.[15]

The prime minister in 1971 was Golda Meir, who had been the minister of labor in 1953 who had negotiated with the religious parties and had failed to reach an agreement with them. She knew from past experience that she must tread with care in the political minefield of national service in order to not fail again. Meir appointed a ministerial committee to discuss the issue. Representing the religious parties on the committee was Minister of Welfare Michael Hazani, who had been a driving force behind the voluntary service program in the north.

Each ministry submitted its manpower requirements to the committee. The Health Ministry needed 2,700 girls to work in the hospitals, the Education Ministry 1,500 to assist in the schools, and the Welfare Ministry 1,000 girls to serve in social services. The committee quickly concluded that a program of national service was vital in order to alleviate the shortages. The more difficult question to resolve was the legal and administrative framework that should be adopted: a mandatory two-year program of service as prescribed in the 1953 national service law or a voluntary one-year program similar to the program started by Rabbi Baharan in the north.

Since the national service law was already on the books, it would have been logical, given the needs of the country, to implement it as written. However, the chief rabbis and many of the rabbis who taught in religious Zionist yeshivas opposed mandatory civic national service. They argued that a program that would "force" the girls to volunteer was clearly an oxymoron and was likely to have a negative impact on their readiness to contribute. A voluntary program would have better results since the girls would choose to serve. The NRP accepted their position and demanded that the program remain voluntary and administered by a nongovernmental agency, headed by an orthodox administrator. Only thus would the girls be ensured a proper religious environment.

The Haredi party Agudat Yisrael opposed all forms of national service and was quite alarmed that the subject was back on the table after 17 years of quiet. The long-ruling Mapai party had promised the ultra-orthodox parties that it would not implement the law. Unsurprisingly, the Haredi response in 1971 mirrored their response in 1953, although more subdued. They again launched mass demonstrations and threatened noncompliance, and they attacked the NRP for rekindling an issue they thought had been effectively "buried." Starting the voluntary program in the north a year earlier was seen as an "irresponsible act," which put all religious girls in jeopardy of conscription. They were particularly incensed at Welfare Minister Michael Hazani (NRP), who had agreed to serve on the ministerial committee.[16] Leading Sephardic rabbis, including Rabbi Ovadia Yosef, also petitioned the government not to institute national service.

The committee recommended a voluntary program. Although the case for implementing the 1953 law was strong (that it was in keeping with the republican ethos of service and would advance the principle of mamlachtiyut, i.e., that state institutions are primary over sectorial or partisan initiatives), political considerations outweighed them. The government did not wish to fail again. The NRP had made its position clear. It would support only a voluntary program, administered by a religious nongovernment agency along the guidelines agreed upon by Mapai minister Pinchas Lavon and MK Binyamin Mintz (Poalei Agudat Yisrael) in 1953. These included hard and fast assurances that the girls would be permitted to live at home if they wished and, if serving outside their homes, would be provided with a suitable religious environment.

The committee accepted the NRP conditions in part. It recommended the establishment of a voluntary program but under the aegis of a government ministry, with the length of service to be a minimum of 18 months up to two years. The government, however, accepted the NRP position almost in full. On October 31, 1971, it announced the establishment of a voluntary national service program in coordination with the Ministries of Health, Education, and Welfare and in cooperation with representatives of the religious sector. Service would be a minimum of one year with the option of serving two.[17]

Prime Minister Golda Meir assigned the implementation of the program to Welfare Minister Michael Hazani (NRP). He had been on record as having proposed that universities stop accepting girls who did not serve in either the IDF or in national service.[18] Hazani set up a religious NGO, Aguda Le'hitnadvut Ba'am (Association for National Volunteering), to set up and administer the program. While formally nonpartisan, the nonprofit maintained close ties to the NRP, which ensured its funding and represented its interests in the government and in the Knesset. In the first years several hundred girls served in national service and the numbers increased each year.[19]

The NRP had succeeded in defusing the political conflict surrounding national service, at least for a few years. The Labor Party continued to pay lip service to the 1953 law. It wrote in its platform in December 1973 and in May 1977 that the party would "consider the possibility" of implementing the 1953 national service law, a relatively noncommittal phrase.[20]

After the Yom Kippur War in October 1973, Israel again faced another severe shortage of manpower in essential services and the subject of mandatory national service was raised again. The government extended the length of service of women soldiers by four months and directed the IDF to reassess its criteria for conscription to allow more men to serve. It also decided to break with tradition and to call women to reserve duty.

This shortage in manpower prompted Ministers Moshe Kol and Gideon Hausner (Independent Liberal Party) to again renew the call to implement the national service law still on the books.[21] Minister of Health Victor Shemtov (Mapam) proposed that the government draft religious girls to serve as nurses' aides in the nation's understaffed hospitals.[22] Unsurprisingly, the NRP defended the voluntary program and opposed this proposal. Then–prime minister Yitzhak Rabin decided to continue the status quo rather than face another showdown with the religious parties.

The Political Upset of 1977: The Debate over National Service Resumes

The political debate over national service reignited in 1978 after the defeat of the Labor Party in the 1977 national elections. Menachem Begin, leader of the right-wing Likud party formed a government with the Haredi and religious Zionist parties, sending Labor into the opposition after almost 30 consecutive years in power. The Haredi Agudat Yisrael party conditioned its joining the coalition on gaining assurances on several issues, among them an increase in the number of yeshiva students receiving deferments from military service and no change in the status quo on national service. They demanded an end to the system of quotas initiated by the Labor government that limited the number of deferments granted to yeshiva students and to eliminate completely the exemption committees that determined whether a girl was eligible for an exemption from IDF service on religious grounds. The Likud agreed to end the quotas on deferments, and to change the law on exemptions for religious girls so that a simple "declaration of religiosity" submitted to a civil or religious court (Bet Din) would suffice. It also agreed not to implement the 1953 national service law. Article 36 of the coalition agreement specifically stated, "There will be no change in the implementation of the National Service Law 1953." This proviso made explicit what had been left unwritten by previous governments.

Now in the opposition, the Labor Party and other parties on the left began a campaign to force the government to implement the 1953 national service law.[23] In February 1978, Naamat, the women's organization affiliated with the Labor Party, passed a resolution calling on the government to implement the 1953 law without delay. In June 1978 12th-grade high school students in Tel Aviv and Ramat Gan submitted a petition signed by hundreds of students from all over the country calling on the government to limit the number of religious girls exempted from the army and to implement the national service law forthwith.[24]

Within the National Religious Party there were also renewed discussions about national service. The number of girls serving in national service had increased steadily each year, yet still most female graduates of state religious high schools did not serve at all. Girls graduating from state religious high schools in 1977 numbered 5,600; the overwhelming majority was observant or traditional in its practices. Among them only 2,000 were conscripted to the IDF and 800 served in national service; 50 percent of the girls (2,800) did not serve at all.[25] At the NRP Actions Committee meeting in July 1978, the religious kibbutz movement put forth a resolution in support of two years of mandatory service for religious girls either in the IDF or in national service. It also proposed that the NRP call on universities and employers to give admission and job preference to girls who completed service. Neither proposal was accepted.[26]

The Knesset too saw increased legislative activity in favor of mandatory civic national service. In February 1978 MK Shulamit Aloni from the opposition Ratz party proposed a law to institute mandatory national service for all religious girls exempted from IDF service. At the same time, MK Haike Grossman (the Labor Alignment-Mapam) proposed an amendment to the 1953 national service law that would require the government to implement the law within six months. Although the Likud government held a majority, it was hard-pressed to maintain coalition discipline on this "republican" issue that had across-the-board Knesset support with the exception of the religious parties. The law passed in preliminary reading and squeaked through a first reading in a tie vote, with some members of the government (the Democracy and Change Party, DASH) voting with the opposition.[27] During the debate, opposition parties denounced the government for failing to implement the law. Its policy, they charged, was particularly objectionable in light of the recurrent shortage of nurses and social service workers in the country. The army had had to assign 500 female soldiers to work in hospitals because of the shortage.[28] The government countered that the very same parties who accused the government of collusion with the ultra-orthodox at the country's expense were those who, when in the government, made no effort to implement the law because of their own agreements with the religious and ultra-orthodox parties.[29] The Likud presidium invoked coalition discipline to defeat the law and threatened sanctions against any party or MK that voted in favor or abstained. The proposal was defeated 61 to 47.[30]

The defeat of Grossman's national service proposal prompted satirist Efraim Sidon to publish a poem in the newspaper *Davar* mocking what he considered to be the hypocrisy of the religious parties on the question of service. The poem reflects the wide chasm between the religious and the secular. Sidon expresses his utter disbelief that national service could ever be considered a threat to a girl's modesty, particularly when many of the same girls were employed outside their homes:

> Is our sister to be like a whore?
> The pure daughter of Israel
> To trudge her path in sin
> As a teacher or nurse
> Before she is wed?
> To depart her parents for a year
> To care for the old or sick.
> Is our sister to be like a whore?
> As are the tens of thousands of girls
> Beneath each hill and shrub
> In the field, outposts, and camps.
> Is our sister to be like a whore?
> We will not be silenced; we will struggle and shout
> Her glory as a king's daughter is from within.
> She will work in a bank.[31]

There was growing discontent with the exemption of religious girls from service, even among religious students, and protests were held regularly against it.[32] In January 1979 a young woman, Anat Fuchs, was arrested after she refused to report to reserve duty, maintaining that it was unfair that she was being compelled to serve in the reserves while religious girls were excused from all service. Her fight became the cause célèbre of a new NGO called Sherut Shaveh (Equal Service), which held several protest demonstrations in support of Fuchs and against the exemptions for religious women. Naamat, the Labor Party's women's organization, held a mass demonstration in support of mandatory national service for religious girls, and the Bar Ilan University student council (a university that had a majority of religious students) petitioned the university administration not to accept students who did not complete either military or national service.[33] The demonstrations were indicative of a growing discontent with the exemption policy, even among religious students. But they had little effect since the government was committed to its agreement with the Agudat Yisrael Party not to alter its policy.[34]

The religious Zionist youth movement Bnei Akiva aligned with the NRP was also troubled by the blanket exemption given to religious girls and with the NRP's position against mandatory national service. As staunch supporters of the republican nationalist ethos, it found it difficult to defend this exemption from service and the fact that most girls in national service served only one year. The general secretary of Bnei Akiva, Amnon Shapira, issued a statement in support of the "Sherut Shaveh"(equal service) movement and in April 1980 senior members of Bnei Akiva called on NRP members of the Knesset to take action to implement the 1953 national service law. They wrote:

> It is our view, that there should not be different treatment for religious girls and irreligious girls because then we will be seriously endangering the unity of the Jewish people and our very existence as one people. . . . We must not allow religious girls to escape their obligations. . . . National-religious girls must stand in the forefront of those who serve the people and the homeland.[35]

Later that month the Bnei Akiva National Council adopted a resolution calling on the government to implement the 1953 national service law straightaway as written. At the time approximately 50 percent of the girls who had belonged to Bnei Akiva served in national service, many for two years; 25 percent served in the IDF in the religious Nahal framework; 5 percent served in the IDF in regular units; and 20 percent did not serve at all.[36]

At the NRP national convention in May 1980 the religious kibbutz movement advanced a resolution supporting two years of mandatory national service for religious girls. The party leadership was torn between support for the republican stance presented by the kibbutzim and Bnei Akiva, to which they were clearly sympathetic, and deference to the opinion of the chief rabbis and to the views of their religiously conservative members who opposed mandatory national service. The ideologues of the NRP, its leadership, and the idealistic Bnei Akiva youth movement regarded service to the state as a nonnegotiable citizen obligation. At the same time as "religious" Zionists it was incumbent on them to respect the rulings of the chief rabbis. Furthermore, the NRP was bound by the coalition agreement with the Haredi Agudat Yisrael party that stipulated that the law would not be implemented. Satisfying no one, the NRP passed a watered-down resolution, "calling on" all religious girls to do national service and "recommending" that they serve two years.[37]

Service Becomes the Norm

Civic national service gained increasing popularity within the religious Zionist sector in the 1980s and 1990s. By 1984 there were 2,500 girls in national service, a number that rose significantly each year.[38] The voluntary nature of the program, the classes in religious studies provided to the girls, and most importantly, the supervision by religiously observant personnel had reassured the rabbis and the parents that the girls would serve in a religious environment that would not have a negative impact on their observance. Among religious Zionist youth, service in the military and, for girls, national service, became the sine qua non for love of country and the unquestioned obligation of republican citizenship. National service agencies were invited to the religious high schools to present a range of placements so that each girl could find the assignment she wanted. The religious high schools laid the supportive ideological groundwork for service, teaching the virtue of contributing to society, but only within a safe religious environment. They discouraged the girls from serving in the IDF and most did not allow IDF recruiters to come to the schools to address the girls. While a minority of girls still chose to go to the army, the overwhelming majority served one year in national service and in later years a minority (25%) served two.

National service remained the exclusive domain of the nationalist religious Zionist sector and was closed to those from outside until 2001.[39] (See discussion in chapters 4, 5, and 6.) NRP ministers over the years were given exclusive administrative authority over the program. They ensured that adequate monies were allocated by the Treasury and other ministries to fund the volunteers' service placements, their travel expenses and allowances. Allocations for national service were usually not itemized in the state budget but rather came from special appropriations to the different ministries. Often government ministers from rival parties would announce cutbacks in funding for the volunteers or in the number of placements available. NRP ministers pushed back to rescind the cutbacks and even threatened to resign from the government if the funds were not restored.[40]

For over three decades the NRP (today the HaBayit HaYehudi party)[41] was the "unofficial" guardian of national service within the government. The Administration for National-Civic Service (ANCS) established in 2007, and today a statutory authority, is still under the control of a minister from the NRP (HaBayit HaYehudi), regardless of which ministry he heads (e.g., in 2015–2019 the Authority moved to the Ministry of Agriculture!). The ANCS moved to six different ministries in 2007–2015.

Over the years, the NRP advanced legislation to give the volunteers a similar status to noncombat soldiers and to ensure them the same rights and benefits from the National Insurance Institute[42] and the Tax Authorities and the same after-service grants and stipends. In December 2015, the Ministry of Transportation agreed to give national service volunteers free passes on public transportation similar to those given to soldiers.[43]

Civic national service is still the only service program approved by the Religious Education Division at the Ministry of Education for girls in state religious schools and ulpanot. Service in the IDF is still officially discouraged. In the policy directive issued in 2007 by the Religious Education Division, it states that one of the goals of state religious education is:

> To educate male students to the obligation of active service in the IDF and its female students to two years of civic national service. The Religious Education Division will encourage the girls to volunteer in education . . . and in frameworks that ensure continuance of a religious lifestyle. It is the religious education agency's position in principle . . . to oppose army service for its female students.[44]

The religious education division discouraged girls from serving in the IDF and, even more importantly, did not *permit* state religious high schools for girls to invite IDF representatives to present its programs to the students. The schools were instructed to present national service as the *only* acceptable option. Girls who were interested in army service had to make their own private inquiries, often without the knowledge of their teachers. This policy helped make national service the primary choice of most of the girls.

Statistics from 1989 indicate that among the graduates of the ulpanot 86.1 percent volunteered to national service and only 12.8 percent served in the IDF. (Only 1.2 percent did not serve at all, probably because they got married soon after high school.) In the state religious schools, the numbers were more varied and were determined by the nature of the school. In the academic track schools, 47 percent of the girls chose to serve in the IDF, 52.4 percent in national service, and only 0.6 percent did not to serve at all. In the general track, where many of the students were from a traditional Sephardic background, more girls chose to serve in national service (62.5%) and only 36.1 percent served in the IDF. The religious education system, in its formal and informal capacity (schools and religious Zionist youth organizations such as Bnei Akiva, Ezra, and Tsofim Datiim) had clearly succeeded in inculcating the ethos of service (99% serve after high school), although most of the girls in national service served only one year. These numbers far exceeded the national averages for service and were an indubitable expression of the sector's strong commitment to a republican ethos of citizenship.[45]

Civic National Service, 2010–2018

Recent statistics show a similar picture. In 2002 6,940 girls graduated from religious high schools, among them 5,158 volunteered for national service (74%) and 1,570 (22.6%) served in the IDF.[46] In 2010 fewer girls chose to do military service (935) and 8,816 served in national service.[47] Less than 3 percent of the girls did not serve at all.[48]

Many religious high schools and ulpanot still bar IDF representatives from meeting with the girls and actively discourage their female students from considering army service. Some of the more liberal high schools started to present both options, service in the IDF and civic national service. In the last decade, the IDF has made a concerted effort to encourage religious girls to serve in the army, particularly graduates of ulpanot. The IDF found that girls from ulpanot who did serve proved to be excellent, highly motivated soldiers. The IDF established a special office for the purpose of recruiting more religious girls. It agreed to establish two *Hesder midrashot* (post–high school seminaries that combine religious studies and IDF service) in Ashdod and in Yerucham to allow girls to postpone service for the purpose of religious studies, and several pre-army preparatory *mechinot*, which offer the girls a year of intensive religious studies and pre-army training and then two years of service in the IDF or in national service, programs similar to the Hesder yeshivot and pre-army mechinot for religious boys.[49] It also agreed to place religious soldiers together if they requested, particularly in the education and intelligence corps.[50]

The IDF began to offer new and more challenging opportunities for religious girls in military intelligence and in cyber security. This posed serious competition to civic national service. A growing number of girls preferred these assignments in the IDF to placements in social work and education in national service. The number of religious girls choosing to serve in the IDF more than doubled in 2010–2016, from 935 in 2010 to 2,499 in 2016. In the more liberal religious schools such as Pelech (91%) and Hartman in Jerusalem (83%), the vast majority of the girls chose service in the IDF while in religious state high schools on the periphery, where IDF service is still discouraged, only 19 to 28 percent served.[51] The vast majority of girls who graduated from one of the Hardal (an acronym for Haredi nationalists) ulpanot, which are religiously conservative, still serve only in national service.[52]

A study conducted by the Religious Division of the Ministry of Education in 2012 asked religious girls serving in the IDF why they chose to serve in the IDF rather than in national service. They gave two main reasons: the first, altruistic and ideological, the second pragmatic. The first response given by many was that service in the IDF was their mission, to prove to themselves and to others that religious girls could serve with secular youth and still maintain a high level of religious observance. They saw themselves as serving as role models to others and by serving in the IDF increasing respect for the religious.

The second reason was a critique of the arduous placement process in national service. They told how difficult it was to get accepted to a challenging placement in civic national service. There was stiff competition and not enough opportunities. Each girl had to apply separately to each placement and then to undergo a series of personal interviews for each. The procedure in the IDF was much simpler. After testing their aptitude, soldiers were assigned according to their preferences and abilities.[53] Like other young people their age, these idealistic girls sought personal fulfillment in service and not just merely to serve, and for that reason they chose service in the IDF.

Another factor that accounts for the rise in the number of religious girls serving in the IDF is a change in IDF policy regarding exemptions. In the last few years the IDF has stiffened its policy of exemptions, which it believed was too lenient and often abused. It began to summon girls who it suspected were not particularly religiously observant to appear before a committee to prove that they were religious. It also sent investigators to their homes. More girls were denied exemptions than in the past.[54]

The Authority for National-Civic Service realized that its programs would have to be more attractive and challenging if it were to compete with the IDF. It expanded its programs to include assignments in Israel's Secret Services and in cyber security to attract the most intelligent and competent girls.[55]

A second innovation simplified the procedure for getting an exemption from military service. The ANCS persuaded the judges in the Rabbinical Courts, who according to law had to certify the girls' exemption requests, to come to the high schools with the necessary forms and certify their requests there and then instead of requiring the girls to go to the court. This change shortened the exemption procedure and allowed the schools to ensure that all their students, except perhaps for a "rebellious" few, applied for exemptions under the watchful eye of their teachers and principals.[56]

While the number of religious girls serving in the IDF has increased slowly but steadily in the last few years, the overwhelming majority (over 72–75%) still prefer civic national service. A growing number weigh both types of service and decide where to serve according to the placement they receive. Still only 25 percent serve a full two years in civic national service rather than the minimum of one. This anomaly remains a bone of contention with movements dedicated to service equality. The ANCS promotes two years of service and the more challenging assignments it offers require a commitment of two years.

The most idealistic girls serve two years as a matter of principle, to serve the equivalent time as service in the IDF. Others view a second year of service as impractical given the pressures on young women in the religious community to study in academia, to marry young, and to raise relatively large families. In order to achieve real change in this issue, rabbis and teachers in the religious state schools and the ulpanot would have to take a unequivocal stand in support of two years of service and inculcate in their students the principle of "equality of obligation" in addition to love of country.

Conclusion

As we have seen, the national service initiative in 1970 was part of the patriotic, republican ethos that swept most of Israel's Jewish population after the 1967 war. It had been anomalous that religious Zionist girls, who were taught love of country and to contribute to society in their schools and youth movements, did not serve at all during the first two decades after independence. Only girls from the religious kibbutz movement and a few others served in the IDF during this period. This jarring incongruity between ethos and practice was the by-product of the conflict over national service in 1951–1954 when Prime Ministers Ben-Gurion and Sharett sought to impose national service on religious girls on terms unacceptable to the rabbis. Ben-Gurion's stubborn refusal to accept a compromise that would have allowed religious girls to serve under the terms and conditions the rabbis could accept allowed the more rigid, ultra-orthodox approach against service to become the de facto policy, that is, no service at all. Moreover, the understandings forged by the Haredi Agudat Yisrael party with the ruling Mapai (Labor) party prevented the implementation of the national service law all the years Mapai was in power.

The initiative to establish a voluntary program of national service for religious girls was the result of a confluence between the desire of the girls to contribute and circumstance, the real shortage in manpower that plagued health and social services in Israel after the 1967 war. At the start of the project, the girls themselves, with the support and encouragement of their principal and the leadership of the National Religious Party, organized a group of volunteers to assist in the schools and in social services in towns on the periphery. The new program met the stringent religious stipulations established by the rabbis and, even more importantly, was voluntary and did not force the girls to serve against their parents' wishes. It also removed the Haredim from the heart of the controversy since the program, which they opposed, had no impact on their girls who continued not to serve as before.

The national service program was embraced by the political leadership of the national religious sector and most importantly by the girls themselves because it gave them the opportunity to put into practice the values they were taught. Although the program was left voluntary, it succeeded in recruiting almost all the girls from the state religious high schools and ulpanot who did not want to serve in the IDF. As we have shown, the percentage of religious girls serving in both programs in recent years is about 98 percent, three-quarters of them in national service. These numbers can be attributed to the republican values religious Zionists inculcate in their schools and youth movements and to the consequent social sanctions placed on those who choose not to serve. Paradoxically, however, despite this strong commitment to service, no more than 25 percent in national service serve two years.

In this chapter we saw that how civic national service became national policy in 1971 but remained the exclusive domain of the national religious sector. No other sector was allowed to join its ranks; boys and girls not conscripted to the IDF for health or other reasons were not offered the opportunity of civic national service.

In chapter 4 we will see how the monopoly of the national religious sector over civic national service was broken to include youth not accepted to the IDF. This opened up new opportunities for youth who failed to meet the IDF conscription standard, those with physical or mental disabilities, youth at risk, and youth from disadvantaged populations.

4

Fighting to Serve

Youth Excused from Military Service

As we have seen, the republican ethos of service was strongly entrenched in the national Zionist ideology in the first decades of the state. Service in the IDF was the primary obligation of citizens, to serve in compulsory service and in the reserves. As a "citizen-army," the IDF was also assigned nation-building tasks external to those of defense, that is, as soldier-teachers in development towns on the periphery and as aides in immigrant absorption.

Civic national service was first instituted in 1971 and was restricted to religious girls who were excused from military service for religious reasons. As described in the previous chapter, the government agreed to establish civic national service at the urging of the religious girls themselves and with the strong political support of the National Religious Party. This program however was specific to religious girls and was closed to conscientious objectors and to those determined by the IDF to be unsuitable for service. This second group included youth with physical impairments, personality disorders, or mentally impaired, as well as youth from so-called "disadvantaged backgrounds" who were often school dropouts, youth with a history of drug use, or those with criminal records.

Until 2001 those rejected from service by the IDF had no service alternatives open to them and were in effect denied the opportunity to serve. This was particularly consequential in Israel, considering the importance of service in Israeli political culture and tradition. Army service was a rite of passage into adult life and, in the case of males, a benchmark of masculinity. Failing to serve impacted the youth's sense of self and self-worth and affected how they were perceived by their peers. It was also a black mark when seeking employment. In the case of disadvantaged youth, rejection by the IDF condemned them to life on the periphery of society.[1]

Recognizing the severity of the problem and its long-term effects, the IDF in 1980 introduced a special remedial program to integrate a limited number of "disadvantaged youth" into service. The initiative, popularly known as "Raful's boys" (the Center for the Advancement of Special Populations, Mak'am), was promoted by then–chief of staff Rafael Eitan (Raful) who had made it his personal project. It was directed primarily to youth from development towns who were immigrants themselves, or the sons of immigrants, from poor and often dysfunctional families. Many had been dropouts from schools that were often themselves substandard. The program established in the Havat Hashomer army compound gave these boys a second chance to complete their studies and to serve in the military. It taught the recruits basic learning skills and the subjects they had failed to learn at school, Hebrew language, English, and mathematics, all under the strictest military discipline.

"Raful's boys" gave a new start to about 20 percent of the disadvantaged youth of recruitment age.[2] It reflected a greater government awareness of the widening gap that existed between the youth growing up in the center of the country and those in development towns, an issue that had figured prominently in the elections of 1977 and 1981.[3] The political upset of the Likud party in 1977 and the defeat of the Labor Party after 30 years of consecutive rule can be traced to the revolt of the Mizrachi[4] voters on the periphery who were fed up with the Labor Party that had perpetuated their second-class status and ignored their problems. Many Mizrachi young men with promising potential had failed to meet the recruitment standards of the IDF because of the difficult circumstances in which they were raised. The "Raful's boys" program gave them a second chance to complete military service and by doing so to be "normative contributing citizens" as expected in a society where the ethos of republican citizenship was still very strong.[5]

Republican Obligation and Equality in Service

As described in chapter 1, the 1990s ushered in a new neoliberal ethos in Israel that placed greater emphasis on individualism, citizens' rights, and equality. The Knesset passed two new Basic Laws in 1992 that provided constitutional guarantees of citizens' rights and freedoms. The Basic Law Human Dignity and Liberty and the Basic Law Freedom of Occupation prohibited the Knesset from passing laws that infringe on the dignity or freedom of citizens or on their right to an occupation unless the law "was befitting the values of the State of Israel, enacted for a proper purpose, and to an extent no greater than is required." The Basic Law Human Dignity and Liberty was interpreted by the Court to mean that laws must be fair and applied equally to all citizens.[6] The neoliberal model of citizenship that emerged in Israel in the 1990s placed greater emphasis on the equal rights and obligations of all citizens than did the earlier republican ethos that had been exclusive to Zionist Jews, religious and secular. During this period there were numerous initiatives in the Knesset to extend the obligation of service to the Haredi and to the Arab population in the name of equality. These proposals were rejected by the government and by a majority in the Knesset but they reflected the new discourse, the demand for an equitable service policy in addition to the timeworn appeals to patriotism and sacrifice.

Consequently this new emphasis on equality of rights and obligations put into question the government policy that offered the option of alternative service exclusively to religious girls. Men and women excused from service by the IDF were left with no recourse if they wanted to serve. A small group of youth rejected from service by the IDF argued that as citizens they had a right to serve, even if the IDF had excused them. Their wish to serve stemmed from their identification with the republican ethos, but the legal argument they put forward was actually one of equality. They enlisted in civic national service in 1994 through the organization Shlomit, a new nonprofit.

Until that time, civic national service had been restricted to religious girls alone. The girls were assigned to placements by the Aguda Lehitnadvut Ba'am, a nonprofit agency that held a monopoly on placements. In 1986 the Aguda was joined by a second placement agency, Aminadav, and in 1993 by a third, Shlomit. Shlomit defined itself as a pluralistic agency that would accept volunteers from all sectors, male and female, Jews and Arabs, religious and irreligious. This was a groundbreaking change since until then neither youth excused from military service nor Arabs were accepted to civic service.[7]

In 1995 Shlomit placed 12 Arab girls and 10 Jewish boys in civic national service. Several months later it was informed by the Ministry of

Labor that these volunteers were ineligible for the benefits paid by the National Insurance Agency. Its guidelines stated clearly that the benefits were for "religious girls performing national service."[8] Shlomit teamed up with the Association for Civil Rights in Israel (ACRI) to challenge the law in the High Court of Justice. ACRI petitioned the High Court to revoke the ruling of the National Insurance Agency, arguing that by refusing these volunteers the benefits that come with civic service they were being denied in effect "the right to serve," which was discriminatory and unfair.[9]

The Court issued a show cause order requiring the government to explain its policy to the Court. The government wanted to avoid High Court interference on the politically volatile question of equality of service, which could have consequences on yeshiva student deferments or conscription of Arabs. It sought a quick out-of-court agreement with ACRI, promising to "study" the question and establish new guidelines if ACRI would agree to withdraw the petition. The petition was subsequently withdrawn.[10]

The government assigned the task to Minister of Labor and Welfare Eli Yishai, who appointed a committee headed by Yigal Ben-Shalom, the director general of the ministry, to study the issue. The committee came back with several far-reaching proposals. It recommended that the option of service in civic national service be extended to all youth rejected by the IDF or who were not called up for service at all, for example, Israeli Arabs, and it should be voluntary, similar to that of religious girls.[11]

These recommendations were a clear departure from the existent policy. For the first time they suggested giving legitimacy to an alternative service program for men that would be independent of the IDF. They also extended the option of civic service to Arabs, recommending that through service they could be integrated further into Israeli society. It is important here to note that the committee discussed these issues during a relatively optimistic and peaceful period in Jewish-Arab relations, when the peace process with the Palestinians was promising, after the Oslo Accords and before the Second Intifada and the October Events in 2000.

While these recommendations seem moderate, in principle they were really quite far-reaching. They were the first crack in the IDF's monopoly on service for men and gave legitimacy to a form of alternative service not under its control. It is true that the religious girls were the first to serve outside the IDF, but they were a small sectarian group outside the mainstream. The Ben-Shalom recommendations opened up a civic service alternative to all youth excused from the IDF for whatever reason. It is important however to note that under the Ben-Shalom plan the IDF would still be the first and single authority to decide who should be accepted to military service. Conscripts would not be allowed a choice between military service and national service. Most significantly, civic service would remain closed to conscientious objectors, who would still face incarceration in a military prison if they refused to serve.[12]

The IDF had traditionally been opposed to proposals that offer youth an alternative to military service. It was resolute that the IDF must have primacy in decisions determining who should be drafted and into which units. Evidence of this can be seen in the military's response to the Shafir report, written by an internal committee appointed by the IDF in 1992 to analyze the manpower needs of the IDF, current and future. The report warned that due to the large number of immigrants that had arrived in Israel from the former Soviet Union in the 1990s the IDF would soon have a large surplus of conscripts, which would prove costly. The committee recommended that the government establish a separate track of national civic service in order to siphon off surplus recruits to civic tasks where they would be needed. The IDF, it wrote, should become a small and more professional force.[13]

The IDF top brass rejected the Shafir recommendations. The IDF was unwilling to relinquish its monopoly over service and its hegemonic status as the one and only "people's army." It was a national symbol, which gave Israel's youth a clear mission of service and love of country. Support for the IDF was ubiquitous among Jewish Israelis, a fact that gave it precedence in appropriations. It was not interested in an alternative track of service that could compete with it for the hearts and pocketbook of Israel's citizens. As long as civic national service remained a sectorial program for religious girls, it had posed no serious threat to the dominant status of the IDF; an alternative independent service track for noncombatants was another story.[14]

To answer the problem of excessive manpower anticipated by Shafir, the IDF expanded the range of assignments comprised in "military" service to include a variety of civic tasks. It added assignments in the police and in military prisons and distantly related "security" assignments in government offices and other institutions, as well as assignments in education, immigrant absorption, and health services.[15] This so-called "embedded service" enabled the army to retain its monopoly over conscription and at the same time to export soldiers to essential services outside the military.[16]

The government dragged its feet implementing the recommendations of the Ben-Shalom committee and when it did act chose a path of minimal change with relatively low political cost. It did not tackle the more sensitive question of Arab volunteers, postponing that issue entirely. It followed a policy strategy of "layering," introducing minor modifications to existing policy without having to overhaul policy.[17] The Knesset, at the government's initiative, passed the Voluntary National Service Law (Experimental-Boys) in 2001 four years after Shlomit and ACRI petitioned the High Court. It authorized a pilot program of civic national service for 250 boys excused from IDF service, along the same guidelines established for religious girls. Over the next two years 300 boys participated in civic national service, some doing one year of service and others two.[18]

Unsurprisingly, the IDF was concerned that the new program may impact negatively on conscription and on the morale of the soldiers. During the discussions in the Knesset Labor, Welfare, and Health Committee in 2003 regarding the renewal of the law, the representative of the Ministry of Defense expressed concern that conscripts may use the alternative of civic service to avoid military service. The IDF, he said, wanted it written clearly in the legislation that those who apply to civic service may do so only after they have been excused from service by the IDF. Moreover, he said, it was critical that the monetary benefits that accrue to youth serving in civic national service be purposely less than those given to noncombat soldiers so as not to equate the two services.[19] The IDF was clearly worried that in time civic national service might become a socially acceptable and attractive alternative to military service, as it was in Germany.[20] This was a consequence it wished to prevent from the start.

The Ivri Committee: A Break with Past Policy

In 2004 the minister of defense appointed a committee of experts headed by retired Major-General David Ivri to study how to expand national service, particularly in the Haredi sector. The Ivri Committee adopted a broad perspective on civic national service, seeing it as a way to promote better citizenship and greater commitment to the state in all sectors. It saw service to the community as a basic right of citizenship as well as an obligation, which should be open to all.[21]

According to information made available to the committee by the IDF, in 2004 about 50 percent of the youth of conscription age actually did full military service. This low percentage was the catalyst for the Ivri Committee's reassessment of service policy. In 2004, 21,500 youth were excused from service by the IDF, among them 16,500 girls and 5,000 boys.

Religious Zionist girls excused from service numbered 6,500 and served instead in civic national service.[22]

The committee estimated that among those excused from service for medical or socio-psychological reasons there were approximately 2,400 youths who would be suitable for civic service if given the proper supervision and guidance. An additional group excused from service was "youth at risk." These were youth from difficult family backgrounds, for example, those who grew up in poverty, children of single parents, children with a parent in prison, or those who had suffered abuse, violence, or neglect.[23] Another group was "disadvantaged youth," who were often from poor immigrant families that had failed to adjust to life in Israel. Many were from the Ethiopian community. Since the committee considered service to be a basic right and obligation of citizenship, it recommended that youth from these three groups be *required* to do alternative civic service if they were found suitable.

This was a far-reaching recommendation and a substantial departure from previous service policy, but it was consistent with the committee's conviction that all youth should serve if they were capable. It was in a sense an amalgamation of the republican ethos that emphasizes service to the state and to society with the liberal ethos of equality, extending the opportunity to serve to all youth, including those with special needs. While similar in many ways to the alternative service policy that existed at the time in Germany, Switzerland, and Sweden, it differed in that it did not equate military and civic national service, or give the youth a choice between them. The committee cautioned:

> The implementation of civic service must be by an independent state authority in order that it be an appropriate alternative to military service, while at the same time preserving the preference and priority given to the IDF, in order that civic service will empower socially those who serve as well as those who benefit from their services.[24]

Service in the IDF was to remain mandatory and the IDF would remain the singular authority to determine if a youth was suitable for conscription. Only after the IDF rejected a conscript would he or she be referred to civic national service and that service too would be mandatory. This was a clear departure from the Ben-Shalom recommendations that had seen civic service as voluntary.

The Ivri Committee also discussed soldiers discharged from the IDF during their service for lack of suitability. According to statistics provided by the IDF, in 2004 there were 8,900 soldiers who were discharged in their first year of service for lack of motivation, adjustment difficulties, disciplinary infractions, personal problems, and other issues, 7,000 boys and 1,900 girls. It was estimated that about 1,350 of them would be suitable for civic national service. The committee recommended that the state require those whose service was terminated midterm by the IDF to complete at least one year of civic national service instead. Civic national service, it reasoned, was a more flexible, personalized kind of program that was less demanding in discipline and endurance. With the proper supervision and assistance, these army "dropouts" could make a significant contribution to society in national service. The committee recognized that this recommendation was a radical departure from previous policy and as such would require a change in the Defense Service Law. In the meanwhile, it proposed that the government extend to these youth the option of civic national service on a voluntary basis.

The final issue discussed by the Ivri Committee was the "recognized" or "embedded" services in the IDF, which were civilian in nature and not connected to the state's defense, for example, assignments in immigrant absorption, education, and health services. As we noted earlier, many of these assignments were identical to those performed by volunteers in civic national service. The committee estimated that there were approximately 2,665 soldiers in 2005 assigned to tasks that were essentially civic service jobs. It questioned the logic of keeping these assignments as part of the IDF mandate and recommended that, as part of a second stage of civic service reform, these assignments be transferred from the IDF to the Administration for National-Civic Service when established. Service in those assignments would be mandatory.[25] This recommendation was in keeping with those of the Shafir committee mentioned earlier. Predictably, this recommendation met with resistance from the IDF and was never implemented. Recommendations to professionalize the armed forces and to eliminate many of these auxiliary assignments have been proposed in several forums but have failed to become policy.[26]

The Ivri recommendations regarding those excused by the IDF and those discharged early from its ranks were implemented only in part. Civic national service was not made mandatory for youth excused from the IDF. However, following the committee recommendations, the government decided to authorize and fund civic service placements for youth with special needs. With the establishment of the Administration for National-Civic Service (ANCS) in 2007, programs were introduced for youth with physical, sensory, or emotional disabilities; youth at risk; and for disadvantaged youth, mainly for new immigrants from the Ethiopian and Caucasian communities who lacked the minimum educational and social skills required by the military. In addition to the regular training and supervision that were provided to all volunteers, youth at risk and disadvantaged youth received added hands-on training and supervision, leadership training, and remedial courses so that they could earn their high school diplomas and prepare for college entrance exams. Youth with a juvenile criminal record were given the opportunity for a new start in civic national service. In a recent development, after completing service successfully they will be eligible to apply to the Ministry of Justice to have their criminal record erased.[27]

The ANCS worked with different placement agencies and with private philanthropic funds to create the infrastructure and the support necessary to integrate youth with special needs into civic service. For example, a program entitled Meshalvim (Integration) was established to assist youth with physical or mental disabilities to serve. It offered a preparatory pre-service course to prospective volunteers and provided support services and guidance during service. It saw as its mandate the integration of special needs populations in civic service because it is "their full right" as citizens to serve society according to their capabilities, here again motivation that combines both republican and liberal egalitarian values.[28]

Meshalvim operates in conjunction with another nonprofit organization, Gevanim (Hues), which coordinates between government offices, placement agencies, and disabled youth in civic service. Gevanim established a communal living facility in the south ("Knafayim," literally, wings) for youth with physical and sensory disabilities. Disabled youth reside in the facility and travel from there to their civic service assignments and to studies at the Sapir Academic College. It also operates programs without living arrangements in conjunction with the Bat Ami placement agency. Together they place about 350 youth with disabilities in civic service each year.[29]

Volunteers with disabilities took pride in the fact that they too could stand proud together with other youth their age. One volunteer said:

> The special placements for youth like me allow us to contribute to society, develop skills and independence and to get work

experience in a normative framework, to prepare for "real life" and to keep up with our friends who are serving in regular army units or in civic service. These placements allow us to "build and to be built." They assist us to fit into society and at the same time to contribute to society.[30]

Other volunteers gave less credence to the republican aspects of service and viewed it mainly as an opportunity for personal development and independence. Civic national service provided new opportunities to develop new skills and to gain work experience and also financial benefits. In the words of one volunteer:

I feel like I have where to go because of civic service. It's great. As I am wheelchair bound I am always being cared for. Service allowed me to live independently, and to give something back to the state that gives me so much. I wish there were more placements for young people like me because there are many who want to leave home, to have a change, to feel adult, to do something different and not just to wither away at home.[31]

Gevanim also runs a civic national service program (Hed-haver) for youth with a history of mental illness. Here too the program includes assigning personal counselors to these youth to assist them in completing civic service, and to encourage their reintegration into society.[32]

The Aguda Le'Hitnatvut placement agency established a similar program called Otzma (power) in nine locations throughout the country as did the Shlomit placement agency. The latter offers a special civic service program for youth with Asperger syndrome and another for high-functioning youth on the autism spectrum (Shalhevet).[33] In all these programs, volunteers with special needs are assigned to the placements of their choice that are appropriate to their needs and capabilities.[34]

Youth at risk are offered a special program, entitled Tmura, run by the Aguda Lehitnadvut Ba'am placement agency. Similar to the other programs, Tmura provides a supportive framework for youth from difficult home backgrounds. It offers workshops and an individual guidance program to empower volunteers to develop their independence and self-confidence so they can integrate into normative society and prepare themselves for the challenges they will face after completing service.[35]

There is great demand for civic service programs from youth with special needs. While in 2010 there were less than a hundred volunteers with disabilities in civic national service, in 2015 there were over 800 volunteers with disabilities and 400 youth at risk.[36] There were many more applicants than placements available and pressure was put on the government to increase funding. The cost of each special placement is more than twice that of a regular volunteer because of the additional hours of guidance and supervision. Moreover, youth at risk and youth from dysfunctional families usually need to be provided with housing in apartments away from their homes.[37]

The government turned to philanthropic funds to provide the additional funding. Today it funds the basic package of costs and allowances provided to each volunteer and the philanthropies pay for the additional expenses required for those with special needs.[38] The largest fund is the Opportunity Fund for Civic Service founded in 2012. It receives contributions from eight different philanthropic funds in Israel and the Diaspora to support volunteers with special needs.

Civic National Service: Win-Win for the State and for the Volunteer

Civic national service by youth with special needs is a win-win project for the state and for the volunteers. Particularly in the case of disadvantaged populations and youth at risk, the state has a clear interest in integrating them into normative Israeli society. Alienated youth are a breeding ground for crime and other social ills, problems that continue throughout their adult lives. Civic service is an opportunity to connect with these youth and to head off their further decline.

Cost–benefit analysis of the economic payback of civic national service by the disabled and youth at risk indicates that in the long run the state gets a positive return on its investment. The government spends between 23,000 and 35,000 shekels per volunteer with special needs to cover living expenses, travel, insurance, and the cost of the coordinating staff. The philanthropic funds pay another 11,000 or 12,000 shekels, the total cost reaching an average of 43,000 shekels per volunteer. A comprehensive study by the Adalya consulting firm in 2015 commissioned by the Civic Service Forum to study the cost effectiveness of civic national service by special and at risk populations found that the government will have a net gain of between 200,000 to 320,000 shekels per volunteer in their lifetime. The study looked at the long-term impact of civic national service on the volunteer and calculated the probability that he or she will live a normative life after service and will be gainfully employed. It concluded that civic national service is a good investment that will reduce dependence on state resources in the future and the need for more costly rehabilitation. An investment of funds at this early stage in adulthood will pay off significantly in the long run because it will produce self-sufficient, competent adults.[39]

In the short term, the Adalya study found that disabled young people found jobs at a significantly higher rate after their year of service than did their disabled peers who did not volunteer. Sixty percent of the disabled young people ages 20 to 24 after a year or more of civic national service were employed as compared to 42 percent of those who did not serve. This advantage was also found to be true among disabled adults ages 25 to 29. Among youth at risk (girls) 88 percent were either studying or working after they completed service, a rate significantly higher than those at risk who did not serve.[40]

Among Ethiopian immigrants the difference was even more pronounced. The Adalya research found that 73 percent of the girls who had completed national service were working and 94 percent were working, studying, or doing both.[41] This was a significant achievement when compared to the number of Ethiopian young women ages 25 to 34 (46%) reported to be working according to a study done by the Adva Center.[42] The study concluded that the work experience and the confidence that the girls had gained in national service had had an empowering effect and had given them an advantage in finding employment. The girls themselves also thought that their service experience had been an important factor in finding a job. Forty-eight percent of the girls agreed that "a year of civic national service was an entrance ticket to the job market."[43]

An in-depth study conducted among youth at risk and immigrant Ethiopian youth from difficult family backgrounds found that at the end of a year of civic service a majority of the volunteers saw their civic service experience as having been both positive and self-empowering, despite the difficult challenges and even failures they had faced while serving. Most regarded their service as having been meaningful both to their service recipients and to themselves as service providers. Some expressed surprise and great pride in how well they had coped and said that they had gained more self-confidence and self-esteem from the experience.[44] A similar study among youth at risk found that the majority of volunteers found the experience to have been personally gratifying and, despite the many difficulties they faced, the more challenging and meaningful their assignment, the greater their personal growth.[45]

A continuing problem faced by the programs for youth with special needs was the failure of the government to allocate sufficient funds for the many who wish to volunteer. ANCS director general Sar Shalom Gerbi told the Knesset Committee for Public Appeals in 2013 that he was forced to restrict the volunteers with special needs and youth at risk to only one year of service and to place those at risk in assignments close to home in order to save on the expense of service apartments.[46] This presented a particularly serious problem for volunteers with special needs who wanted to serve a second year and for whom civic service served as a transition period toward adult independence. For youth at risk, it was untenable to require them to live at home since their homes were often difficult and dysfunctional, which was the reason they had spent most of their childhood in children's homes or dormitories. To expect them now to live at home was impracticable and counterproductive.[47] After heavy pressure from the committee, government offices agreed to set aside 10 percent of their civic service slots for disabled and disadvantaged youth and the government agreed to fund another 400 placements for them.[48]

There were 700 youth at risk serving in civic national service in 2018 and an additional 100 youth at risk with criminal records. The National Insurance Agency increased the living allowances of these volunteers by 1,000 shekels a month, recognizing that unlike other volunteers, these youth usually had no other source of income.[49] In another initiative to further integrate youth at risk, the Justice Ministry in 2018 launched a pilot project to erase the criminal records of volunteers who successfully completed a year of civic national service, similar to one adopted not long before by the IDF.[50]

The Knesset in 2017 adopted a new national civic service law to replace the National Service Law 1953 that had never been implemented. It listed the special programs for youth with disabilities, youth at risk, and disadvantaged youth, in the "national" track of civic service, together with the program for religious girls and Haredi service and Arab service in different tracks. The placement of these programs in the "national" track recognizes that these populations share in common a commitment to the republican ethos, identify with the state and its institutions, and are entitled to an equal opportunity to serve as do others.

Conclusion

The expansion of civic national service in the first decade of the 21st century to include youth with disabilities and other youth excused from service by the IDF was the result of the overlap between two ethea of citizenship, republican and liberal. For many youth who were excused from the IDF because of a physical or mental disability, this "rejection" was a denial of their dream to serve the country and to contribute. Imbued with the same republican values and responsibility as their able-bodied friends, they were frustrated that they were denied the opportunity to serve. In the words of Neta, age 19, "I could not serve in the army for health reasons. . . . I view service in civic national service as a central and meaningful way to fulfill my civic obligation to the state. I believe that both society and I have benefited from my service."[51] For Neta and for many disabled youth it was important and personally gratifying to be able to give back to society rather than just receiving. And the opportunity to do civic national service and to utilize their skills and talents reinforced their sense of self-worth.

It was however only after the ethos in the country changed from republican to a more liberal ethos of rights and equality that civic service opened up to these marginalized populations. Until then, the disabled and the disadvantaged were an overlooked segment of society, for reasons that include insensitivity, paternalism, and discrimination. In theory, many of these youth shared the same republican values as other Israelis. However, until 2001, they were seen as dependents and not as individuals with talents and capabilities who could contribute to society. In effect they were marginalized together with those groups who did not share an ideological commitment to the Jewish state, the Arabs and the Haredim. In rejecting youth who did not fit the requirements of the IDF, it turned IDF service into something exclusive and "selective," a position of status that only the fit can occupy. This instilled pride and a sense of purpose in those accepted to the IDF, particularly to combat units, but at the same time placed a lifelong stigma on those who were found unfit for service. And the latter could not take pride in having contributed in an alternative framework of civic national service. It was only with the introduction of the liberal ethos of rights and equality for all citizens that this injustice was recognized and remedied. This alternative ethos required equal access for those with special needs and equal opportunities with the enabled, which included the right to serve.

The placement of a small number of youth with disabilities in national service by the Shlomit agency in 1995 and its appeal to the High Court in 1996 on their behalf was the first stride in their struggle to serve. As part of the reassessment and redirection of Western society's attitudes toward people with disabilities at the end of the 20th century, new emphasis was placed on ensuring mobility and equal access to services and job equality rather than care, dependence, and paternalism. It required breaking down stereotypes and taking note of capabilities rather than limitations. This change toward greater inclusion evolved over time in Israel as well, supported by organizations in the third sector and by philanthropies devoted to the advancement and social integration of people with disabilities and special needs. Civic national service was an important milestone in this process.

This dualism of ensuring equality for these youth and the promotion of republican values of service found expression in the national civic service law adopted by the Knesset in 2017. Youth with disabilities, youth at risk, and disadvantaged youth were incorporated into the law. This inclusion was a step toward achieving greater integration of these youth into Israeli society by giving them the opportunity to serve.

In the next chapter we will take a close look at the Haredi sector in Israel and its attitudes toward service, both military and civic. We will explore how the policy of draft deferments for yeshiva students came into being, which in effect exempted Haredim from all forms of service, and the difficulties faced by Israeli governments when they attempted to alter this policy. Most importantly, we will assess to what extent amendments to the defense law and rulings by the Israel High Court of Justice have succeeded in getting Haredim to serve in civic national service and in the military.

5

The Haredim

Will a Communitarian Approach Bring Them to Serve?

As discussed in previous chapters, the republican ethos of citizenship was shared by most Israeli Jews in the period after independence. The new nascent state could not meet its objectives of absorbing immigration, building an economy, and providing security without the willingness of its citizens to contribute and sacrifice. From the start Israel faced serious security challenges on its borders, which required the institution of three years of mandatory military service as well as long-term service in the reserves. The "citizen-soldier" became a significant component of Israel's national culture. The obligation to serve was clearly a survival requirement that needed little explanation or justification. Those who fell in service were commemorated as heroes for they gave their lives so that Israel could survive.[1]

While military service strengthened the republican ethos and generated bridging social capital among those that served, those who did not serve remained "outsiders," apart from society. This was certainly true of Arab citizens who were not called to service and was true as well of the ultra-orthodox sector, known in Hebrew as Haredim, those who are God-fearing. The Haredim in Israel number about 1,000,000 and compose approximately 14 percent of the Jewish population.[2] They are rigorous in their religious observance and endogamous in their marriage patterns. They reside in separate neighborhoods, and generally avoid contact with secular culture and the popular media.[3] Most do not engage in secular studies and only a small minority have academic degrees.[4]

For many years, the overwhelming majority of Haredim in Israel did not serve in the military nor was civic national service open to them. Since 1948, conscription regulations permitted a limited number of students in religious seminaries (yeshivas) to defer service on a yearly basis, while they engaged in Torah study. After the Likud came to power in 1977, limitations were lifted on the number of yeshiva students receiving deferments, creating the anomalous situation where the overwhelming majority of Haredi males ages 18 to 34 avoided conscription completely. By 2009, the number of yeshiva students deferred from service had reached 54,300. In 2015, 64,605 were deferred from service.[5]

This "carte blanche" that in effect exempted Haredim from service became an issue of contention in Israeli politics and a major cause of hostility and resentment toward the community.[6] To choose not to serve is regarded by most Israelis as shirking one's republican obligation to the state and to society, particularly in light of the country's continual state of war and the many soldiers who have lost their lives in the line of duty (about 22,000). Most Israelis resent this differentiation "between blood and blood" and argue that the sacrifice must be shared by all sectors. Moreover, because yeshiva students with deferments are not permitted to work during their studies, support for them and for their relatively large families fell on the government, which gave them subsidies and grants at the taxpayers' expense. The Haredim's long-standing refusal to share the burden of conscription or to do any alternative service remains a continual source of tension between religious and secular Jews in Israel, and impacts their social and economic integration into Israeli society.[7] Successive Israeli governments, the Knesset, and the High Court of Justice have wrestled with this question with limited success.

It is important to clarify from the start that our discussion here will pertain to Haredi men alone and not to women. Haredi women were excused from military service in the Defense Service Law of 1949 for reasons of religiosity and since that time do not participate in any form of service. As seen in chapters 2 and 3 Haredi rabbis opposed civic national service for religious women, which they thought would lead to sin. Haredi women were expected to live sheltered lives, first under the jurisdiction of their fathers, later that of their husbands. They were expected to finish high school and then to attend perhaps a religious seminary, to marry early and raise a family, all within the community. In later years when Haredi women took upon themselves the burden of supporting the family, they went to work outside the home but in work environments that were religiously suitable. This was true in the first decades of the state and is just as true today. Since civic national service is voluntary and does not impact national security, their nonparticipation is not an issue of contention.[8]

In this chapter we will explore the complex issue of service for Haredi young men, both military and civic. It is important here to note that it is not possible to discuss civic national service for Haredim without placing it within the context of military service since in Israel military service is the primary obligation of citizens; civic national service as an option becomes a possibility only after being excused from the IDF. We will discuss the conscription policy of Haredim both in light of the change in ethos in Israeli society, from a dominant republican ethos of service to a more liberal egalitarian ethos, and how this change has impacted service policy. We shall see that there were several attempts by the government to adopt a service policy that would be politically viable and would meet the principles of equity stipulated by the High Court, but they failed. At the close of the chapter we will suggest that a communitarian approach to service may prove to be more constructive in order to advance Haredi integration into Israeli society and we will examine the possible pitfalls to such an approach.

In order to understand the current debate over service for Haredim, both military and civic, we must take a closer look at how Israeli conscription and deferment policy of Haredim evolved since the early years of the state.

"Blanket Deferments" to Haredim

In 1948, shortly before independence but still during the hostilities, leading Haredi rabbis approached the head of the Jewish Agency and the designated head of the Provisional Government, David Ben-Gurion, with a special request. They asked that yeshiva students be excused from army service so that they could continue their religious studies uninterrupted. Rabbi Avraham Yeshayahu Karelitz (the Hazon Ish) appealed to the prime minister's sense of historic justice, explaining that the deferments were critical to the very survival of Torah scholarship in light of the terrible decimation of the yeshivas in Eastern Europe in the Holocaust a short time earlier. Thousands of Torah scholars had been killed, leaving Torah scholarship all but destroyed. It was imperative for the Jewish people, he argued, that Torah study be restored. This could be accomplished only if yeshiva students would be allowed to engage in continuous study. Great scholars could not be produced if yeshiva students were obliged to interrupt their studies for three years in order to serve in the armed forces.

Ben-Gurion, in a historic decision, agreed to grant deferments to 400 yeshiva students, most of them married, providing they engaged in full-time study in a religious seminary. In March 1948 the Executive Committee of the Center for Service to the Nation authorized a temporary army service deferment for yeshiva students whose "occupation" was Torah study.[9] A second reason for exempting these yeshiva students was practicality. Many of them opposed Zionism and were against the establishment of a Jewish state, particularly those from the Old Yishuv and those affiliated with the Neturei Karta, an extremist ultra-orthodox group. It would have been a Sisyphean task to conscript them to the army by force, particularly during the war.[10]

It is clear that Ben-Gurion had no intention to exempt an entire sector of the population from military service. In fact, in the pre-state period and in the first decade of the state many who identified as Haredim served in the military. Evidence of this can be found in the records of the IDF from this period, where there are numerous requests by religious soldiers for kosher food and letters telling of their problems relating to Sabbath observance.[11]

The Labor government in 1968 decided to limit the number of yeshiva student deferments. It adopted a policy of quotas to curtail deferments to 800 a year and to limit the number of yeshivas recognized by the Ministry of Defense as eligible for this purpose. The Haredi party Agudat Yisrael was in the opposition at the time and so its angry protests had little effect. The election upset of May 1977 changed the political balance. The voters ejected Labor from power after almost 30 consecutive years in office. The Likud party headed by Menachem Begin formed the new government and Agudat Yisrael entered the coalition. The latter made the cancellation of the hated quotas a condition for entering. The quotas were canceled and were never reinstated. As a result, the number of yeshiva students with deferments climbed over the years. Deferments were also extended to others involved in religious work, teachers in yeshivas in the Haredi school system, municipal rabbis, and religious judges.[12] By 1980, the number of deferments had reached 10,000 and by 2009 it had reached over 54,000. Among all the eligible conscripts in 2009, 14 percent were deferred because of full-time yeshiva studies.[13]

Since the historic decision by Ben-Gurion to allow deferments to yeshiva students, the population of the Haredim has grown exponentially, and the number of students deferring service has multiplied as well. In effect, Torah study has become the "trade" of Haredi men. There were 114,000 Haredim ages 18 to 45 and older engaged in full-time Torah study in 2018.[14] In order to understand how the number of students grew, it is important to take a closer look at the Haredi community in Israel.

A "Society of Scholars"

Haredi life in Israel is centered in the yeshivas. That is where the yeshiva student spends most of his waking hours; it is an all-encompassing social framework. There he studies and prays and shares in community celebrations and misfortunes. The head of the yeshiva, a rabbi, has a dominant influence on the student's life. He is selected for his extensive knowledge of Jewish sources, primarily the Talmud, and for his proven commitment to living the exemplary life of a God-fearing Torah scholar. He is asked to rule on issues of Jewish law and is consulted by the students on important personal life decisions.

The Haredi community maintains its own separate network of educational institutions from pre-K to adulthood, segregated by gender. Much of its early success can be attributed to the 1953 national education law that established free mandatory education for all Israeli children, in separate state school networks, for secular, national-orthodox, and Haredi (the independent religious school network). Friedman attributes the "revolution" of the "society of scholars"[15] largely to the establishment of this separate and independent school system, which was funded by the state but controlled and supervised by Haredi rabbis who had a strong influence on its contents and tone.[16] Particularly in the first decades of the state, children who attended these schools were taught to observe Jewish law even more rigorously than did their parents, and boys were encouraged to continue their Torah studies long after high school. The rabbis set a very high standard, teaching their students that the true ideal of a Haredi Jew was to devote his life totally and exclusively to the study of Torah. Their parents, they were told, who generally worked for a living, were to be viewed as the victims of circumstance, not to be emulated. Accordingly, Haredi schools did not teach sciences, mathematics, English, or other secular subjects, and if taught at all, then only at the most rudimentary level, making their students grossly unprepared for the modern postindustrial job market. State high school matriculation requirements were not met and university studies were forbidden. This is still true in Haredi schools today. A recent report released by the Education Ministry in 2014 placed Haredi cities Bnei Brak, Beitar Elite, and Modiim Elite at the top of the list of Israeli cities with the lowest percentage of high school matriculation.[17]

Haredi males are expected to engage in Torah study from early childhood. After marrying young (the average marital age is 21), the yeshiva student continues full-time study in a *kollel*, a yeshiva for married men, where he can continue to study for as long as he wishes and where he will receive a monthly living allowance. These stipends are provided by government grants and by donations, primarily by Jews living abroad. Understandably, the representatives of the Haredi parties in the Knesset throughout the years have devoted their efforts toward obtaining increased government funding for these allowances that sustain thousands of yeshiva students and their families. In 2009–2010 there were 83,055 yeshiva students ages 19 to 45 and older, 20,000 were over the age of 40, 26,350 were ages 30 to 39, and 22,289 ages 25 to 29. Recent studies estimate that only 51 percent of Haredi men are employed.[18] (It should be noted that some may work part time and have unreported income.) This phenomenon of a "society of scholars," according to Friedman, is unprecedented in Jewish history and singular among ultra-orthodox communities worldwide.[19]

Women make an important contribution to the maintenance and strengthening of the "society of scholars." They are educated in a vast network of girls' schools, the largest being Beit Yaakov, that extends from kindergarten to teachers' seminaries. The girls are taught that the greatest virtue is to marry a Torah scholar (or a young man with the potential to be a Torah scholar) and it is their privilege to shoulder the burden of supporting the family while he continues his studies indefinitely. This is evidenced in the preference given to yeshiva students as prospective sons-in-law rather than young men who will work in a trade or profession.

Haredi women are encouraged to have large families[20] (the average number of births is 7.1 per woman)[21] and family planning is discouraged. Many found work teaching in the Haredi school system or in cottage industries in the home. In recent years, because opportunities to teach have become scarce as many more women seek jobs as teachers (50% of

Haredi women in 2016 were teachers, down from 65% in 2006),[22] Haredi women began to study technological subjects such as programming (10%) and have begun working in hi-tech companies where the salaries are higher and the opportunities for advancement greater. According to recent statistics, 74 percent of Haredi women work, many of them only part time.[23] Families also receive child support subsidies (as do all Israeli citizens) from National Insurance, sums that for very large families are substantial, and small stipends from the yeshiva. The main burden however falls on the women.[24]

Studying the Torah Is Our Service

As previously noted, the republican ethos prevailed in Israel during the first decades of the state and military service was an important component. Failure to serve was ideologically and socially unacceptable in the eyes of most Israelis. Haredi rabbis present an ontological justification for yeshiva students studying in yeshiva rather than serving in the military. They assert that it was the study of Torah throughout the ages that had ensured the existence of the Jewish people despite its afflictions. Its very survival then as well as today was dependent on the continual study of Torah. Torah study shields the Jewish people from adversity and is therefore as important for Jewish survival as service in the armed forces. The IDF may protect the physical existence of the Jews but the yeshivas ensure their soul. In order to assure Jewish survival, both must be maintained. It is their belief therefore that yeshiva students who are diligent in their studies are actually contributing to the national defense. Could anyone say to what one should attribute Israel's victories in war? Was it to the valor of the soldiers or was it due to the thousands of yeshiva students who study the Torah and pray to the Almighty for the welfare of Israel?[25]

The rabbis also equate the challenge of devoting one's entire day to the study of Torah to the rigors of army service. Studying Torah day and night is a difficult task; it too requires sacrifice, discipline, and dedication equal to if not greater than that of the soldiers.[26] This contention is actually a reformulation of the republican ethos. According to the rabbis, they who study Torah are fulfilling an obligation to society equal to if not greater than service in the military. Since many Jews do not study Torah, the obligation to maintain Torah study falls on the yeshiva students, who shoulder the "burden" for the rest of society. Needless to say, this argument enrages secular Israelis who find it all but impossible to equate the studies and prayers of yeshiva students to the contribution and sacrifice of combat soldiers.

Haredi rabbis discourage and even prohibit service in the IDF for other reasons as well. They fear that the conditions of service and the easy camaraderie with secular soldiers, male and female, will negatively influence the Haredi soldier and cause him to abandon his strict standard of observance. The easy mix between male soldiers and female, the rugged coarseness of the military environment, the threatening secular Zionist ideology that encouraged the conscript to disregard his past and become a new "Israeli," and the spiritual challenges facing the religious soldier in an environment of scoffers make conscription a serious challenge for the religiously observant in general and for the more sheltered Haredi in particular. Even separate units for Haredim would not protect them from the seductive influences of secular society. From the perspective of the rabbis, the only formula for religious continuity is to seclude young men in yeshivas, marry them off at a young age, and allow them only minimal contact with secular society. This isolation by choice is reinforced by maintaining separate neighborhoods and even having segregated whole towns (e.g., Beitar Elite, Elad, Modiin Elite, Emanuel) exclusive for Haredim.

In addition to the Haredi ethos that extols those who study the Torah, there was an important structural factor that had encouraged Haredi men in Israel to remain yeshiva students until 35 to 40 years of age and that was, paradoxically, the conscription policy itself. It is well known that Haredim in Israel differ significantly from ultra-orthodox communities in the Diaspora. Haredim in the United States and Western Europe generally end their studies in yeshiva in their mid-twenties and then go out to work. This however was not the case in Israel where approximately 50,000 men were still studying in yeshivas after the age of 30.

The difference between the communities rests in Israel's Defense Service Law first passed in 1949.[27] The law requires military service for all men and women age 18 (citizens and permanent residents) and authorizes the minister of defense to exempt from service those in specific categories, for example, Arab citizens, Druze women, married women, and religious Jewish women if they so request. Section 36 gave the defense minister the authority to give discretionary exemptions or deferments based on "reasons relating to the size of the IDF, or reasons of education, defense settlement, national economy, family or other reasons." Among "the other reasons" are requests by yeshiva students to defer service so they can continue their studies, students for whom "the Torah is their craft." The defense minister was authorized to defer their service on an individual basis, renewable each year. The conscription requirement applied to all males until age 35, with the actual length of service determined by the IDF in accordance with the age of the recruit, marital status, and number of children he has. If a Haredi wished to avoid the draft completely, which they did, he had to study in the yeshiva at least until age 35.[28] During that period he was prohibited from working (legally). In effect, the deferment policy combined with the stalwart determination of the Haredim not to serve created an entire society of long-term yeshiva students who did not work and lived in poverty off government stipends, child assistance, and the meager salaries of their wives.[29]

The Haredim were also poorly prepared for entering the workforce after ending yeshiva studies. Because of the limited general education offered in the Haredi school system, they lacked proficiency in mathematics and computers and had almost no knowledge of English. Their options for employment were limited to jobs relating to "religious studies" (teaching or editing) or to low-paying jobs that did not require formal education or skills. In 2003, 59 percent of the Haredim were living in poverty and only 36.9 percent of the men were employed (among them only 25% at full-time jobs) and 48.4 percent of the women.[30] In 2009, 55 percent were living in poverty (360,800 people, 57,500 families).[31] In 2018, there was an improvement because of changes that have taken place in the Haredi community, which will be discussed later. 45 percent were living in poverty.[32]

Family size was usually very large, averaging 7.1 children per family, a fertility rate almost three times that of the general Jewish population.[33] Families with 10 or even 14 children were not unusual. Understandably, the national insurance child allowances paid differentially for each additional child were an important source of income for these families. The size of these allowances fluctuated according to the policy of the ruling government coalition and was subject to negotiations. It was therefore important for the Haredi parties to belong to the government coalition. They often conditioned their membership on increased allocations for large families and larger stipends for yeshiva students. The decision of many men in the Haredi community not to be gainfully employed, and instead to live on government stipends and welfare, is seen by economists as a serious drain on Israel's economy and a factor holding back growth. This situation is even more worrisome in light of demographers' prediction that the Haredi sector will become a bigger portion of the population in the future because of its high birthrate. These two factors were among the motivating factors behind the government's interest in conscription reform.[34]

The deferments granted to the Haredim were challenged unsuccessfully in appeals to the High Court of Justice in the 1970s and 1980s. In the earlier appeals, the Court refused to intervene, ruling that the appellee lacked standing and because the Court considered the question of deferments to be a political matter that should be resolved by the legislature, not by the Court.[35] However, in 1986 a more activist High Court determined that it did have jurisdiction to hear the case. However, it ruled against the appellate, who argued that the defense minister abused his authority in granting deferments to yeshiva students. The Court decided that the minister had acted within the authority granted to him by law since the number of deferments, although on the rise, was still only 5.4 percent of the age 18 cohort. This percentage was still reasonable and as such within the discretionary authority of the defense minister. The Court warned, however, that it might amend its ruling in the future if the number of deferments kept rising.[36]

The mood in the country in the 1990s became increasingly hostile toward deferments for yeshiva students. This was a period of transition in the dominant ethos, from republican values of service and obligation to a more liberal ethos that placed the individual citizen at the center, his personal aspirations and success.

In the Knesset, members of the opposition parties proposed legislation to cancel the deferments entirely and to institute mandatory military or civic national service for all citizens, including Haredim.[37] The debate over deferments and service for all dominated the public discourse. Reservists organized several mass demonstrations to protest yeshiva deferments. They presented a different discourse than had been heard previously. They emphasized "sharing the burden" rather than contribution and sacrifice. Were they "suckers" to give three years of service while Haredim the same age sat and studied? The republican ethos that had extolled sacrifice and contribution was less popular in the late 1990s, particularly in the center of the country. The new discussion was clearly liberal, emphasizing equal rights and obligations for all citizens, and rejecting the special concessions made to the ultra-orthodox as a community.[38]

Several members of the Knesset, reserve military officers, and student organizations appealed again to the High Court in 1997 against the deferment policy (*Rubinstein v. Minister of Defense* 3267/97). They argued that the defense minister's authority to grant an unlimited number of deferments to yeshiva students was disproportionate and unreasonable since it violated the principle of equality. This time the Court decided to intervene and in a groundbreaking decision canceled the government's deferment policy. It ruled that the defense minister had in fact exceeded his authority when he had granted such a large number of deferments. This large number, now 7.4 percent of those age 18, was grossly inequitable, and as such unreasonable, wrote Chief Justice Aharon Barak for the majority, and exceeds his administrative authority. The Court assigned to the Knesset the task of remedying the situation in primary legislation that would regulate conscription, deferments, and exemptions more fairly. It accorded the Knesset one year to rewrite the legislation, and if it failed to do so, the Ministry of Defense would have to draft all yeshiva students.

To comply with the Court's ruling, Prime Minister Ehud Barak (Yisrael Ahat)[39] appointed a special government committee (the Tal Committee) to study the conscription issue in depth and to design legislation that would meet the requisites of the High Court. The ruling had brought relations with the Haredim to a crossroads, but it was also an opportunity for lawmakers to transform national service policy, military and civic. The lawmakers, as we will see, chose to proceed with caution and to introduce gradual change, rather than confront the Haredim head-on.

The Tal Law and the Introduction of Civic National Service for Haredim

The Tal Committee submitted its recommendations in April 2000, after hearing seven months of testimony. It accepted in principle that all citizens should be obliged to perform some form of service to society and it concurred with the High Court that the previous policy of unlimited deferments was inequitable. It noted that young artists, authors, athletes, scientists, and computer whizzes were all required to postpone fulfilling their personal goals and aspirations, their talents notwithstanding, and to serve.

At the same time, the committee accepted the IDF's caveat that conscription must be by consent. It was unrealistic to try to force 50,000 Haredim to serve against their will. If the government were to draft all Haredi men under 35, it would be met with violent protests and would cause a severe rupture with the community. A draft by force policy would serve neither the interests of the IDF (who would have to confront unwilling recruits) nor the nation.⁴⁰ Moreover, in their testimony before the committee, IDF top brass admitted that Israel's defense did not require drafting all yeshiva students. While it is true that an increase in the number of conscripts would allow the IDF to reduce the number of reservists called up each year, failure to induct them would not impact in any way Israel's defense capabilities.⁴¹ The committee therefore concluded that it was unrealistic to legislate a mandatory draft applicable to all that could not be implemented.

After hearing testimony from IDF generals past and present, economists at the Bank of Israel, rabbis, and representatives of nongovernmental organizations, the Tal Committee recommended that the existing deferment policy continue but with some modifications. It called on the IDF to create special programs designed for Haredim that will attract them to service and enable those who want to serve to be in a totally religious environment. Until then, there was only one small army program created in 1999 designed specifically for Haredim, the Nahal Haredi unit. This combat unit was composed of youth from Haredi homes who had dropped out of yeshiva studies and had been living on the margins of Haredi society.⁴² Soldiers in this unit were assigned only male instructors, provided with special glatt kosher food, given daily Torah classes, and were completely segregated from women soldiers and nonreligious recruits. The committee noted that while the Nahal Haredi program was a positive first step toward the inclusion of the Haredim in the military, the number of real hard-core Haredim serving in it was actually quite low.⁴³ Additional programs, although not necessarily in combat, were needed if the IDF was to increase conscription among the Haredim.

The committee gave considerable weight to the testimonies of sociologist Menachem Friedman and *Haaretz* journalist Shachar Ilan, both of whom had studied the Haredi community for decades. Both described the widespread poverty that pervaded the community as a result of the "society of scholars" and the heavy burden it placed on the national economy. The Israeli public paid high taxes not only for defense but also for the entitlements and stipends to yeshiva students. Friedman and Ilan suggested that many Haredim would end their studies sooner and would seek out gainful employment if not for the fear of conscription. Their testimony and that of others convinced the Tal Committee that the government must loosen the Gordian knot that had linked yeshiva study to deferments, in order to allow those who were not serious "Torah scholars" to serve briefly and then to go out to work.

The committee recommended continuing the policy of granting unlimited deferments for committed Torah scholars. No quotas would be set; no excellence standards would be required. The minister of defense should be authorized by law to grant deferments to those who engaged in full-time Torah study. And, as in the past, yeshiva students from age 18 would be allowed to defer army service until they reached the age or had the size family that would make them eligible for a full exemption. They would be required to reapply for the deferment each year at the draft office and would have to bring a letter from the head of their seminary attesting to their full-time studies.

The innovation proposed by the committee was at age 23. Students after age 22, and a minimum of four years of study at a yeshiva, would be allowed a "year of decision" during which time they could leave the yeshiva and study secular subjects, work or engage in vocational training, without endangering their entitlement to a draft deferment. The deferment would be placed on hold for a year. At the end of the year, the students would have a choice of three courses of action: to resume their studies at the yeshiva and regain their draft deferment; to serve in the IDF for an abbreviated tour of duty, dependent on their family status;[44] or to serve a year in civic national service, which would be recognized as an alternative to military service. While serving in civic national service, they would be permitted to work or study part time.[45]

The proposed "year of decision" was based on studies brought before the committee of the work/study patterns of ultra-orthodox young men in Great Britain and in the United States. The studies showed that in both countries the men married young and by ages 24 to 25 most leave their yeshiva studies in order to go out to work or to study. The main reason Haredim in Israel followed a different pattern and studied in yeshivas until age 40 was the draft law. If the threat of the draft were removed, Haredim in Israel would leave yeshiva studies earlier and would join the workforce.[46]

The "year of decision" was intended to test this hypothesis. Yeshiva students could try "life outside" the yeshiva without endangering their draft deferment. If the IDF and civic national service would set up supervised "kosher" programs for Haredim where the "spiritual dangers" would be mitigated, more of them may choose to serve. The ultimate goal was to encourage more Haredim to leave a life of study and to join the workforce. Service in the military and in civic service would serve a dual purpose: it would have them serve the country like others their age and would also be a transition or training period to prepare them for academic studies or employment.

The Tal Committee made far-reaching recommendations regarding civic national service. As we saw in previous chapters, civic national service had been an option open only to religious girls. Boys and girls excused by the IDF were able to do civic national service only in 2001. The Tal Committee proposed expanding civic national service to include Haredi men. Married yeshiva students over the age of 26 would be offered the option of doing one year of civic national service in their communities instead of service in the IDF. Service could be done in health, welfare, firefighting, and remedial education, all within a suitable religious environment. The committee took special care to uphold the primacy of the IDF. Single men ages 18 to 26 and married men under the age of 26 with only one child would be ineligible for civic national service, unless they were excused by the IDF on a case-by-case basis.

The government accepted the committee's recommendations and the so-called Tal Law (its full title, The Service Deferment Law for Yeshiva Students for Whom "the Torah Is Their Trade") was passed by the Knesset in July 2002, for a provisional period of five years, at which time it was to be reassessed. The law disappointed secular activists who had hoped that it would put an end to deferments for yeshiva students. MK Yosef Lapid, from the secularist Shinui party, called the law "a law for shirkers." Meretz MK Mussi Raz derided the law, saying that it basically claimed that "Haredi blood is redder than secular." A new student movement called Hit'orerut (Awakening) organized in protest.

Haredi rabbis had a mixed reaction. On the one hand they were relieved that it had allowed the existing deferment policy to continue without quotas or selectivity. Those who wished to study could continue to do so without fear of conscription. However, they were not happy about the "year of decision" offered to yeshiva students.[47] They saw this as part of a diabolical government plan to induce yeshiva students to leave their studies, which in fact it was. They feared that the "year of decision" and the attractive option of one year of civic national service instead of military service would open the floodgates for those contemplating leaving the yeshiva.

The Haredi newspaper *Yated Neeman* condemned the proposals as a "dangerous precedent. . . . a diminution of the value of Torah" and as a plan "to promote their assimilation into secular society." Posters in Haredi neighborhoods accused the committee of "bringing a Holocaust" (*sic*) upon the world of the yeshivas.[48]

In effect, the Tal Law sowed the seeds of a more communitarian approach toward citizenship and its obligations. Rather than adopting a liberal, culture-blind policy of service equality that would have forced the Haredim to serve as called for by the reservists or reinstating the hated quota system enacted by the Labor Party in the 1960s and 1970s, the committee chose to accommodate the community and to offer it alternatives that respected its norms and values and yet allowed for the beginning of change. By providing yeshiva students with the options of a shortened military service or one year of civic national service in a Haredi environment, it encouraged those contemplating leaving their yeshiva studies to do so without fear. At the same time, serious students who wished to continue to study would not have to worry about the draft. While it did not satisfy those who wanted an egalitarian conscription policy, it did offer new avenues for gradual change within the Haredi community.

Implementation of the Tal Law: The Government "Drags Its Feet"

The implementation of the Tal Law got off to a slow start. Neither the government nor the Haredim were particularly eager to set up the new programs. With some of the political pressure off, and with the High Court temporarily contained, the government headed by Ariel Sharon did little to establish a civic service program for Haredim, nor did it allocate it any funds.[49] It also did not take steps to publicize the provisions of the Tal Law within the Haredi community. Most yeshiva students were unaware that they were now being offered a "year of decision," to leave their studies for a year without losing their deferments. Haredi newspapers too did not report the new options.[50] The few who knew about the program and asked about it at the draft office were told to leave their names and contact information and then nothing happened.

The government was slow to create the administrative infrastructure needed to operationalize the civic service program. In 2004 the minister of defense appointed yet another committee (the Ivri Committee) to study how to implement civic national service in the Haredi community. It issued its recommendations in 2006 (four years after the Tal Law was passed) after over a year of discussions. It too concluded that while mandatory service, military or civic, for all citizens, was in fact the optimal policy, it would not be feasible, given the strong opposition in the Haredi sector.

It recommended instead that the government establish a separate track of civic service for Haredi men, the prototype being the veteran program of voluntary national service for religious girls. Innovatively, the Ivri Committee also recommended setting up a separate track of voluntary service for Arabs, a development we will discuss at length in chapter 6. Most importantly, it recommended establishing a quasi-independent agency to administer all three tracks of service, religious girls and youth excused from the IDF, Haredim, and Arabs.[51]

The government adopted the Ivri Committee recommendations in December 2006 and began their implementation in August 2007. It established the Administration for National-Civic Service (ANCS) in the Prime Minister's Office and allocated funds for 200 civic service placements for Haredim.[52] The Knesset in 2007 extended the Tal Law for another five years. The government's delay in operationalizing the Tal Law provoked petitions to the High Court. An impatient High Court, in 2007, unimpressed by the government's halfhearted steps to implement the law, warned that it would nullify the law in the future if the government failed to significantly increase the number of Haredim inducted to the IDF and serving in civic national service.[53]

After the reprimand of the High Court, the IDF accelerated its implementation of the Tal Law. It expanded the Nahal Haredi combat unit Netzach Yehuda from one company to two.[54] Taking note of the growing number of yeshiva students studying in evening programs in computer programming,[55] it established technology units for Haredim where the skills they would gain in service would be an advantage when seeking employment after service. The IDF set up a program called "Shachar," a Hebrew acronym meaning "integrating Haredim," made up of technology-related programs in the air force, navy, intelligence, and logistics corps. Only married Haredim ages 22 to 27 who completed four years of yeshiva study were eligible to apply.[56] The programs also included intensive remedial courses in English and mathematics to close the gaps in Haredi education.

"Blue Dawn," for example, is the technology program established by the air force for Haredim. Recruits complete basic training and are then given short remedial courses in mathematics, English, and computers, followed by courses in electronics, computer programming, and information systems. Others are trained as technicians and mechanics and then assigned to maintain the most sophisticated aircraft and weapons systems of the air force.[57] Similar courses for Haredim were offered by the navy, and by military intelligence. The IDF Logistics Corps trained Haredim as auto mechanics, truck drivers, and electricians.⁵⁸ The conscripts were permitted to live at home in all of these programs and were provided with a "sterile" work environment, that is, no contact with women soldiers.

The soldiers in the Shachar programs, all of whom are married with families, receive a generous living allowance from the IDF during their service. It is estimated that the cost of a Shachar soldier is double the cost of a regular conscript, estimated to be about 9,500 shekels a month in 2013 compared to 4,000 shekels paid to a regular conscript serving in a noncombat unit.⁵⁹ Take-home pay was estimated at seven times the pay of a regular conscript.⁶⁰ In 2016 there were 2,850 Haredi conscripts serving in the IDF, 805 in the Shachar programs.⁶¹

Civic Service in the Haredi Community, 2007–2012

The civic national service program had mixed results at best. On the positive side, the Administration for National-Civic Service became an operational unit with significant funding. Haredim serving in civic service were paid a monthly allowance in accordance with their family situation, a sum significantly higher than that which was paid to religious girls. At the outset, in order to induce non-profits to accept Haredi volunteers, the government promised them extra funding.⁶² To induce them to serve, Haredim were given the option of serving full-time (40 hours a week) for one year or half-time, 20 hours a week spread over two years. The latter option allowed them to work while doing service, to continue their studies in yeshiva, or to learn a vocation.

The ANCS faced a formidable challenge marketing civic service in the Haredi community. Unlike religious girls who were motivated by Zionist republican values, a sense of commitment, and a desire to contribute, most of the Haredim rejected the Zionist discourse and had strong reservations about service to the secular state. Some viewed their service as *hesed* (a charitable deed); others had clear instrumental goals, that is, to do some easy type of civic service so that they would have on their record that they had "served." With this, they could go out to work without penalty and without the threat of conscription.⁶³

The ANCS chose a low-key marketing strategy and refrained from advertising the program in Haredi neighborhoods in order to prevent a backlash. Leaflets describing civic service options were made available at the military recruitment centers but were not distributed in yeshivas or synagogues. The ANCS avoided all publicity, both good and bad. It purposely did not approach prominent rabbis in the Haredi community for their approval for fear that they would issue a directive forbidding all service. Recruitment was done mostly by word of mouth and the rabbis' approval was achieved quietly, on a case-by-case basis.[64]

The ANCS framed the program differently in the Haredi sector in order to reduce the ideological antagonism to service. It rebranded the Haredi program "civic service" rather than "national" service in order to disassociate it from nationalism or Zionism.[65] It also conceded to the rabbis that most of the placements would be in Haredi communities or in Haredi nonprofit organizations,[66] under the most stringent religious standards. For example, a Haredi would not be assigned to service in a general Israeli hospital so that he would not be required to assist a female patient. He would be placed instead in Laniado hospital in Netanya, which is under Haredi auspices. Haredim were placed as counselors in Haredi institutions for disturbed youth, in children's homes, and in programs to assist Haredim that were elderly, handicapped, or mentally impaired. They were also assigned to charity organizations run by Haredim that provide meals and food packages for the needy and to other programs serving the Haredi community. This insular range of placements failed to achieve one of the fundamental goals of civic service, the creation of bridging social capital between groups in Israeli society.[67]

Nonetheless, the seeds of change began to take root in the Haredi community, albeit slowly. The overwhelming majority of yeshiva students (51,000) in 2009 chose to continue their studies and to defer service as before. Only 3,800 yeshiva students took advantage of the "year of decision" in 2003–2009, 1,254 served an abbreviated period in the IDF, and 1,752 served in civic service. This was indeed slow progress, but it is important here to note that social change takes time if it is to be achieved without coercion. The number of Haredim serving in the military and civic service did increase each year. The insular community that had shunned all forms of service now had several thousand families with a member that had served in the military or in civic service. This could cause a ripple effect in the community, generating a change in attitude toward the state and its institutions and toward service. Moreover, studies among those who served in either civic service or in the military indicated that a greater percentage of those who had served then went out to work than among those who did not, giving support to the Tal Law's premise that service would lead more Haredim to enter the job market.[68]

Policy Displacement and Confrontation: The High Court Intervenes

Opponents of the Tal Law petitioned the High Court again in August 2009, challenging its constitutionality. The Court decided not to intervene but warned the government that it would strike down the law in the future if it failed to achieve greater equality. In effect it put the government on notice that failure to significantly increase the number of Haredim who serve will invite High Court intervention.

In February 2012, the Court did just that. In response to yet another petition against the Tal Law, an expanded panel of justices struck down the law 6 to 3 on constitutional grounds, and ruled that it could not be extended after August 2012 (*Resler v. Knesset*, HCJ 6298/07). Chief Justice Dorit Beinish, writing for the majority, criticized the law's design and the results achieved. She expressed the Court's disappointment with the low number of Haredim serving in the IDF in 2011 (1,280) and in civic service (1,070) and at the very limited progress that had been made since the law was passed. While she recognized the need to proceed gradually and cautiously on this particularly volatile issue, she concluded that the law had failed to achieve a *reasonable* rate of change.

The Tal Law, Beinish concluded, was inequitable and therefore unconstitutional, in violation of the Basic Law: Human Dignity and Liberty, which required equality before the law. Tens of thousands of yeshiva students were still receiving deferments and only a very small number chose to serve. While the chief justice acknowledged that some progress had been made and that the number of recruits in both the military and in civic service was increasing each year, it was far from sufficient. The low numbers were the result of inherent flaws in the law and not due only to the slow and faulty implementation by the government, which admittedly was also a contributing factor. The Court determined that the law in effect perpetuated a policy that discriminated against the many soldiers who do serve. While the Court recognized that the issue was complex, where two fundamental rights conflict, the right to freedom of religion and the right to equality, as derived from human dignity protected under Israel's Basic Law, it ruled that, in this case, the right to equality must take precedence.

It is interesting to take note of the view of the three justices in the minority. While they shared their colleagues' dissatisfaction with the limited progress achieved under the Tal Law, they concluded that it was too early to determine that the law was a failure. They emphasized that societal changes take time and would not be achieved overnight. In their view, more time was needed before the effectiveness of the law could be determined, particularly since for the first five years after the law was passed the government did little to expedite its implementation.

By nullifying the Tal Law, the High Court in effect compelled the government to adopt a more aggressive approach, a move that foretold a head-on confrontation with the Haredim. Israel held elections in January 2013. A new party, Yesh Atid, headed by journalist and television personality Yair Lapid, entered the political fray with a strident campaign against yeshiva student deferments and stipends. Lapid framed his party as the party of the secular middle class that was fed up with the government's continual sellout to the Haredi parties. He excoriated the government's reluctance to confront the Haredim, end their deferments, and reduce their dependency on government handouts. His message was clear: young, educated, secular, middle-class Israelis had been shouldering an unfair share of the military burden for far too long and had been paying the lion's share of taxes. The government must change its priorities and stop subsidizing those who do not work, that is, the Haredim, and instead strengthen the secular middle class who contributes most to society. Lapid's message was directed at young secular couples who worked hard but could not finish the month without debt, not to mention buying an apartment. He pledged that if elected, Yesh Atid would not sit in the government with the Haredi parties.

Lapid's message struck a chord among middle-class secular Israelis. Yesh Atid garnered 19 seats and became the second largest party in the Knesset, a meteoric achievement for a new party. Benjamin Netanyahu (Likud–Yisrael Beteinu), with 31 seats, formed a coalition with Yesh Atid and with the religious Zionist party Habayit Hayudi (12 seats), and for the first time in 25 years left the Haredi parties Shas (11 seats) and Yahadut Hatorah (7 seats) in the opposition. Lapid became minister of finance. He immediately announced that he would cut stipends to yeshiva students and reduce child allowances to large families, many of whom were Haredi.[69]

Military and Civic Service for Haredim: Service Law #2

The new government was left without a law regarding conscription and deferments after the Tal Law expired in August 2012. Prime Minister Benjamin Netanyahu appointed a special ministerial committee (the Peri

Committee) to write a new law. It held hearings, consulted experts, and put together legislation that was more far-reaching than the previous law. The Knesset approved the new law, Amendment 19 to the Defense Service Law ("The Equal Sharing of the Burden" Law) in February 2014, by a vote of 67 to 1. The opposition, including the Haredi parties Yahadut HaTorah and Shas, boycotted the vote.

Amendment 19 introduced a new concept to conscription policy, one of collective community responsibility. Unlike the Tal Law that had related to the individual yeshiva student and had presented each with several options (a year of decision, military service, civic service, or to continue yeshiva studies), the new law related to the Haredim as a community and placed on it the collective responsibility to provide a target number of recruits to both civic national service and to the military. Community leaders, that is, rabbis and yeshiva heads, would determine who should continue to study and who should serve. If the quotas were not met, the minister of defense would have the authority to conscript all but a few select yeshiva students and to penalize those who failed to comply.

Conscription targets were not something new. Already in 2013 the government had set nonmandatory conscription targets for Haredim, 2,000 men in the military and 1,300 in civic service. The targets were increased each year, reaching 5,200 in 2016, 3,200 to the military and 2,000 to civic service. New were the punitive sanctions that would be applied if the community failed to comply. This new "community approach" should not be seen as a step toward greater communitarianism in Israel. Instead of encouraging the integration of the community into society, as central to a communitarian approach, it instead put the community on notice that it would be collectively responsible and collectively punished if it did not meet the dictates of the majority.

Amendment 19 included two periods of adjustment. During the first period (2014–2017), there would be no punitive actions taken if the conscription targets were not met. However, if during the second period (2018–2021) the targets were not met, the minister of defense would have the authority to draft all yeshiva students over the age of 21 and to apply punitive sanctions to those who refused to comply.

There were innovations in the law that negatively impacted civic national service. During the first period of adjustment, yeshiva students who would be age 22 and older when the law came into effect (March 20, 2014) would be given a full exemption from all service, unless they *chose* to serve in civic national service or in the military. The rationale for this provision was the government's real interest in encouraging Haredim to enter the workforce. Since these men would be exempted from service anyway when conscription targets became mandatory if they studied in yeshiva until age 26, the framers of the law decided they should be offered the option of leaving their studies without penalty already at age 22. This new policy gave hundreds of men ages 22 to 26 carte blanche already in 2014 to do no service at all (men who would have been required to serve under the Tal Law). Also under Amendment 19, younger yeshiva students ages 18 to 22 on the day the law went into effect (March 20, 2014) would be eligible for a complete exemption from army or civic service if they continued to study until age 24. If they left their studies before age 24, they would be required to serve in the army or in civic service. In effect, the law gave wholesale exemption to all yeshiva students over age 24 during the first adjustment period, 2014–2017.

During the second adjustment period (2017–2020) Haredi youth ages 18 to 21 could study in yeshiva, the targets notwithstanding.[70] After age 21 their deferments would be conditioned on whether the targets set by the government were met. If there was sufficient conscription among Haredim, the defense minister was authorized to defer the service of others. If the target were not met, the defense minister would be required to conscript all yeshiva students ages 21 to 26 except for the 1,800 top scholars recommended by the rabbis. Those the IDF determined not suitable for military service would be obliged to do two years of civic national service instead. The law included criminal sanctions, including imprisonment, for those yeshiva students who refused to appear before military authorities when called.[71]

The Haredim were incensed by Amendment 19, particularly at the criminal penalties for noncompliance. A very embittered MK Moshe Gafni of the Yahadut HaTorah party declared after the law was passed:

> The Haredi sector will not forget and will not forgive Netanyahu and his partners for the harm they have caused it, for the public attack on Torah scholars and the damage done to the delicate relations that had existed between the different sectors. This is a black day for the state and for this evil government. No yeshiva student will enlist in the army, not today and not in the future.[72]

The law was denounced by the Haredim and several prominent rabbis forbade compliance. Rabbi Shmuel Auerbach, leader of the so-called

Jerusalem faction (an estimated 10–15% of Lithuanian Haredim[73]) called for acts of civil disobedience. He instructed his students not to report to the induction office when called up, not even to register for deferments. Auerbach directed them to go to jail rather than comply and lauded imprisonment "as an act of heroism that would sanctify the name of God."[74]

The debate over the law deepened the schism within the Lithuanian faction of Haredim that had begun with the death of Rabbi Yosef Shalom Elyashiv and the ensuing succession struggle, a struggle that Auerbach had lost to Rabbi Aharon Leib Steinman. Rabbi Steinman, although also opposed to the law, instructed his students to comply with the law and to report when called, hoping that the Haredi parties after the next elections would return in even greater force to the government and cancel the law. Mass demonstrations were organized by Haredim against the law, the largest of which was a mass prayer vigil and demonstration of 300,000 held in Jerusalem.[75]

While the immediate impact of the law on the Haredi community was negligible since the quotas and penalties in the law were scheduled to take effect only in 2017, it generated much anger and hostility within the community. If under the Tal Law there had been slow but gradual change, with more Haredim starting to serve in the IDF and in civic national service, the new law with its threat of forced inductions and sanctions reversed much of the progress that had been made. Haredi soldiers in uniforms were threatened and even attacked physically in their neighborhoods. They faced verbal abuse; Haredi children called them a new epithet, *hardakim*, an acronym that stood for "a Haredi who is feeble minded." Dolls portraying Haredi soldiers were hung in effigy in Mea Shearim, a Jerusalem neighborhood inhabited by the more extreme Haredi sects.[76]

Huge banners were hung on streets in Haredi neighborhoods, warning Haredi soldiers not to enter. They read, "Have you become weak? Have you fallen into the hands of the army? Do not enter our neighborhood with your repulsive uniform!" "Banishing the hardakim is the only guarantee we have to save our children" was written at the bottom.[77] Army recruiters who were themselves Haredi faced threats of violence; their names and pictures were plastered on billboards that labeled them "dangerous traitors."[78]

Secular Israelis who had hoped for a more far-reaching conscription law were also disappointed by Amendment 19, particularly because it was rife with exemptions. They realized that only a small percentage of the Haredim would actually be required to serve and then only starting in 2020.[79] The enlistment target of 5,200 set by the government for both civic and military service together included a broad range of ages and would impact only 13 percent out of an estimated 40,000 yeshiva students ages

21 to 26. Moreover, it was clear from past experience that many of the so-called Haredim who did serve in the IDF were not in fact "hard core" but those who had been raised Haredi but were not Haredi today. The designation of a recruit as "Haredi" was determined by his having been registered for two years in a "Haredi" secondary school and not by the extent of his religious observance upon conscription.[80] If the targets would be filled with former Haredim, the law would change little.

Amendment 19 offered yeshiva students the option of doing civic national service starting at age 21. However, there was no statute that stipulated the terms of civic service, its regulations and benefits, nor were there legislative guidelines regulating the participating agencies. In March 2014, the Knesset passed the National Civic Service Law relating specifically to civic service in the Haredi community. The law gave statutory status to the Administration for National-Civic Service, henceforth to be called the Authority for National-Civic Service. The law branded the tracks for Haredim "civic" service rather than national service in deference to the stance of many of the Haredim against Zionism and Jewish nationalism. It required those conscripted to the IDF and then excused from service to serve two years in civic service, rather than one year as required previously under the Tal Law. It included two tracks of service: civic service in social services[81] or civic service in defense-related services, in intelligence, prisons, police, fire, or health and rescue services. Those in the social services would be required to complete 30 hours of service per week for a period of two years or 20 hours of service per week for three years, the latter plan offering the option of working or studying in yeshiva during part of the day. Those signing up for the defense track were required to complete 36 hours of service per week for two years and would receive a higher stipend. They would receive professional training that would be useful in finding employment after service, often in the same organization. Placements in the social service track were mainly in Haredi welfare organizations that serve the general public or in government offices that serve the community. In both tracks, married men with families would receive a larger monthly allowance than those who were single.[82]

The Haredim Return to the Government: Service Law #3

As Haredi leaders had hoped, Prime Minister Benjamin Netanyahu called new elections less than two years after taking office, claiming that the coalition with Yesh Atid was unsustainable. After the election, Netanyahu turned to the Haredi parties Yahadut HaTorah and Shas to form a government without the secular Yesh Atid party. Predictably, the Haredi parties conditioned their joining the government with the removal of the noxious sanctions clause in Amendment 19 within six months and postponing the law's implementation. Additionally, they demanded that the defense minister be given discretionary authority to grant deferments to yeshiva students even if induction targets would not be met entirely. Netanyahu agreed to their terms and a government was formed.

In March 2015, the Knesset passed revisions to the defense law (Amendment 21) in accordance with the promises made to the Haredi parties. The first adjustment period when targets would not be mandatory was extended for three more years until 2020; the second period, with mandatory targets, would take effect in 2020 and then only for three years.[83] Amendment 21 in effect postponed implementation of the law until after the tenure of the government. It also assigned discretionary authority to the defense minister to decide whether to draft yeshiva students if the quotas were not met. Clearly this authority would allow coalition politics to influence his decision. Finally, the criminal sanctions clause was removed from the law.

The results were to be expected. If in 2014 after the Tal Law was not renewed 18,900 yeshiva students had received deferments from military service, in 2016 the numbers deferred or exempted reached 26,000 and in 2017, 37,200, an increase of 43 percent over the previous year. Despite the angry rhetoric of Haredi leaders against Amendments 19 and 21, in reality a greater number of yeshiva students were in fact able to defer service under the new laws or to be exempted from service completely.[84] The gap between the "non-mandatory targets" set by the government and the number of Haredim actually serving in the IDF and in national service widened as fewer yeshiva students chose to serve.[85]

The High Court Intervenes Again, September 2017

The Movement for Quality Government, the Forum for the Equal Burden of Service, the Yesh Atid party, and the Israel Students' Union filed petitions to the High Court asking that Amendments 19 and 21 be struck down because they perpetuated the inequitable system of deferments and exemptions given to yeshiva students.[86] The High Court chose to respond to all the petitions together (September 2017). An expanded panel of nine justices ruled almost unanimously (8 to 1) to strike down Amendments 19 and 21 because they continued and even widened the inequality between those who serve and the Haredim. The Court stated the obvious: the latest version of the law would increase the burden on those who serve, quite the opposite of its stated intent and the grounds for its constitutionality.

The Court reasoned that the law's discriminatory aspects could be justified only if they were necessary to achieve a higher purpose. If the inequality allowed in the law (deferments for some yeshiva students) would result in a greater number of Haredim serving in the military and civic service, then its inequities would have been acceptable under clause 8 of the Basic Law: Human Dignity and Liberty. (Clause 8 prohibits a violation of rights except by a law "befitting the values of the State of Israel, enacted for a proper purpose and to an extent no greater than is required.") However, Amendments 19 and 21 will create even greater inequality in conscription and will not achieve a higher purpose.

In the majority opinion, Chief Justice Miriam Naor carefully reviewed the enlistment numbers among Haredim since Amendment 19 had taken effect in 2014 and concluded that it had achieved the opposite of what was intended. Fewer Haredim than anticipated had enlisted in the IDF and in civic national service; the targets set by the government were not met. While the Court recognized that a law that would eliminate all yeshiva student deferments would be unrealistic and unenforceable in current circumstances and while it understood and valued the study of Torah in a Jewish state, it could not overlook the serious discriminatory aspects of the law. In effect, Amendments 19 and 21 had increased the number of yeshiva students exempted from service. And the elimination of punitive sanctions had removed the pressure on the yeshivas to meet the enlistment targets. The amendments also failed to stipulate what would happen in 2023 when the law was scheduled to expire. This, in the view of the Court, exposed the real motivation of the government: to "buy time" and avoid conflict rather than to confront the equality issue head-on. The Court, wrote the chief justice, had no choice but to invalidate the law. It gave the Knesset a period of one year to devise a law that was more equitable.[87]

The revoking of the law by the court created even greater ferment and anger in the Haredi community. Rabbi Shmuel Auerbach who had led the protests against the law in 2014 again urged his students to go out and demonstrate and to ignore their induction notices. When his students were arrested, he declared them "martyrs in the struggle for the Torah." Many of the demonstrations turned violent; police and protestors were injured. There were also more incidents of Haredi soldiers being physically attacked in Haredi neighborhoods.

This researcher interviewed the administrators of the civic service program for Haredim at the Administration for National-Civic Service in 2009 when the Tal Law was in effect and again at the Authority in 2018. While the directors of the program had not changed, their perspective and mood had altered considerably. In 2009 the directors saw the program as full of promise and took pride in describing how they succeeded in enlisting hundreds of Haredi volunteers to civic service. They expressed confidence that civic service would have a significant impact on Haredi integration into Israeli society and their entrance into the workforce. In 2018 they were noticeably devoid of enthusiasm and cynical. They were resigned to a diminishing number of volunteers, which, in their view, was a consequence of the annulment of the Tal Law by the High Court, the adoption of Amendments 19 and 21, and their subsequent annulment by the Court. In their view, the Tal Law had started a path of positive change, sowed the seeds of a revolution, and its invalidation by the Court had caused a serious setback whose effect they see up until today. The number of Haredim joining civic service declined significantly starting in 2015. Only half of the expected number of volunteers signed up.[88] In 2016 only 70 young men signed up each month, less than 900 for the year. This was a far cry from the target of 2,000 set by the government.

Amendment 19 had put a spoke in the wheel of civic national service, because it offered full exemption from all service at age 24. Moreover, the threat of criminal sanctions had succeeded in uniting the Haredi community against service and put strong pressure on those who intended to serve to reconsider. The dire warnings of the ANCS administrators to lawmakers that the proposed amendments would totally undermine civic service had failed to prevent their adoption. The sharp reduction in the number of volunteers therefore was to have been expected.[89]

Avinoam Meir, the administrator of Haredi programs at the ANCS pointed to some additional factors that discouraged civic service. Those who did serve saw military service as a more attractive option since it gave valuable job training and held promise for future employment in industry and hi-tech. For married recruits with families, the living allowances paid by the IDF were substantially higher than what they were offered in civic service, particularly in the social services track.[90]

An exposé that appeared in the national daily *Yediot Ahronot* in March 2018 exposed serious irregularities in civic service in the Haredi sector.

Not surprisingly, there were many cases of absenteeism, false reporting, and misuse of funds in some of the social service programs. Investigators found duplicity and collusion between the "volunteers" and the organizations where they had been placed to serve. Several organizations allowed participants to not show up at all or to come to work only on the days when there was an inspection by the supervisors from the placement agency. The "volunteer" was registered in civic service and as such was eligible for subsidies for day care, free public transportation, a reduction in property taxes, and at the end of service to receive a stipend and benefits amounting to 17,000 to 24,000 shekels; yet he did no service at all or just minimal service. He would also have on his record that he had completed civic service, which would give him an added advantage when seeking employment. There were cases where the organization pocketed a participant's living allowance in return for his not having to serve or divided it with him half and half. In some cases, "volunteers" received the allowances and benefits while continuing to study full-time in yeshiva, civic service being just another scheme to gain an additional stipend from the government.[91] These irregularities were able to take place beneath the radar of the Authority because of its lack of supervisory personnel and the derogation of service by the volunteers and their organizations where they served.[92]

Another blow to civic service came from the rabbis. In January 2018, the Rebbe of the Gerer Hassidim, the largest of Hassidic sects, issued a ruling forbidding his male followers under the age of 30 from serving in the police or in paramedical services, such as Magen David Adom and Hatzala, because, he said, the conditions of service were unsuited to the Haredi lifestyle. He alleged that some of those who served had experienced a "spiritual decline" while in service. The announcement came with a threat of punitive action: those who defied the ruling will pay a heavy price—their children would be expelled from all Ger education affiliates. Parents enrolling their children would be asked to sign a declaration that they did not serve in any of these forbidden organizations. The ruling was clearly a setback to civic national service since a ruling by the Ger leader would likely have a ripple effect on other Hassidic sects.[93]

The number of Haredim serving in civic service in 2018 fell far below the target set by the government (2,000). Only 800 men signed up (40% of the set quota) and among them less than 400 served in a full-time program.[94]

At the time of this writing, Amendments 19 and 21 are still in effect since the High Court granted the government additional extensions to the one year it gave the government to pass a new conscription law. Failing to design a law that would meet the Court's stipulations and also the demands of the Haredim, Prime Minister Netanyahu decided to call new elections in December 2018, leaving to the next government the task of rewriting a conscription law. Netanyahu also faced the prospect of an indictment brought by the state attorney general on charges of bribery, fraud, and breach of trust and it is assumed that a major reason he chose to go to elections was to postpone the preindictment hearing. The Likud party received the largest number of seats in the election and Netanyahu was again assigned the task of forming a government. However, he failed to achieve a majority with just the religious parties (Hayamin Hameuchad) and the Haredi parties (Yahadut HaTorah and Shas) who together only had 60 seats. The center and left parties, Kahol Lavan and the Labor Party, had announced straightaway they would not sit in a government headed by Netanyahu because of his imminent indictments. The only likely candidate to join the coalition was the Yisrael Beitenu party with five seats. But its leader, Avigdor Lieberman, after weeks of negotiation conditioned his party's entrance into the coalition on getting hard and fast assurances that the government would pass the conscription law he had proposed while serving as defense minister in the previous government, a proposal that had been summarily rejected by the Haredi parties. Netanyahu could not give these assurances and keep the Haredim in the government. Unable to budge Lieberman or the Haredi parties into a compromise, Netanyahu asked the Knesset to vote to disband and schedule new elections, which it did, leaving the country with a caretaker government until a new government is formed after the election held in September 2019. Netanyahu and his Haredi and national religious partners failed to achieve a majority after the September elections and were unable to form a government. The country went into a third election again in March 2020 with the issue of Haredi deferments left unresolved.

Conclusion

As we have seen, efforts to design an equitable service policy in Israel that would include the Haredim have proven elusive. Twenty years of legislative efforts failed to devise a policy that was politically acceptable to the government and would meet the standards of the High Court. While special programs in the military and in national service designed specifically for Haredim were instituted, they remain relatively limited and involve only a small minority. The majority of Haredim continue to study in yeshivas at least until the age of exemption from conscription.

The Tal Law (2002) had been the most auspicious plan for incorporating Haredim into military and civic national service and from there into the job market. It had adopted a moderate approach that appealed particularly to those young men who were mostly "roaming rather than learning" while permitting the more serious students to continue their studies. It offered those who were not serious scholars the opportunity to leave the yeshiva, serve for a short period, and then join the workforce rather than remain yeshiva students until age 35 in order to evade the draft.

The designers of the Tal Law acknowledged the religious and cultural sensibilities of the Haredim and had treaded carefully. They did not try to impose a republican Zionist ethos of "devotion to country," nor did they adopt a liberal ethos of requiring all to serve. Instead they adopted a multicultural communitarian approach that was moderate in its aims and considerate of the Haredim and their special lifestyle.

Civic national service programs were designed to meet strict community norms and standards. The military too created special programs and separate units specific to Haredim that conformed to community requirements. This more communitarian approach encouraged Haredim to serve in civic service by offering the option of serving in their own communities, and created for them a special "kosher" environment in the military. Most importantly, it gave Haredi young men the option of "a year of decision" to consider options other than yeshiva study without losing their deferments. While there was much Haredi opposition to the law (clearly from their perspective the optimal policy was no service at all), it was in retrospect a moderate law that could effect change.

The High Court's revocation of the law set the stage for more acrimonious controversies over service, both civic and military, which at the time of this writing (April 2020) have not yet been resolved. The passage of a more contentious conscription amendment (Amendment 19) in 2014 when the Haredi parties were out of government, its subsequent modification in 2015, with the Haredim back in the coalition (Amendment 21), and the invalidation of the amendments by the High Court in 2017 have left the state without a service policy in regard to the Haredim and with an increasingly disaffected, angry Haredi community.

As a result, progress in civic national service has been disappointing. When this research began, there was greater interest in civic national service and optimism among the programs' administrators that change, albeit slow, was taking place. There was hope that with the Tal Law there would be a gradual change in Haredi attitudes toward service and it would become more acceptable. In the long run, more Haredim would enter the job market and get off government subsidies.

Unfortunately, we can characterize progress since civic national service policy was instituted in the Haredi community as having gone one step forward and then two steps back. This can be attributed to the slow start by the government to implement the law, insufficient supervision of the programs, the recurrent interventions of the High Court, and the repeated negotiations and renegotiations of the service law. Rather than allow the government to implement a service policy however imperfect that in the long run could have achieved significant change, the High Court intervened repeatedly to cancel the legislation. The conscription laws that had been born out of political exigencies and compromise and that impacted directly on civic service could not but fail to meet the high standard set by the Court. Their invalidation left the country without a policy for the third time in eight years and has aggravated intercommunal relations.

The invalidations by the High Court were a setback to communitarian citizenship. In order to succeed, communitarian citizenship requires that lawmakers and political leaders be committed to the integration of the minority communities into the nation while recognizing that the community must be able to maintain and protect its cardinal norms and beliefs. The minority community must be willing to take steps to integrate further and to contribute more to the general society while upholding its communal norms and values.

The concept of communal responsibility included in Amendment 19 was a radical idea that changed conscription from the obligation of an individual to an obligation assigned to an entire community. However, it also threatened the community with collective punishment and punitive sanctions if it failed to meet its obligation, that is, to meet the conscription target. This negative use of community was clearly counterproductive. In order for a communitarian approach to work, it must be based on consent and cooperation. In the case of Amendment 19, its punitive sanctions infuriated the Haredi community and unified it against the government and against service.

Past experience has shown that when the Haredi parties are members of the coalition and the stability of the government depends on their support, legislation to radically change conscription and national service policy will not be adopted, the rulings of the High Court notwithstanding. The subject of conscription of Haredim was an issue of contention in 2019–2020 during three rounds of elections, and will be back on the new government's agenda. There will not be a radical change in service policy if the Haredi parties are members of the government. And if legislation is passed without their agreement and they leave the government, we will witness protests and demonstrations and greater alienation of the Haredim from Israeli society.

In 2015 Israel's President Reuven Rivlin described Israel's social divide as being composed of four separate tribes that have different and often conflicting ethea, norms, and values—the national religious, the secular, the Arabs, and the Haredim—and each has few opportunities to encounter the other. In previous chapters we have discussed the politics of national service in reference to the national religious community, youth excused from service by the IDF, and the Haredim. In chapter 6 we will turn our attention to another one of these tribes, Israel's Arab community, and we will ask what its attitude toward civic national service and toward greater social and economic integration into Israeli society has been. We will begin with a discussion of the status and citizenship of Arabs in the Jewish state and then we will examine conscription and civic service policy as it has related to Israeli Arabs over the years.

6

From National Service to Community Volunteering

Israel's Arab Citizens and the Controversy over Civic National Service

Integrating Israeli Arabs[1] into the national fabric has been one of the most difficult challenges facing Israel as a Jewish state and a democracy. Exempted from service in the IDF, they were excluded from the citizen obligations required of Jews and Druze and were not eligible for the post-service benefits. Arabs make up 20.8 percent of the population and are divided into several religious and ethnic groups. Approximately 1.5 million are Muslims (82%), 139,000 are Druze (9%), and 134,130 are Christians (9%).[2] Bedouins make up about 18.7 percent of the Muslim population. During the War of Independence in 1948 it is estimated that 80 percent of the Arabs residing in Palestine emigrated, fled, or were expelled from the country. Many of the Arab elites left the country to other Arab countries or to the West with the onset of hostilities. The majority of the Arabs who remained within the armistice lines after the War of Independence were averse to living under Israeli rule and Jewish leaders suspected them of being a fifth column.[3]

Arab cities and villages were put under military rule after the armistice, a policy that continued until November 1966. Throughout the 1950s there were numerous attempts by Palestinians to infiltrate into Israel. Some of those who fled sought to return to the homes they had abandoned, which were now occupied by other Arabs or, more likely, by Jewish immigrants. Fedayeen terrorists supported by the neighboring Arab states regularly wreaked havoc on the civilian Jewish population. Israelis and Arabs alike anticipated a second war, and, in this tense environment, Israeli leaders feared that "Israeli" Arabs would provide an intelligence network for their enemies, harbor terrorists and returning refugees, or engage in terror.[4] Ben-Gurion stated the problem as he saw it: "The IDF seeks to deter the external enemy, and the [military] administration seeks to deter the internal enemy. Do you really believe the internal enemy does not exist? . . . I see three dangers to the Jewish people in its land: the armies of Nasser, the refugees, and the Arabs in Israel."[5]

Given these doubts about the loyalty of the Arabs citizens, it is not surprising that Israeli governments failed to extend them true equality. In the first decades of the state, improving the quality of Israeli democracy took second place to nation-building, and quick absorption of new Jewish immigrants took priority over the needs of the Arab minority. In those years, the republican nationalist ethos that prevailed fell short when relating to the Arab minority. The Arab sector, which identified neither with the "return to Zion" nor with the ingathering of the exiles, was excluded, by definition, from the national endeavor. Government expenditures for infrastructure development were directed toward building new Jewish settlements and development towns. Contributions from Jews in the Diaspora to the Keren Hayesod, the Jewish National Fund, and the United Jewish Appeal went to projects in the Jewish sector alone. Although the Arabs were granted full political citizenship, the government paid them little attention except with reference to security. There were few attempts to engage them in a dialogue regarding their needs and development.[6]

As discussed in earlier chapters, Israel's first prime minister, David Ben-Gurion, was a strong proponent of the republican ethos, and of the idea that the state of Israel was the nation-state of the Jewish people. He expressed these views on many occasions. In a speech in 1962 he declared, "In Israel, the Jews are the nation; they are the people and they are the state."[7] He made no mention of Israel's Arab citizens. In line with this Zionist nationalist approach, development projects during the first decades were directed exclusively to the Jewish sector and many Arab-owned lands were expropriated in order to create Jewish agricultural settlements or to construct new Jewish towns and cities.[8]

Military Service and Citizenship in the First Decades

In those early years, there was an internal debate among Israeli leaders on whether to conscript Arab citizens to the IDF. Many regarded the Arabs as a serious security threat, among them Israel's first prime minister, David Ben-Gurion, and for that reason thought they should not be conscripted. Ben-Gurion was concerned that they would become a fifth column and threaten Israel's security.[9] Military rule was established over Arab villages and towns in order to keep the Arabs under surveillance and to limit their access to Jewish centers. Permits were required to travel from their villages to other locales in the country. Extensive surveillance was imposed to prevent the formation of terrorist rings and a network of informers within Arab villages and towns was recruited and rewarded.[10]

A second reason raised by government leaders against conscripting Israeli Arabs was on so-called "humanitarian" grounds. It was argued that since Israel was at war with the surrounding Arab states, it was unfair and even callous to require Israeli Arabs to take up arms against their "brothers." The history of the Jews of having been combatants in the armies of both the Allied and Central powers in World War I and having to fight one another was recalled as a tragic circumstance that should not be imposed on Israeli Arabs. This on the face of it was an expression of sensitivity and accommodation toward the Arabs but in effect reflected a lack of trust, questioning whether Arabs could ever be truly loyal to a Jewish state. This assumption, that Arabs should not be expected to fight against their "brothers" reflected the leadership's supposition that the Arabs were primarily loyal to each other and in effect constituted one nation, disregarding the fact that Arabs had engaged in armed conflict against other Arabs in the past, and Muslims had fought other Muslims.[11]

Bauml suggests that Israeli leaders over the years had an additional motivation for the exclusion of Arabs from any kind of conscription. The challenge of nation-building obliged the state's founders to set the boundaries that would define the Israeli nation. It was necessary to find that which would unite within it the diverse mass of Jewish immigrants that were arriving in Israel. Service in the IDF was that integrating litmus test. Jews of all colors and cultures were to be embraced and conscripted; Arabs, by definition, would be excluded. Exempting them from conscription would achieve three goals: first, it would identify Israeli Arabs with the enemy, a measure that allowed the government to maintain a hardline approach toward them and to justify the retention of the military government; second, it would portray Israeli Arabs as a sector that did not serve and as such was ineligible for the special "advantages" that service extended to those who serve, that is, easy entry into the job market and access to government housing; and third, it would make them ineligible for the material benefits granted to those who completed service, that is, assistance with college tuition, mortgages, and child allowances. Thus by not being called to serve, Israel's Arabs were kept segregated from Israeli society and without the benefits that accrue from membership, while the ties binding Jewish Israelis to each other and to the state were fortified.[12]

Ben-Gurion's supposition of Arab disloyalty underpinned the retention of the military government in Arab areas throughout the years of his premiership, 1948–1954 and 1956–1963. His hardline position, however, was not shared by all Mapai leaders. Pinchas Lavon, for example, who was the secretary general of the Histadrut and later served as defense minister, supported greater integration of the Arabs and wanted to grant them full equality. Already in 1952 he proposed ending military rule in the Arab sector.

Lavon had an opportunity to implement this proposal when he became minister of defense in January 1954, with the resignation of Prime Minister Ben-Gurion. Soon after his appointment, he proposed instituting general conscription of Arabs into the IDF as an expression of their full citizenship. Prime Minister Moshe Sharett concurred, hoping that conscription would improve Arab-Jewish relations. In July 1954 Defense Minister Lavon asked the IDF chief of staff, Moshe Dayan, who had been on record against the conscription of Arabs, to design just such a program for the recruitment of Arabs, Muslims, Christians, and Druze.[13]

The Arab response to conscription at the time was mixed. Many youth responded positively to the initiative and signed up for service, sometimes even requesting to be assigned to particularly challenging fighting units. The older generation was less enthused; some suggested that their sons should devote their time to earning a living rather than wasting time in the army. Since they were living under military rule, it is not surprising that they were cautious in what they said so as not to express support for Arab nationalism or opposition to the Jewish state. About 4,000 Arab youth (male) signed up for military service in response to the call up, about 90 percent of those who were eligible. The initiative was short-lived. Soon after, Lavon was dismissed as defense minister (February 1955) in the wake of a failed espionage mission in Egypt that occurred on his watch. He was replaced by Ben-Gurion, who canceled the conscription plan immediately after returning to office, with the strong backing of the IDF chief of staff Moshe Dayan.[14]

For many years, Israeli policy toward the Arab population reflected a divide and control approach. Policymakers rejected the idea that the Arab population was of a single identity. Following the advice of the prime ministers' advisors for Arab affairs and the intelligence agencies, they differentiated between Christian Arabs, Muslims, Druze, and Bedouins when making policy.[15] A report prepared by the prime minister's advisor on the Arab minority in the 1950s described quite openly the purpose of the divide and rule policy:

> The policy of the government in the last decade has sought to divide the Arab population into communities and regions. . . . the communal policy and clan divisions in the villages have served to prevent the Arab communities from forming one unit. . . . It is possible to retard the pace of Arab progress with a policy of communal and clan divisions and with other artificial means. . . . This policy has caused communal leaders to be preoccupied with communal matters rather than in general Arab issues.[16]

The Druze for example received special consideration. Starting in 1956 the government began to integrate the Druze into Israeli society by extending mandatory conscription to Druze males. At the same time, it granted official recognition to the Druze religion and began to fund Druze religious institutions. It also lifted their remaining travel restrictions while maintaining them for Muslims and Christians.[17] It is interesting to note that while the Druze were encouraged to volunteer to the IDF even before 1956, once inducted to the armed forces they were assigned to a special minorities unit and were stationed in the Negev in order to distance them from the northern front, where there were Druze villages, in Syria and Lebanon.[18] In 1971 the IDF amended this policy and allowed Druze soldiers to join regular units (the tank corps, Golan Brigade, the military police, or the navy) if they so requested and in 1991 integrated them completely into all IDF units.[19] In 1958 the government extended conscription to the small Circassian community and in the 1960s Christian Arabs and Bedouins were permitted to volunteer.[20] While there is no statute that specifically exempts Israel's Arabs from military service, the Ministry of Defense recruitment regulations state that Muslim and Christian Arabs as well as Bedouins will not be drafted but will be permitted to volunteer on a case by case basis.[21]

Arab Civic National Service: Committee Recommendations and Legislative Proposals, 1968–2000

The subject of civic national service by Arabs came up periodically in the Knesset and in the relevant government offices only after the 1967 war. The military government in the predominantly Arab areas ended in November 1966, allowing Arab citizens greater freedom of movement. The first discussions relating to service were in December 1968 when the Labor government under Levi Eshkol appointed a ministerial subcommittee headed by Justice Minister Yaakov-Shimshon Shapira to study the possibility of instituting mandatory civic service in the Arab sector. The committee rejected the idea, determining that for "reasons of national security" civic national service in the Arab sector was not advisable at this time.[22]

After the upset election of Menachem Begin in May 1977, the subject of civic national service in the Arab sector was raised again, this time by the prime minister's advisor on Arab affairs, Moshe Sharon. The civic service program for religious girls had already been in progress for six years and could serve as a precedent (see chapter 3). Sharon prepared a policy paper in regard to Israeli Arabs several months after the violent protests that had erupted in the Arab sector in March 1976 on what came to be called Land Day. Arabs had held mass demonstrations to protest the confiscation of Arab lands by the government. Several protestors were killed by the police during the events, exacerbating an already tense situation. Sharon thought it important to take steps to integrate the Arabs into Israeli society, while recognizing that they could neither be expected to share the Zionist republican ethos nor identify with the state and its Jewish symbols. Nonetheless, he thought they wished to be loyal law-abiding citizens and, as such, would be amenable to government initiatives to assist their integration. He recommended initiating civic national service in the Muslim sector and, in the Christian sector, military service. Sharon also urged the government to improve living conditions in the Arab sector and narrow the social and economic gap between Arabs and Jews. None of these recommendations were ever discussed by the government and

Sharon resigned his post in frustration soon after.[23] At the same time the Knesset Subcommittee on Arab Affairs headed by Amnon Rubenstein (Shinui) discussed the possibility of establishing a program of national service in the Arab sector and invited community leaders to appear before it. This initiative too failed to result in any concrete recommendations.[24]

In 1984, Yosef Ginat, the government advisor on Arab affairs, presented to the government a program similar to that recommended by Sharon, that civic national service be introduced in the Arab sector. This time the government did discuss his recommendations but decided to postpone taking any action. It reasoned that the situation in the Arab sector was relatively quiet and therefore did not require any government intervention.[25]

The subject of civic national service for Arabs came up again in 1990–1991 during the premiership of Yitzhak Shamir. Government officials held concrete discussions with Arab leaders regarding the establishment of a national emergency services corps in the Arab sector, but these discussions ended abruptly with the onset of the Gulf War in 1991.[26]

The Knesset was the primary venue for discussions regarding civic national service in the Arab sector during the years 1984–2000. Private member legislation instituting civic national service was often initiated by MKs from parties in the opposition, given the government's general lack of interest in such programs. MKs from small ideological parties on the left and right of the political spectrum (Mapam, Meretz, Shinui and Tehiya, Moledet and Tsomet) regularly proposed legislation to extend civic national service to all citizens, Arab and Jew. It is interesting to note that these same parties, when they were themselves members of the government coalition, became "strangely inactive" on this issue, for example, in 1992–1996 when the Meretz party was a member of the Barak-led Labor coalition, 1996–1999 when Tsomet participated in the Netanyahu Likud government, and in 2001 when the Moledet party entered the right-wing coalition of Ariel Sharon.[27]

The first private member bill relating to civic national service for Israeli Arabs was submitted to the Knesset by Labor MK Edna Solodar in October 1984, who proposed legislating mandatory civic national service for Arab boys, similar to the civic service program of religious girls. They would be required to serve two years in civic service in agriculture, industry, health, and welfare. She explained that she had been approached by Arab citizens who expressed interest in serving in a civic capacity.[28] Civic service, she suggested, would further Arab integration into Israeli society. Her proposal never reached the plenum for discussion.

Several months later, opposition MK Raphael Eitan from the small, far-right Tehiya-Tsomet party (five seats) proposed legislation that would require all Israeli citizens, men and women, exempted from military service for whatever reason to do civic national service, three years for men and two for women. While the proposal purported to promote republican values, requiring all citizens to fulfill their civic obligation, and was ostensibly equitable in that it would apply to all, it also included far-reaching punitive measures: those who failed to serve would lose their right to vote and their right to serve in the Knesset; they would be ineligible for government-sponsored student scholarships and for jobs in the civil service. They would also not be allowed to study in the university until age 21. While Solodar's proposal had been intended to further Arab integration into Israeli society, Eitan's proposal was intended to be provocative and to arouse Arab opposition. The bill, in republican guise, was directed against Israel's Arab citizens. It did not apply to Haredim since it included within it an appeals procedure for exemptions based on religious lifestyle and special family circumstances. Ultra-orthodox yeshiva students and religious girls would have been eligible for exemptions.[29]

As expected, Arab MKs regarded Eitan's bill as a provocation and voiced strident objection to it. The Labor and Welfare Ministry, which had ministerial authority over national service, rejected the proposal as being discriminatory against Arabs because it would require them to engage in menial labor in agriculture and industry. It agreed that a program of civic national service in the Arab sector was vital and in the national interest and it suggested that the government draft Arabs to noncombat units in the military or to the police force rather than to serve in agriculture and industry.[30] The Eitan proposal failed to garner support in the Knesset. The very same legislation was submitted at least seven more times between 1986 and 2004 by MKs from parties on the far right. The government majority voted them down; others remained declaratory, never reaching the plenum at all.[31]

Eitan again proposed instituting civic national service in the Arab sector during the second Rabin government in 1993. This time he proposed amending the Basic Law: The Knesset[32] to require service in either military or civic national service as a condition to the right to vote. This provocative proposal would now target two populations: Israeli Arabs and ultra-orthodox yeshiva students. The bill also set a ceiling on yeshiva student exemptions: no more than 500 exemptions a year.[33]

As expected, Arab and Haredi MKs were incensed by the proposal. Speaking for the government, Justice Minister David Libai (Labor) rejected the proposal unequivocally because it set conditions on political rights that, he said, should be independent of any and all citizen obligations. It implied that the Arabs were at fault for not serving, which was not in fact the case. All of Israel's defense agencies, he said, were opposed to conscripting Arabs to the IDF. This had been their position in the past, during the right-wing governments of Menachem Begin and Yitzhak Shamir and was still their recommendation under Labor in 1993.[34]

The government showed little interest in instituting civic national service in the Arab sector throughout the 1990s. Prime Minister Yitzhak Rabin (Labor) had been on record opposing civic national service in the Arab sector because he thought "it would turn them into 'hewers of wood and drawers of water,'" a biblical reference to those assigned to perform menial tasks. While he supported equal rights and obligations for all citizens, it was in his view counterproductive to force Arabs to do national service and would widen the divide between Arabs and Jews.[35]

The subject of civic national service in the Arab sector came up often during debates in the Knesset relating to the difficult social and economic conditions in the Arab towns and villages. Inevitably, when the need to extend more aid to struggling Arab municipalities was raised in the Knesset, their high unemployment rates or the disproportionate number of Arab children living in poverty, there would be an outcry from MKs on the far right who would link improving social services to requiring Arabs to do civic national service. This would trigger a furious response from the Arab MKs who rejected any linkage between social equality and service. Civic service became a regular point of contention in the incendiary exchanges between MKs on the far right and Arab and Jewish MKs on the left.[36]

Proposals to institute national service for all citizens were not however only the province of the right-wing parties. Proposals also came from parties on the left (Labor) and far left (Meretz) who wanted to advance Arab integration and achieve greater equality in services.[37] In 1996–1999 MKs from the Labor Party and from Meretz, then in opposition, submitted eight legislative proposals regarding national service. Several called for the establishment of voluntary programs open to all youth, Arab and Jew, others a mandatory program.[38]

MKs Yossi Beilin and Yona Yahav (Labor) proposed even more far-reaching legislation. They proposed that all youth at age 18 be given a choice whether to serve in the IDF in a combat unit, in the IDF in paramilitary duties, or in national civic service. Those who for reasons of religion or conscience would wish not to serve would be excused. The Beilin-Yahav proposal was revolutionary in that it gave youth a choice where to serve and would have ended the long-established prerogative of the IDF to determine who would be conscripted and in what capacity.[39]

The government regarded the Beilin-Yahav proposal as a serious threat to the IDF, whose interests and manpower requirements should take precedence over the wishes of the draftees. The very fact that such a proposal was seriously proposed indicates a changing ethos toward service on the left and greater support for more liberal values that put the choices and the wishes of the individual ahead of that of the collective.

The government strongly opposed the proposal. Responding in the Knesset, Deputy Defense Minister Silvan Shalom (Likud) asked MK Beilin with undisguised sarcasm why he failed to propose this law a year before when his party was in the Rabin-Peres government. He warned that the proposed policy would weaken the IDF as the "army of the people" and give legitimacy to those who sought to avoid military service. Unsurprisingly, the Knesset rejected this proposal as well.[40]

It is clear that successive Israeli governments in the 1980s and 1990s were not really interested in creating an alternative service track that would compete with the IDF, nor did they want to take on the challenge of drafting Arabs into any form of service, military or civic. They preferred to continue the status quo, leaving military service to Jews (other than the Haredim) and civic service to religious girls, all of whom shared the Zionist republican ethos.

The Impact of the Liberal Ethos: "A State of All of Its Citizens"

The harbinger of change came from Shlomit, a new nonprofit service placement agency that began accepting a small number of Arabs and boys rejected from the IDF into civic national service in 1995. This was a trailblazing challenge to service policy since until that time only religious girls were accepted to service. In February 1996, the National Insurance Authority informed the agency that these volunteers would not be eligible for benefits since its guidelines limited benefits to religious girls doing civic national service (see chapter 4). This led to a petition to the High Court by Shlomit and by the Association for Civil Rights in Israel in the name of the volunteers and an out-of-court agreement that included a government commitment to study the question and to create a more inclusive civic service policy (*Eyal Daniel v. the Director of National Insurance*, HC9173/96).

The government assigned the question to the minister of labor, who set up a committee (the Ben-Shalom Committee) to study the issue. After months of research and discussion, it recommended that the option of civic national service be extended to all citizens not conscripted to the IDF, including Israeli Arabs. This was the first of several government committees that would recommend instituting civic national service in the Arab sector.

The mid-1990s was marked by a gradual shift in values among Israeli intellectuals, political elites, and the more educated middle class, a shift from republican norms of contribution, sacrifice, and obligation to themes of equality, individualism, and self-expression. As a part of this shift to more liberal values, there were increased demands by reservists and others that all should "share the burden" of service.[41] The republican ethos that had glorified service and stressed the duties of citizenship as patriotic duty were slowly being replaced by a narrative of fairness, that is, to "share the burden" equally by all. This was especially the case when considering the inequality of draft deferments for yeshiva students, but some broadened the issue to include Israeli Arabs as well. Speaking in the Knesset, MK Eliezer Zandberg (Tsomet) said:

> In my view full equal rights should be matched with full equal obligation. . . . Israeli Arabs must take part in either national service or military service. There is no possible reason why a young Arab man who completes high school at age eighteen can go straight to the university and at age twenty two will be an engineer while a Jewish young man during the same time period will not be able to do so.[42]

In July 1997, the Labor Party initiated a no-confidence motion in the Knesset against the Netanyahu government charging it with a list of policy failures. Prominent among them was the government's "failure to enact national civic service legislation" applicable to all youth not conscripted to the military. The theme of mandatory national service for all citizens was embraced by MK Ehud Barak (Labor), then leader of the opposition, as part of the "citizen revolution" he promised to lead. Barak declared that if he were elected prime minister, he would initiate legislation requiring all citizens to do some form of service, civic or military.[43] True to his word, upon his election in May 1999, he instructed the National Security Council to set up a committee to study the issue and bring him policy recommendations.[44]

As discussed previously in chapter 5, the High Court in 1997 became the address for the liberal challenge to the "unfair" distribution of the "burden" of service. The Court was asked to rule whether the defense minister, who until then had been the sole authority to grant deferments to yeshiva students, had in fact the constitutional authority to do so, considering that the number of deferments had reached the tens of thousands (*Rubenstein v. Minister of Defense*, 3267/97). While the Court deliberated about yeshiva students, a similar petition was submitted regarding the legality of the government's policy not to conscript Arabs. The parallel with the Rubenstein petition was clear. If all must serve, then why was the Arab minority excused from all forms of service?[45]

The High Court issued a show cause order requiring the government to respond to the petition. The government responded that the court's intervention on this matter was redundant since the government was already preparing primary legislation regarding the conscription of Arabs to civic service that it would introduce soon in the Knesset. In light of the government's response, the Court turned down the petition. The petitioner submitted the petition again several months later after it became clear that the committee that had been appointed to devise a formula for the conscription of yeshiva students (the Tal Committee) did not have a mandate to discuss service in the Arab sector. The Court rejected the petition again, citing government assurances that it would enact a service policy in the Arab sector after it completed the plan for the conscription of yeshiva students.[46] The High Court's decision not to intervene showed its clear reluctance to take on this politically charged issue, preferring to leave it to the government and the Knesset.

The National Security Council assigned by Prime Minister Ehud Barak to study the question of civic national service submitted its recommendations in 2000. As did the Ben-Shalom Committee before it, it too advised introducing civic national service in the Arab sector in order to advance its integration into Israeli society. It suggested that the program be voluntary in order not to foment protests among the Arabs. The volunteers were to be assigned mainly to placements within the Arab community, at least at the start. It also recommended changing the name of their program from "national" service to "civic service" in order to emphasize that service was an act of good citizenship rather than an expression of "national" identity. "National" service, it said, was a title appropriate to religious Zionist girls but was problematic for youth bearing a strong Palestinian identity.[47]

However, violent events in the Arab sector in October 2000 postponed any government action on the issue. Palestinians in the West Bank and Gaza Strip began a second uprising, later known as the Second Intifada. In sympathy with them, Israeli Arabs in the north held mass demonstrations, some of which became violent, resulting in the deaths of 13 Israeli Arabs at the hands of the police. In response to the violence and loss of life, the government appointed an investigatory commission (the Orr Commission), to study what came to be called "the October events" and the circumstances that led up to them, and placed on hold the plan to engage the Arab leadership in a dialogue over civic national service.[48] In the interim, Prime Minister Ehud Barak, who was on record in favor of extending civic national service to the Arab sector, lost his bid for reelection to Ariel Sharon and retired temporarily from politics. In 2001 the Knesset passed legislation extending civic national service to boys rejected from the IDF. Civic service in the Arab sector was not included.[49]

The Arab Response to the Civic National Service Proposals, 1990–2000

Before addressing the government actions and recommendations after the October events, it is important to examine the Arab leadership's response to the numerous proposals regarding civic national service proposed in the Knesset and by the various government committees up until then.

In 1989 and 1991 there was still a modicum of flexibility in the Arab position; Arab MKs from the Mapai party were willing to discuss the possibility of civic service and even participated in a delegation of Jews and Arabs that traveled to Germany in 1989 to study the German *Zivildienst* program.[50] And in 1991, Arab leaders seriously discussed options of civic service with Prime Minister Shamir's advisor for Arab affairs, Alexander Bligh.[51] However this was not the case in later years, after there was a generational shift in the Arab leadership and more radical leaders took over.

The number of Arab representatives in Zionist parties in the Knesset decreased sharply in the 1990s and more radical parties such as the Communist Hadash party, the United Arab List, and Balad (1996) gained the vote of the majority of Arabs. These parties identified strongly with Palestinian nationalism and were committed to the Palestinian struggle for independence in the West Bank and Gaza. They opposed all proposals that required Arabs to give any form of national service, military or civic, and all voluntary programs as well, which they argued were merely the first step toward mandatory military service.

The Arab leaders gave several reasons why they opposed civic national service, the first and foremost being inequality. Arab leaders pointed to the deep-rooted economic and social inequality that exists in Israel between Arabs and Jews. The state had inflicted historic injustice on the Arabs and therefore had no moral justification to ask them to serve. It had adopted a deliberate policy of discrimination and neglect that had created and perpetuated social inequality, that is, low allocations for Arab municipalities and local governments, substandard conditions in Arab schools, and a disproportionate number of Arab families living in poverty. There were almost no building and development plans for the Arab sector in the 1990s and those that were formulated were not approved. As a result, many houses were built without permits and then demolished by the authorities.

Arab towns were at the top of the charts in unemployment figures. Thirty-eight percent of the Arabs were living below the poverty line in 2001–2002, compared to only 16.6 percent below the poverty line among the general population.[52] Arab leaders contended that if the proponents of national service were serious about achieving social equality, they would first need to address the social and economic disparities between Arabs and Jews and only then ask them to contribute. It was totally unacceptable to assign them obligations without giving them equal rights. Arab leaders frequently brought up the socioeconomic conditions in the Druze villages as a sorry example of a minority that did serve in the military and yet got little in return. The same conditions of neglect that persist in the Muslim villages were found in the Druze villages as well.[53]

A second argument raised by Arab leaders against civic service was intrinsically connected to military service. They would not serve in what was an essentially "Jewish" army serving a "Jewish" state at war with their nation, the Palestinians, and was the oppressor of their people in the West Bank and Gaza. Service in the IDF was contrary to their very identity as Palestinians. Arab leaders contended that participation in civic national service, which at first glance may seem innocuous and even beneficial to the Arab community, was in fact the first step in a government scheme to conscript Israeli Arabs to the military. The government, they maintained, would begin with a voluntary program of civic service that would soon become mandatory and then move from there to mandatory service in the military. Civic service was just a ploy to get Arabs to serve. This claim is still widely accepted in the Arab community despite the government's efforts to refute it and indicates the Arab leaders' lack of trust in the government and its promises.

The establishment of the Administration for National-Civic Service (ANCS) in 2008, which was an administrative agency completely separate from the IDF, did nothing to dispel this distrust.[54] "Proof" of the linkage between army service and civic service, Arab leaders said, was in its conception. Civic national service began as an alternative to military service, applicable to religious girls exempted from the IDF. The starting point of service was the obligation to serve in the military and civic national service was the substitute. Arab leaders were quick to point out that the benefits received by those who complete civic national service came from the Discharged Soldiers Fund allocated by the Ministry of Defense. This, they contended, was proof of the intrinsic connection between civic national service and the military. This procedural "detail" was dismissed by the ANCS as merely "an administrative procedure employed for efficiency purposes,"[55] but for those opposed to civic national service it was further evidence of the "unholy" connection between civic and military service.[56]

More recently, Arab leaders point to the fact that the initiative to institute civic national service in the Arab sector originated out of the recommendations of the Ivri Committee, which had been established by the Defense Ministry (discussed in the next section). This was yet another indication of the civic-military connection.[57]

A third argument questioned the very concept of "national" service because it was essentially an expression of patriotism, and attachment to the state. Arab leaders questioned the "national" aspect of civic national service. Which "nation" were they expected to serve, the "Jewish nation," with whom they do not identify? They argued that civic national service was a ruse by the government to strip the youth of their Palestinian identity and to further their "Israelification." Since the express purpose of national service was to strengthen the youths' ties to their community and to their country, it was a sellout to the Palestinian cause. An Arab youth with a proud Arab identity could not serve a "Jewish" state that discriminates against his people and oppresses his Palestinian brothers in the territories. So long as the occupation of Palestinian lands continues, Arabs must not serve.[58]

MKs from the Balad party raised a different argument, that of control. Balad is a secular nationalist Arab party that supports replacing Israel as a "Jewish" state with a "state of all of its citizens." It advocates establishing a binational state that would give equality and recognition to the Arab minority as the "indigenous" residents of the land and would recognize their national rights. Former Balad MK Azmi Bashara called on the state to recognize the national rights of the Arab minority and give it complete control over its own institutions.[59] Civic national service would be acceptable in the Arab sector only if it would be taken out of the government's hands and placed under the full control of the Arab municipalities and regional councils.[60]

An additional concern raised by some Arab leaders was the negative effect civic national service may have on employment. They questioned whether the introduction of volunteers into hospitals, schools, and welfare services would create greater unemployment in the Arab sector, particularly since many Arabs are employed in low-level jobs that do not require professional training. They argued that civic service would reduce the number of jobs available and replace workers in basic services.[61] For all these reasons, Arab leaders opposed civic service and, as we shall see, continue to oppose service today.

The October 2000 Events: A Catalyst for Policy Change

The October 2000 events sent shock waves throughout Israeli society. Thirteen Arab citizens were killed by police fire when the police tried to control mass demonstrations that had turned violent. Some Jewish citizens were the targets of rock throwing and one Israeli lost his life as a result.[62] This was indeed a watershed event in Jewish-Arab relations. The government appointed a special commission headed by retired High Court judge Theodore Orr to investigate the events and to recommend measures to prevent their reoccurrence.

The Orr Commission adopted a broad perspective on the events, ascribing them to a response to the long-term discrimination and alienation that had characterized the Arab community's relations with the state and its institutions. It concluded:

> The events, their unusual character and serious results, were the consequence of deep-seated factors that created an explo-

sive situation within the Israeli Arab population. The state and generations of government failed to comprehensively address the serious problems created by the existence of a large minority inside the Jewish state.

Government handling of the Arab sector has been primarily neglectful and discriminatory. The establishment did not show sufficient sensitivity to the needs of the Arab population and it did not allocate state resources in an equal manner. The state did not do enough or try hard enough to create equality for its Arab citizens or to uproot discriminatory or unjust phenomena. Meanwhile, not enough was done to enforce the law in the Arab sector and illegality and other undesirable behavior took root there.[63]

While the commission had harsh words for the Israeli political leadership, it also placed some of the blame squarely on the shoulders of the Arab leadership, which, it wrote, had contributed to the escalation of tensions and did not take "precautions to prevent the deterioration into violence" when they saw where the protests were leading. It also faulted the police for using excessive force in its efforts to quell the protests and restore order. It recommended that the government take immediate steps to "give true equality to the country's Arab citizens. . . . and initiate, develop and operate programs . . . that will close the gaps in education, housing, industrial development, employment and services."[64]

In September 2003, Prime Minister Ariel Sharon appointed a ministerial committee headed by Justice Minister Yosef Lapid to recommend specific operational measures for improving relations with the Arab community based on the Orr findings. Arab leaders were invited to join the committee but they refused. The Lapid committee recommended among other things the immediate establishment of a voluntary program of civic service in the Arab sector, with assignments mainly within their own communities, at least at the start. The program was to be voluntary in its early stages and then made mandatory at a later time.[65]

Arab leaders rejected this recommendation out of hand. They maintained as they had in the past that the state must provide the community with full equality before it could ask it to contribute.[66] MK Muhammad Barakeh (Hadash-Taal) said in the Knesset:

The recommendation to require Arab citizens to do national service under conditions of structured deprivation, extreme marginalization and systematic discrimination is outrageous and unacceptable. The essential principle of civic democracy is that rights are absolute and unconditional, derived from citizenship itself, while obligations are relative, circumstantial and dependent on the ability of the citizen to fulfill them.[67]

Following the Lapid Committee recommendations, the government in December 2005 approved in principle the establishment of a voluntary program of civic national service for all youth, Arabs and Jews, who were not conscripted to the IDF.[68]

During this same period, Minister of Defense Shaul Mofaz in August 2004 appointed a committee headed by retired air force commander David Ivri[69] to study how to operationalize civic service in the Haredi sector as authorized in the Tal Law. In February 2007 it submitted its recommendations. (Its recommendations regarding conscription of Haredim were discussed earlier in chapter 5.) The Ivri Committee, like the Orr Commission and the Lapid Committee that preceded it, recommended that a voluntary program of civic national service be established for both Jews and Arabs for all youth not conscripted to the military. It did not adopt a mandatory program because of the strong opposition of the Arab leadership.[70] A voluntary program, it wrote, would have a "positive impact on the status of Arabs in Israel and on relations between Jews and Arabs."[71]

The Ivri Committee recommended setting up separate civic service administrative tracks for each sector, religious girls, Arabs, and Haredim, within one central authority. The government adopted the Ivri recommendations in August 2007 and announced the establishment of the Administration for National-Civic Service (ANCS) in the Prime Minister's Office. It appointed Reuven Gal, the former chief psychologist of the IDF and a member of the National Security Council, to set it up and head it.[72]

Upon entering the job, Gal described the goals of the new Administration for National-Civic Service:

> We are talking about a civilian governmental program, in which young citizens, men and women, from all groups in the population, Jews, Arabs, young women and men, religious and secular and ultra-orthodox will contribute a year or two of their time to service in the community. This service will bring notable benefits to society in general and to weaker populations

in particular. . . . The program has three goals: to strengthen young citizens' bond and identification with their community, society, and with the state; to develop professional skills and readiness for the job market; and to develop and achieve personal empowerment and leadership skills.[73]

At the outset, Gal sought to include Arab leaders in the initiative. He invited them to join the Civic Service Advisory Committee but was firmly rebuffed. He invited the heads of the Arab Regional Councils to meet with the ANCS and advise it of their needs, but they too refused.[74]

Immediately after the establishment of the ANCS, the Higher Arab Monitoring Committee[75] issued a statement denouncing civic service and began an active campaign against the program within the Arab community. It appointed Ayman Odeh, a lawyer and a young rising activist in the Hadash party to head the Coalition against Civic Service.[76] The coalition organized mass rallies against service, produced internet videos, and even commissioned rap songs that denounced service and condemned anyone who served.[77] Those that volunteered were labeled traitors; parents were warned that their children would be ostracized if they served.

Arab leaders pressured school principals and regional council heads not to cooperate with the ANCS. In Kafr Kana, for example, the head of the regional council cut the phone lines of the local school in order to pressure the principal not to admit volunteers. In Bir el Machsor and El Batuf coordinators for one of the placement organizations, who were themselves Arabs, were threatened and verbally abused. There were several incidents reported of physical attacks on the volunteers and on service coordinators.[78] At a meeting of the Knesset's Education, Culture, and Sport Committee in January 2008, Ataf Karinawi, an ANCS administrator for the Arab sector warned that the atmosphere surrounding the volunteers was extremely tense and volatile. He cautioned that this situation could even lead to the murder of one of the volunteers or supervisors.[79] Yoram Kamisa, head of the Association for Social Equality, one of the organizations that placed Arab volunteers in civic service, told a Knesset committee in 2016 that one of the Arab volunteers chosen to receive the President's Prize for Excellence had had her house set on fire.[80]

At a meeting of the Knesset Education, Culture, and Sport Committee, MK Jamal Zahalka (Balad) was asked to explain why he opposed a program that was voluntary and administered by Arabs, for Arabs, and that offered Arab youth the opportunity to serve their own communities. He responded categorically:

> The program is against the Arab population. The fact that Arabs are marketing it—that is how it always is under occupation. There are always those who assist the colonizer against their own people. That is nothing new . . .
>
> Why are 90 percent of the volunteers girls? This is the establishment's cynical way of taking advantage . . . of unemployment among Arab women. . . . Only 20 percent of Arab women are employed. It comes and takes advantage of their [bad] socioeconomic condition to entice the girls to do this without explaining to them what the [real] goal of the program is. It is a program that is intended to obscure and weaken the national identity of the Arab citizens and youth and it will not succeed.[81]

On another occasion, Zahalka charged that civic service was "a colonialist attempt to weaken the Arabs' national identity,"[82] and he branded those who volunteer "lepers"[83] and threatened that Arab society will ostracize them. He warned ominously that the volunteers will face serious problems when they seek marriage partners.[84]

The Baladna Arab youth organization launched its own vigorous campaign against civic national service, mainly through online media and workshops in Arab schools and in youth movements. The message in the videos and on the posters read, "I am an Arab and not a servant. No, to military and civic service!," linking civic service directly to service in the IDF. Baladna commissioned DAM, a popular Arab rap group from Lod, to write a rap song against national service. The song, entitled "Wanted: An Arab Who Has Lost His Memory," was aired on Arabic radio stations and had wide coverage in the media.

> Civic service will take me backward.
> It will put me in a tank that will threaten my grandfather.
> It will put me in the bulldozer that will destroy my legacy.
> On the way I will take with me 35 unemployed heroes and
> Fall with them into poverty numbering 60 percent.
> Are we really citizens? Will service lead me anywhere?

> Our neighborhoods are erased even from the city garbage truck map.
> What do you want? That I should do national service in a school?
> So that I should teach the pupils how we live?[85]
> . . .

The song mocks the state for failing to give the Arabs a fair share of services, not even decent garbage collection, and for giving preference to Jews in immigration and yet expecting Arabs to serve. Its lyrics include a warning to the youth not to be fooled: their situation will not improve if they do service.

Baladna also organized "anti-service" youth seminars during which civic service was condemned and vilified. Thousands of teenagers attended these seminars and they were often the youths' main source of information about service.[86] MKs from the Balad party often led these seminars. They warned the youth not to be enticed by the benefits offered by the government or misled by the seemingly positive aspects of volunteering. Nadim Nashif, head of Baladna youth, noted that government efforts to recruit Arabs to national service have a historical parallel: when the government in 1956 drafted the Druze to the Israeli army. He warned:

> This matter is no less dangerous than in 1956 when a similar law to do military service was forced on the Palestinian Druze community. . . . We must work to stop this law. Can you imagine 28,000 Arab youth doing national service annually, going through a brainwashing process and regarding the State of Israel as a Jewish state? Where does that leave the Palestinian identity? We cannot let that happen to our youth. We are joining forces as organizations and individuals to stop this law.[87]

The leaders of the Islamic Movement northern faction Ra'ad Salah and of the southern faction Ibrahim Sarsur addressed a Baladna convention against civic service in 2007 and accused the government of using it as a means of sowing division within the Arab community. Salah said, "What I fear is that the intent of civic service is to further empower the Israeli defense establishment by creating conflicts among the Arabs in Israel and even to bring about our physical extinction."[88] Following the same line of argument, Sheik Sarsur told the youth:

> Israel would like us to give up our identity and turn us into a group without aspirations, programs and without a future. It wants to defend itself against the world's indictment of it for its persecution and discrimination (against us). It is trying to cover this up with this project of civic service and by doing so is passing the ball to our court, claiming before the world: we do want the Arabs to succeed but we are correct in what we have claimed for the last 60 years: they (the Arabs) are adamant in their refusal to recognize Israel and it is therefore permissible for us to take steps to defuse this demographic bomb and strategic danger.[89]

Civic service was merely a tactic used by the government to divide the Arabs and weaken them in their struggle against the state. The Islamic leaders warned the youth not to fall into the Israeli "honey trap" of benefits and promises of greater integration.

Arab MKs and regional council heads met with school principals, students, and parents to warn that civic service was in fact a first step toward conscription. The evidence they said was clear: the postservice grant given to the volunteers comes from the Discharged Soldiers Fund. There was no need for further evidence. Clearly, civic service is another form of military service. MK Ahmed Tibi (Raam-Taal) summed it up. "We don't want anything . . . through the state, no military service and no alternative to military service."[90]

Faced with the strong opposition of the Arab leadership, the ANCS adopted a low profile and a cautious marketing strategy to avoid confrontation. It worked behind the scenes with those regional council heads and school principals who were willing to accept volunteers. The policy was not to try to place volunteers by force in a city or regional council where the mayor was opposed. Most volunteers were assigned to jobs in their own communities unless their council head objected. The ANCS advertised the program mainly online, held recruitment fairs in cooperating towns, and worked with supportive principals. Not all the principals who admitted volunteers favored the program. Some agreed after being pressured by their regional council head or by the Ministry of Education. There were incidents where volunteers complained that in the school where they were placed they were obliged to sit and do nothing on the instructions of the principal. Others complained that they had received threats and were subjected to insults.[91] Nonetheless, and despite serious efforts by the

Arab leadership to derail the program, the number of volunteers in the Arab sector continued to climb each year. In a single decade, the number went from 240 volunteers in 2006 to 4,157 volunteers in 2017–2018.[92]

A Communitarian Initiative?
From Civic National Service to "Community Volunteering"

The government was determined to expand civic service in the Arab sector in order to grow Israel's economy. It regarded the high unemployment numbers in Arab communities, particularly among Arab women, as a factor that retards the state's economic growth. Recent studies have shown that Arab young women who complete civic service join the workforce at a higher rate than those who did not serve. Service provided the volunteers with valuable work experience that gave them an advantage with potential employers and it had increased their self-confidence and sense of self-worth.[93] For many, service had been their first step outside the protective environment of school and family and encouraged further independence.

Prime Minister Netanyahu appointed a committee of directors general in government ministries in 2010 to plan the expansion of civic service in both the Arab and Haredi communities and to set enlistment targets for each. The committee adopted a communitarian approach to civic national service, which emphasized service in and to the community and respect for the lifestyle and values of the volunteers. It recommended that the number of Arab volunteers be increased by 500 each year and that the program remain voluntary. In 2017, the targets in the Arab community were met and even exceeded.[94] The committee concurred with the low-key recruitment strategy adopted by the ANCS in the Arab sector in light of the opposition of Arab leaders and recommended that it continue. It called on the ANCS to extend and improve the courses in Hebrew language, mathematics, computers, and college entrance exam preparation offered to the volunteers, in order to boost their chances of acceptance to academic studies after service and give them greater marketability in the job market.[95]

The committee cautioned the ANCS to take steps to ensure that placements in both the Haredi and Arab sectors be respectful of the religious and cultural norms of the volunteers and provide them with an appropriate work environment. It concluded with a clearly communitarian message: while the overriding purpose of national service was to strengthen the connection between citizens and the state, it could only be achieved by strengthening the volunteer's "ties and identification with his community, society and the state."[96] In other words, the adoption of a multitiered, multicultural approach to service was essential if it were to gain acceptance in the Arab and Haredi communities.

In May 2012, the Knesset appointed yet another committee (the Plesner Committee) to suggest service legislation to replace the Tal Law that had been annulled by the High Court. The mandate of the committee was to study how to "share the burden" of service in the Haredi sector, but not surprisingly it extended its purview to the Arab sector as well. While the committee disbanded before completing its deliberations due to new elections, its chairman, Yochanan Plesner, released a preliminary report that included far-reaching recommendations. In a departure from the recommendations of previous committees (Ben-Shalom, Orr, Lapid, and Ivri) the Plesner Committee recommended that the government institute mandatory civic service in the Arab sector, after a transitional period of five years, during which time it would remain voluntary. During the transition, recruitment targets should be increased by 600 volunteers each year until they reached 6,000. It recommended that the Administration for National Civic Service consult regularly with Arab leaders and report to the government if any heads of regional councils took action against the volunteers in their districts.[97] The Plesner Committee was clearly more confrontational than previous committees, being that its members were politicians.

Civic National Service in Arab Public Opinion

Public opinion surveys conducted in the last two decades within the Arab community show a relatively stable pattern of relations between Arabs and Jews, with occasional dips, particularly after violent events in the West Bank or Gaza. Surveys conducted by Sammy Smooha of Haifa University 2003–2009 indicated that most Arab Israelis accepted the existence of the state within the 1967 borders as a given and were interested in coexistence with their Jewish neighbors. Most agreed with the statement that Israel was a good place to live, despite continued discrimination, and they would not consider immigration to another country. Israeli Arabs also expressed strong support for the democratic process and were resolute in their demand for political and social equality.[98]

In 2012 Smooha questioned both Arab leaders and the general Arab public on their attitudes toward the state and toward civic national service. He found a clear difference between what the general Arab public believed and the positions taken by their elected leaders. The former were more pragmatic and moderate, the latter more militant and ideological. For example, 60.2 percent of those who voted for Arab parties accepted Israel as a Jewish and democratic state while only 18.4 percent of the Arab leaders did so. The leaders were also more uncompromising in support of the full right of the Palestinian refugees to return to Israel (65.4%) while only 22.4 percent of their voters supported the refugees' inalienable right to return.[99] A majority of the general Arab public differentiated between support for Arab political institutions (62.7% supported the Arab Higher Monitoring Committee and 61.9% the Arab political parties) and their regard for the politicians who lead the Arab parties. Of those surveyed, 58.2 percent said they did not have confidence in the Arab leadership and 63.2 percent thought that they did not serve the community well in solving its problems. Those who thought that Arab leaders should direct their efforts toward solving the real problems of Arab communities rather than on finding solutions to the larger Palestinian problem comprised 61.1 percent.[100]

This difference between the leadership and the general Arab population found expression in their attitudes toward civic national service as well. In 2007, 78.2 percent of the Arab public said they would support civic national service if the Arab volunteers received the same financial benefits as others, while only 7.8 percent of the Arab leadership supported service.[101] Of Arab youth ages 18 to 22 in 2009, 53 percent said they would be willing to do civic service. This number decreased to 40 percent in 2011, a change that can be attributed to the vigorous campaign waged by the Arab leadership against civic service. Support for civic service was found primarily among those youth who already held relatively positive attitudes toward the state and its institutions. Similarly, support for civic service declined among the general Arab public in 2011 from 78 percent in 2007 to 62 percent.[102] This too can be attributed to the vigorous campaign by Arab leaders against service but also to a general deterioration in relations between Arabs and Jews during this period. The Arabs surveyed in 2011 expressed greater anger about inequality and discrimination and expressed more frustration at the failure of the government to end the occupation.[103]

When Arab youth were asked whether the position of the Arab leadership regarding civic service was important or very important to them, many responded that it was indeed very important. They were then asked whether they would support civic service if they knew that the Arab leadership was opposed: 48 percent answered that they would not support service. Significantly, 78 percent of the Arab public said they would be in favor of civic service if it were run by the Arab leadership, while only 62 percent said they would support a program run by the government.[104] These results give some credence to the leadership's contention that Arabs are not opposed to volunteering as such but rather oppose service designed, controlled, and operated by the state.

It is clear that civic service volunteers are youth who from the start have a somewhat positive attitude toward the state and who are interested in integrating further. For those reasons, they are willing to serve despite the stance of the leadership. In light of these findings, Smooha and Lechtman in 2015 recommended that civic service in the Arab sector continue in its voluntary format and not be made mandatory in the context of "equalizing the burden." A mandatory policy, they warned, would be viewed by the Arab leadership and by most of the Arab public as crossing a red line and would likely lead to civil disobedience among the youth.[105] A study conducted in 2017 by the Guttman Center for Public Opinion and Policy Research confirmed these findings. When asked whether civic service should be made mandatory for all Israelis, Arabs and Jews excused from the military, only 27 percent of the Arab respondents answered in the affirmative while among the Jews, 67 percent supported service for all.[106]

Civic National Service 2018:
Evolutionary Change and the Seeds of Communitarianism

Despite the determined efforts by the Arab leadership to derail civic national service in the Arab community, significant, slow incremental change is taking place. In 2006 there were only 240 Arab volunteers in civic service; in 2018 there were 4,140. This is still only a small percentage of the eligible 18 year olds, estimated at 35,000, but the numbers mean that in over 4,000 Arab households one member of the family is doing service, and that an increasing number of Arabs have a relative or friend who is doing service. In 2018 7.8 percent of the volunteers were Christians, 36 percent Muslims, 33.3 percent Bedouins, and 22.5 percent Druze. Women comprised 90 percent of the volunteers.[107] Seventy-five percent served in Arab communities near their homes and 56 percent worked in education.[108]

Clearly there is a self-selection process in those who sign up for civic service. Many of those who volunteer wish to integrate into Israeli society and most have a relatively positive or neutral attitude toward the state and its institutions. Many are interested in engaging in academic studies or vocational training in the future and are eager to gain the skills and the financial benefits given to those who serve. Their parents too are usually supportive of service.[109] For example, Rian Abu Leil from Kfar Ein Maahal had been a member of the General Federation of Working and Studying Youth (affiliated with the Labor Party) while in high school. She said in an interview that it had been clear to her that she would volunteer in civic service after graduating from high school. Her parents too were supportive, despite the pressure placed on them by the Islamic Movement. She said that members of the movement had approached her parents and had warned them that it was forbidden for her to volunteer. Rian said, "I wasn't willing to listen. I wasn't afraid."[110] In some areas, the Islamic Movement has been successful in discouraging girls from serving. According to Amir Abu Issa, the national coordinator of minority volunteers at the Authority for National-Civic Service, there were cases where girls were even offered money by the Islamic Movement not to serve. The movement pressures parents not to let the girls serve and in some cases, particularly among the Bedouin in the Negev, they succeed.[111]

Another volunteer explained that she was attracted to service because of the benefits it offered and because it would help her attain a better future. She decided to serve in order to improve her Hebrew and to have the opportunity to work outside her village so that after service she could find work in sales. She did service working at the reception desk at the District Court in Tiberias.[112]

Most Arab youth sign up for national service for purely instrumental reasons, for instance, to gain job experience, to receive the grants and benefits, or to do something different and challenging after completing high school. For many of the young women, if not for service, they would remain idle at home until the time that they marry, since there are few employment opportunities in their towns and villages. Civic service offers them job training, benefits, and postservice grants in addition to a monthly allowance. At the end of their service, volunteers received a grant of 3,452 shekels and another 6,557 shekels in a savings fund for education, job training, opening a business, buying an apartment, driving lessons, or marriage. They also receive free tuition for the first year of their studies in colleges and universities located on the periphery.

According to Zinav Abu Sayid, deputy coordinator of civic national service in the Arab sector at the ANCS, many of the volunteers begin their service without much idealism; however, toward the middle of service they begin to realize the value of giving and the importance of their contribution. This realization changes their attitude toward service and most of all toward themselves. They become more committed to contributing to the community and, as such, to the state. And many of the volunteers who had not considered higher education or job training before service were now empowered by the volunteering experience and had higher aspirations. This change in attitude, said Abu Sayid, achieves one of the state's goals: to increase the number of Arab women in the workforce. It will also strengthen their communities and in the long run grow the Israeli economy.[113]

Druze women are the newest group to join civic national service. While Druze men have been drafted to the IDF since 1956, Druze women have been traditionally excused for reasons of religion and modesty. Druze religious leaders in the past had forbidden the girls from serving in national civic service as well. They reversed this decision in 2012 after Druze religious leader Sheikh Moafaq Tarif and the Druze religious council met with the director of the ANCS, Sar Shalom Gerbi, and received binding assurances that the girls would not be given firearms or uniforms and, most importantly, would be permitted to live at home and to serve in their own communities. This was a major breakthrough that will have far-reaching consequences for Druze society. Previously, most Druze girls had no vistas open to them after completing high school except for marriage. Civic service offers them new opportunities, more empowerment, better Hebrew skills, and leadership training. Within six years, the number of Druze girls in civic service has increased dramatically. Today about 85 percent of Druze girls do civic national service, similar to the percentage of Druze boys conscripted to the IDF.[114]

Opposition to civic service among Arab leaders remains strong. In some municipalities and local councils civic service administrators still face significant opposition. For example, in the town of Turan the ANCS does not even try to recruit volunteers given the opposition of its leaders. In the Bedouin city of Rahat, the mayor and the deputy mayor opposed service and have pressured the schools and community center not to accept volunteers. At the start of the school year in September 2017, the deputy mayor, Amar Alhozile, went from kindergarten to kindergarten in the city ordering the teachers to expel the civic service volunteers that were assigned to them because they were not "approved" by the city's Office of Education.¹¹⁵ In September 2018 Rahat's Mayor Talal al-Krenawi and Deputy Mayor Amar Alhozile interrupted the training seminar held for the volunteers by the ANCS in the city, cursed at the volunteers, and told them that their services were unwelcome in Rahat. The girls ran out crying as did the coordinator of civic service, who felt personally threatened.¹¹⁶

The administrators of civic service in the Arab sector contend that there is often a discrepancy between what mayors or council heads say and how they act in fact. Some leaders were on public record denouncing civic national service; however, in actuality, they accept volunteers and in some cases are even supportive. In effect, they are part of a conspiracy of silence surrounding service and do not obstruct or discourage the volunteers. Zinav Abu Sayid, the deputy coordinator of civic service in the Arab sector, said that this pragmatic acquiescence to civic service was fairly common, except in towns where extreme nationalists control the local politics, for example, the towns of Arraba and Tur'an. There are also mayors who openly and actively support civic service and welcome volunteers, particularly in Druze, Christian, and Bedouin villages and towns in the north and in cities with a mixed population of Jews and Arabs, like Haifa, Lod, and Ramle.¹¹⁷

In Bedouin communities, 90 percent of the volunteers work in education, in schools, kindergartens, community centers, and 10 percent work in health services, government offices, environmental protection, assistance to the elderly, and so on.¹¹⁸ Most of the volunteers are girls, and most serve within their communities. Some had sought placements in organizations outside the community, for example, in a health fund or in Magen David Adom emergency health services, but were not accepted because of their low proficiency in Hebrew. Insufficient fluency, particularly among the Bedouin in the south, is often an obstacle.¹¹⁹

Another challenge to civic service is a lack of voluntary organizations in the Arab sector. Civic society organizations are relatively few, and many of the nonprofits that operate in the Jewish sector do not operate in the Arab sector. For lack of funds, local councils do not provide afternoon programs or day camps, assignments that occupy volunteers in the Jewish sector. Often schools are pressured to accept more volunteers than they need because there are more volunteers than assignments.¹²⁰

In recent years, particularly in light of the growing number of volunteers, some Arab leaders have modified their stance against civic service. While continuing to oppose service in its present form, some have presented the issue as one of control. In theory, they said, they were very much in favor of volunteering and recognize that it is a positive contribution to the community. However the real problem with civic service is that it is being imposed on the Arab community from outside, by the government, without the input, control, and consent of the Arab leadership. If it were to be placed entirely in the hands of the Arab leadership to manage and control without government intervention, and if it were to remain voluntary, they would withdraw their opposition.

In 2012 the Council of Arab Mayors called on the government to place the Arab program entirely under the administration and control of the Arab local councils. The government, it said, could set the guidelines but should not be involved in the operation of the programs.[121] Nazareth Mayor and Council Chairman Ramez Jerayssi said the mayors were willing to discuss expanding the existing programs if they would be controlled by the local governments and if they would be placed entirely under the aegis of domestic government ministries (education, social affairs, etc.), severing all connection to the Ministry of Defense.[122]

This proposal was rejected out of hand by the government, which raised doubts as to whether the funds for civic service would be directed to the volunteers alone if the municipalities were to gain control of the programs and could distribute the funds at their discretion. It questioned whether the funds would not in fact be diverted to cover the deficits of the local councils.[123] Moreover, there was also an ideological reason behind the government's refusal to transfer control. In many forums, Arab leaders and heads of local councils have articulated demands for local autonomy and recognition of the Arab sector as an indigenous national minority.[124] The government has rejected these demands and seeks instead to integrate Arab communities. It has a clear interest in having the volunteers become better citizens and gaining a greater appreciation of the state and its services, goals it feared would not be achieved if the program came under the exclusive control of nationalist Arab leaders.[125]

After 10 years of deliberation the Knesset finally passed comprehensive national civic service legislation in 2017. The Labor, Welfare, and Health Committee in the Knesset had held hearings and studied the question for almost two years. It received information from the many agencies that operate service programs in the different sectors and heard the testimony of supervisors and volunteers in the field. It also invited members of the Joint Arab list to participate in these discussions but, as in the past, they refused.[126]

The committee adopted a communitarian approach that gave credence to the idea that Israeli society and the state would be stronger if it strengthened each community, including the minorities. It recognized that in order for civic service to succeed, it must take note of the sensitivities of each community and brand the program differently for each.[127] If each community needed to be addressed in terminology it can relate to, then it was incumbent on the government to do so.

The civic service legislation passed in 2017 remedied one of the problems faced by recruiters in the Arab sector. Lawmakers changed the name of the civic service track in the Arab sector to "Community Volunteering" at the urging of the ANCS. This semantic change was intended to alleviate two problems confronting the ANCS when marketing civic national service in the Arab sector. Calling the program "Community Volunteering" eliminated the word "service" entirely since "service" in the Arab community was associated with the military and as such was automatically precluded. "Service" also had a second negative connotation, that of being a "servant" (doing menial work or servitude). Moreover, the committee eliminated the words "national" and "civic" from the title since both implied support for the state and membership in an "Israeli nation," which contradicted a Palestinian identity. The anti-service campaign promoted by the Arab leadership and by Baladna had emphasized the "national" in civic national service as evidence of the unholy connection between Israeli nationalism, the IDF, and civic service. While the change seems cosmetic in nature, it did remove a stumbling block that deterred some Arabs from service.

The civic service law passed by the Knesset in March 2017 lists two tracks of service that are essentially identical but operate in different sectors: "national" service, which in its branding clearly emphasizes the nationalist "republican" dimension of service for Jewish volunteers, religious girls, and those rejected by the IDF from service, and "community volunteering," the track for Arab volunteers that emphasizes the community dimension of service. The law specifies the same conditions and benefits to volunteers in both tracks.[128] A separate civic service law relating specifically to Haredim had already been passed in March 2014.

"Community Volunteering": The Challenges Ahead

The number of volunteers in civic service in the Arab sector continued to rise in 2017–2018 but only slightly. The total number of those doing "community volunteering" was 4,140. This was significantly lower than

4,800, the target set by the government.¹²⁹ A closer look at the numbers reveals different developments within each subgroup. Among the Bedouin, for example, the number of volunteers was lower, 1,057, about 100 fewer than in 2015. There was also a drop in the number of volunteers among Christian Arabs, from 468 in 2015 to 253 in 2018. Among the Muslims there was a small increase in the number of volunteers, 1,639, and a large, steady increase among Druze.¹³⁰

Civic service has become the accepted norm among Druze girls, similar to girls in the religious Zionist sector. In the last few years, the number of Druze serving in civic service has risen steadily and service has become as common among girls as military service among boys. (The Druze have the highest percentage of conscription to the IDF, 83% of males.) Druze leaders frequently state that the Druze have "tied their fate" to the state of Israel and as such to the Jewish people, and because of that commitment they serve in the IDF and in civic national service.

This partnership may be impaired because of a new Basic Law, "Israel as the Nation-State of the Jewish People," passed by the Knesset in July 2018. The law, which was passed by a small margin of 62 to 55, states that Israel is the Jewish state and the "national home of the Jewish people." It designates Hebrew as the official language of the country, demoting Arabic to a "special status," and determines the flag, the anthem, and the national symbol of the state, all Jewish. The law does not mention the minorities at all. Many Druze were deeply offended by the law, which did not include their partnership in the state and, in their view, relegated them to second-class status. The Druze found paragraphs 1c and 7a particularly objectionable:

> (1c) The right to exercise national self-determination in the State of Israel is unique to the Jewish people.
>
> (7a) The state views the development of Jewish settlement as a national value and will act to encourage and promote its establishment and consolidation.

Both paragraphs give exclusive rights to the Jewish people and in effect ignore the minorities who live among them. The Druze questioned whether the state will also encourage settlement by the minorities living in Israel, or whether they will be condemned to living in their towns and villages without hope for development and expansion. Would they be treated with equality in a land that is constitutionally designated as the "Jewish state"?

Particularly affronted by the law were Druze officers and former officers in the IDF who had devoted their lives to serving the country. The law generated impassioned demonstrations by the Druze and a petition to the High Court submitted by Druze MKs and former senior officers to annul the law. The law gave fuel to a small but growing minority of Druze who oppose service because of the failure of the government to improve conditions in their villages.

Amir Abu Issa, the national coordinator of minority volunteers at the Authority for National-Civic Service, himself a Druze, expressed to this writer his serious concern that the Nation-State Law would have a negative impact on the number of Arabs and Druze signing up for civic national service as well as on the number of Druze volunteering for elite units or officer's training in the IDF. If the law was not amended to specify equality for the minorities, he expected a drop in the number of Druze and Arabs serving in the IDF and in civic service. In the meanwhile, at the time of this writing, the law has not yet been amended.[131]

The number of Arab youth enlisting in civic national service is influenced understandably by the political atmosphere in the country and by disputes between the government and the Arab sector. Although the total number of volunteers has risen each year, the rate of increase has actually slowed in the last two years. Recruitment efforts have not achieved a major breakthrough. There is still strong opposition from the Arab leadership, which pressures local mayors, principals, and parents not to cooperate with civic service and warns the youth not to serve.

There are several other factors that influence the number of volunteers in a given year. The political situation in the territories inevitably impacts the number of youth doing service. Clashes between Israel and Palestinians in the West Bank and Gaza influence the political mood among Israeli Arabs and their willingness to serve. Escalation on the border with Gaza, violence at the fence, and bombings by the Israeli Air Force in retaliation incite opposition to the state and to its policies.

Disputes over land are often a cause of confrontation between Arabs and law enforcement officials. One such incident was the events at Umm al Hiran, where the government demolished illegally built houses in an unrecognized Bedouin village in the Negev. In the course of the protests, a protestor was killed by police.[132] The violence that resulted and the controversy surrounding the conduct of the police worsened relations with Bedouins and inflamed the entire Arab sector. In the last few years, the government has doubled the number of demolitions of illegal structures in Bedouin communities in the south, action that has increased tensions. It is not surprising that the rate of increase in the number of Bedouins in civic service has slackened and that more Bedouin volunteers come from the north rather than the south, even though the Bedouin population in the south is significantly larger.

Another factor that discourages youth from doing civic service is the growing influence of the Islamic Movement, particularly among the Bedouin in the south. The movement actively discourages Bedouins from army service and opposes civic service as well. The number of Bedouin boys volunteering to serve in the IDF has dropped precipitously in the last several years, particularly after Operation Protective Edge in 2014, and these same currents also impact the number of girls volunteering for civic service. Until 2014 there were approximately 300 Bedouin boys who volunteered each year to serve in the IDF. This number dropped to 200 in 2016–2017, explained in part by anger at the IDF policies in the Gaza Strip and West Bank and to the increased influence of the Islamic Movement.[133]

Timing is also a factor. The fact that 2018 was an election year in the Arab municipalities and local councils exacerbated the rhetoric of some Arab politicians who sought to gain votes by adopting more extreme positions. Many did not want to appear to be moderate or in collusion with the state in order not to lose voter support. Taking a stand against civic service was politically more advantageous, at least in some communities.[134]

Finally, a factor that continues to discourage Arabs from signing up to civic service is the government's own failure to institute reform. Despite numerous requests by the ANCS to stop payment of the postservice grants to the Arab volunteers through the Discharged Soldiers Fund, a branch of the Defense Ministry, the government continues to do so. The volunteers find it disturbing if not offensive that the payer on their grant checks is the fund. This becomes especially stressful when they go to deposit their benefit payments at their local Arab bank. The connection between civic service and the Soldiers Fund gives fuel to the opponents of civic service who point to the fund as clear evidence that civil national service is just another form of service in the military. Sar Shalom Gerbi, director general of the ANCS, appealed to the government on several occasions to transfer disbursement authority to the ANCS, thus removing from civic service all connection to the IDF and the Defense Ministry. The government understood the problem and in July 2013 instructed the minister of defense to take the necessary measures to transfer disbursement authority to the ANCS for benefits paid to Haredim and to Arab volunteers.[135] However, almost six years after this order, no measures have been taken; the payments are still being paid to the volunteers through the Discharged Soldiers Fund.[136]

Further evidence of government inaction is the failure of the Ministry of Education to take measures against principals in the Arabic state education network who refuse to admit volunteers to their schools. The ministry had been asked by the ANCS on several occasions to intervene on the matter. If it would issue a clear directive to all principals of schools funded by the Ministry of Education that they are required to accept volunteers, it would have an impact, particularly if state funding were conditional on accepting volunteers. It would also give support to school principals who want volunteers but are pressured by Arab leaders and by the Islamic movement not to accept them. The ministry has yet to take action until now.

This failure to act reflects to some extent the secondary importance of civic national service in the eyes of the government and the general lack of interest of the minister. Often the minister from a religious Zionist party takes a keen interest in matters that impact civic service in that sector (religious girls) since that is his natural constituency; he is less attentive to the needs of the minorities whose votes he cannot reap.

Conclusion

We have seen that despite several committee recommendations and many legislative initiatives, the option of civic national service was extended to the Arab sector only in 2006. Similar to the program for religious Zionist girls and for those rejected from service by the IDF, the program is voluntary. It offers Arab youth the opportunity to volunteer in their communities and to receive the same benefits, scholarships, and conditions that other Israelis receive as part of their postservice package. An increasing number of Arab youth, mainly girls, have recognized the benefits of volunteering for their own personal growth, for its financial benefit, and for its contribution to the community. Many who plan to study in the university and to find employment outside the Arab sector recognize that having civic service on their record is an advantage in employment, particularly in the Jewish sector.

Is this the start of a new communitarian model of citizenship in Israel? Recent developments that have taken place in the dialogue and diatribe over civic service leave a measure of hope and optimism to better relations between the Arab community, the nation, and the state. This chapter opened with a description of the first decades of the state when the dominant ethos of citizenship in Israeli society was republican, nationalist, Jewish, and Zionist. While it had united and inspired all those who shared the dreams and aspirations of establishing a Jewish state and justified the absorption of Jewish immigrants from all over the globe, it also served to exclude those who did not identify with this ethos. Israeli Arabs, although granted political rights, were excluded from the national endeavor. With the exception of the Druze, they were not called to army service nor did they wish to serve. The government accepted their alienation from the state as a given (some would argue a self-fulfilling prophecy), in light of the Arab defeat in 1948, and made minimal efforts to improve their conditions or to integrate them into the new society that was being formed.

As we have shown, initiatives in the 1990s and later to adopt a liberal democratic approach that related to each individual citizen in an equal manner also failed to integrate Arab citizens. Liberalism gave emphasis to the rights of each individual citizen and was ostensibly blind to ethnic and religious differences in the name of equality. However, it also introduced a discourse that required that obligations to the state should also be equal, that is, sharing the burden of military or civic service. While Arab citizens who suffered from government neglect and discrimination rallied to the cause of equal rights, they were incensed when their demands for equality were answered with counterdemands that they fulfill citizen obligations, that is, civic service.

The Arab leadership firmly rejected all attempts to link their right to equality with a service obligation. Moreover, as the occupation of the West Bank and Gaza by Israel entered its fourth decade, Arab leaders and the majority of the Arab population identified with the Palestinian population in the territories and its struggle for independence. Their anger at Israeli policies and their feelings of alienation came to a head in the events of October 2000 when protests and demonstrations became violent. The events served as a wakeup call to Israeli governments not to continue to ignore the inferior conditions in the Arab sector. They also obliged the government to reevaluate the nature and meaning of citizenship for groups who did not share the republican Zionist ethos, and to initiate policies of inclusion, while respecting and acknowledging difference. A new kind of citizenship had to traverse beyond the existent policy that gave recognition to Arab cultural needs, for example, an Arabic track of education, Arabic as an official language, Arab regional councils, and so on. The government after the Orr Commission report recognized that it would have to reach out to the Arab sector and encourage it to participate more fully in Israeli society, by extending more opportunities for employment and by offering the youth the option of civic service.

It is this nascent effort by the state to recruit Arab youth into civic service that has incensed the Arab leadership, which fears that by participating in these programs the youth may strengthen its connection with the state and its institutions. Civic service, they feared, could lead to further Israelification, the seeds of which had already taken root. After completing civic national service, volunteers will be empowered to continue on to higher education or job training. More will study in Israeli universities and colleges and will find employment outside their towns and villages, and they will mix with other Israelis in the workplace. The Arab leadership's fear of Israelification is in fact its greatest challenge, particularly if the conflict with Palestinians reaches some settlement. Israel's Arab citizens will demand that their leaders focus on domestic issues, such as community safety, schools, roads, and infrastructure, issues brushed aside because of their preoccupation with the occupation.

Civic national service or "community volunteering" may transform Israel from a country of warring tribes, polarized by nationalist ideology and ethnic strife, into a more tolerant, communitarian democracy where citizens identify both with their communities and with the state and its institutions. A first step toward achieving this two-tiered model of citizenship must include a willingness by all communities, majority and minority, to cooperate with each other and to work together to achieve a better society for all. Civic national service in the Arab sector is a program that can achieve just that. It will improve social and educational services within the community and develop learning skills and leadership among Arab youth. It will also give the volunteers a greater understanding and appreciation of state services. Those who serve will gain the respect of Jewish Israelis, who value those who contribute to the well-being of the country.

The government has a responsibility to find a way to include Arab leaders in the service project and not to reject their proposals out of hand. It should quickly set up an alternative postservice disbursement track separate from the Ministry of Defense and stop postponing this very necessary change. If civic service is to achieve greater integration of Israel's Arab citizens in the body politic, the government must be particularly attentive to those who are willing and even eager to serve. It must continue to reach out to the Arab community while seeking solutions to the conflict with the Palestinians. It is incumbent upon the government to make every effort to incorporate Arab leaders into the decision-making bodies of civic service. If this is not done, the contribution of civic national service to a communitarian model of citizenship in Israel will be limited.

Conclusion

Four Tribes: Is a Communitarian Model the Answer?

We have seen how national civic service policy in Israel evolved parallel to changes in state-citizen relations, from the period of nation-building in the mid-20th century until today. Israel is a relatively young country that is still in the process of defining itself and its democratic processes. It is still in the midst of writing its constitution and has not yet settled the question of its borders. These open but very basic questions of identity, regime, and territory cannot but impact its domestic politics and relations among different groups in society. To what extent should Israel be a Jewish state, that is, a religious state, has plagued relations between the orthodox and the secular. And relations of the Jewish majority with the Arab minority are influenced by the success or failure of the peace process with the Palestinians and by Israel's war on terror. The absence of a completed constitution is but a symptom of the lack of consensus on the question of the religious or secular nature of the state and on the status of the minorities in a Jewish state. Debate on these fundamental issues is often contentious between parties on the left and nationalists on the right, orthodox versus secular, Arab versus Jew. Formally, Israel defines itself as a Jewish and democratic state, a catchphrase that resonates easily in the ears of the listener, allowing each to hear the melody they wish to hear. The orthodox and the nationalists hear the tones of Jewish tradition and history that dominate the composition; Israel's parties on the left and the Arabs, the theme of democracy and liberalism shared by Western democracies throughout the world.

One would have thought that civic national service would not be a topic that posed much interest for students of politics in general or students of Israeli politics in particular. One might have assumed at first glance that the act of volunteering, which is essentially an act of altruism and public spirit and ostensibly devoid of politics would generate little conflict or political debate. However, as we have shown throughout this book, the debate over civic national service in Israel was intensely political and intrinsically connected to different perspectives on the nature of citizenship. As such, it has aroused the passions and conflicts that simmer at Israel's volcanic base. Unresolved fundamental issues relating to integration or exclusion, Zionism or a state of all its citizens, have found expression in the debate over service, military and civic. The debate over civic national service is an integral part of the wider discussion about the rights and obligations of citizenship in a state with multiple and diverse communities.

In this book we have divided Israel's political history since independence into three periods, each with its characteristic ethos of citizenship: republican, liberal, and nascent communitarian. Each includes periods of transition when an ethos overlaps with a previous one. The republican ethos characterized the first decades of the state when nation-building and security dominated Israel's political agenda. It is not surprising that the discussion regarding national civic service at the time mostly ignored the question of drafting the Haredim or of extending national service to Israel's Arabs. The former rejected the Zionist ideology and did not share the ideals and commitment of the secular Zionist majority. They were anxious to rebuild the world of Torah scholarship that had been destroyed in the Holocaust and to strengthen religious observance. Since they were a negligible number among potential conscripts, they could be excused from service without consequence. Israeli Arabs were regarded by Israel's leaders as a potential security threat and a possible fifth column, to be monitored rather than embraced. The government had no interest in forcing them to serve in the military or in any other mode of service. While excluding those who do not serve, Israel's leaders united other Israelis in a covenant of brotherhood and citizenship in support of those who serve and sacrifice for the nation.

As detailed in chapter 2, the Defense Law of 1949 conscripted men and women to service in the military but gave religious girls the option of being excused for religious reasons. This disparity between religious and irreligious soon became the subject of a political conflict between the ruling Mapai party and the religious parties, Mizrachi and Hapoel Hamizrachi, Agudat Yisrael and Poalei Agudat Yisrael. Prime Minister Ben-Gurion advanced legislation to require religious girls exempted from the IDF to do two years of alternative civic national service. The religious and Haredi parties were incensed by the law that had been proposed without consulting with them and without their prior agreement. Since civic national service was used as a truncheon in the hands of the prime minister in his conflict with the religious parties rather than as an idealistic initiative to promote community service, it was doomed to failure. Similarly, in the 1980s and 1990s when members of the Knesset from far-right parties proposed civic service legislation in the Arab sector in order to appeal to their own electoral base, with the clear intent of provoking a vociferous response from Arab representatives, no real policy could result.

Faced with unalterable opposition from the religious parties, Israel's chief rabbis, and the Haredi rabbinical leadership, Ben-Gurion's successor Moshe Sharett let the law rest, never to be implemented. While the law itself had had little difficulty being passed in the Knesset, since it reflected the prevailing republican ethos, it could not be forced upon a Haredi population that did not share these norms and values. Had civic national service been made voluntary as proposed by Binyamin Mintz of the Poalei Agudat party in 1953, the program would have attracted many young women from the religious Zionist sector who would have been happy if not eager to serve the country in a nonmilitary framework. They would have contributed to the general welfare of the country particularly in the early years of the state when the country faced the huge task of immigrant absorption, limited funds, and a serious shortage of social services providers. However for political reasons, neither Ben-Gurion nor Moshe Sharett were willing to consider a voluntary option.

The national civic service program that was successfully implemented in 1971 was a result of a grassroots initiative by religious Zionist girls with the backing of the National Religious Party (NRP). Almost 20 years after the abortive Mapai initiative, this program succeeded in energizing young women in the religious Zionist community to give a year or two of voluntary service. This initiative was driven by the nationalist feelings that pervaded after the Israeli victory in the 1967 war and by a feeling of disquiet among many girls that they had failed to contribute to the nation as they should. Ironically, the voluntary civic national service program that was then established followed the guidelines proposed by MK Mintz in 1953.

The new program was limited specifically to religious girls excused from service by the IDF and, as such, did not challenge the primacy of the IDF. The IDF remained the primary institution of service and was the sole authority to determine who should serve and where. National service extended to religious girls the opportunity to contribute and to fulfill their republican obligations to the nation and in performing civic service, they too would be part of the "normative" community of citizens who serve. As such, civic national service became a rite of passage of religious Zionist girls. While in the last decade a small but growing number of religious girls have opted to serve in the IDF, the overwhelming majority still serve in national service. There are few instances of girls who choose not to serve at all, a choice that is socially unacceptable in the religious Zionist community. Religious girls' high schools without exception imbue in their students the value of contributing to the state and to society and most endorse civic national service over service in the IDF.

From the early 1970s until the mid-1990s, civic national service remained the exclusive prerogative of national religious girls and the exclusive domain of the National Religious Party. It remained closed to youth who were excused from service by the IDF and to Arabs. Ministerial authority over civic national service was held exclusively by the NRP.

The 1990s proved to be a transitional period in the Israeli national ethea. While the republican ethos of service still dominated, particularly among the religious Zionist and traditional Sephardic populations, a more liberal discourse became prevalent among many second- and third-generation Israelis residing mostly in the center of the country. It placed greater emphasis on the freedom of the individual and on self-expression rather than the Mapai inspired republican ethos of service and collective responsibility. Civic and human rights dominated the discourse as well as demands for greater equality of rights. Pursuance of personal ambition and self-fulfillment became more socially acceptable. This transition away from republican values and social responsibility also found expression in the neoliberal economic policies of the Likud governments, which rolled back the socialist state of the Mapai years. The government introduced liberal economic reforms, which succeeded in getting Israel out of a deep recession and out of the high inflation of the mid-1980s.

This new emphasis on human rights and equality was realized in two far-reaching pieces of constitutional legislation, the Basic Law: Human Dignity and Liberty and the Basic Law: Freedom of Occupation. And most importantly, the High Court of Justice interpreted Basic Law: Human Dignity and Liberty as giving it the authority to invalidate laws of the Knesset that do not befit the values of Israel as a democratic and Jewish state, unless they were for a good purpose, and suitably measured.

The High Court that from the outset had been the address for petitions by individual citizens whose civil rights had been violated by government actions became the advocate and protector of liberal values and of citizen equality for the entire society. Moreover, the High Court had earlier expanded the standing of citizen groups in the third sector and others to appeal to the Court and had shown a new readiness to rule on issues of public controversy that were under debate in the political domain.

This change in the public ethos and in the powers of the Court within the Israeli parliamentary system had direct impact on service policy as well. As we have detailed in chapter 4, the court was instrumental in jumpstarting the expansion of civic national service although without a formal ruling. When the government policy that restricted civic national service to religious girls alone came under the scrutiny of the High Court in a challenge by Shlomit and ACRI (Association of Civil Rights in Israel) in the name of a disabled Jewish youth and several Arab girls, it became clear to the government that it would be difficult if not impossible to justify its policy. The motivation of these youth to seek a remedy from the High Court was republican in essence; they were asking for the opportunity to serve despite their physical disability or ethnic identity. However, the premises upon which the appeal was based were those of equality and rights, values that were fundamental to liberal citizenship and consonant with the Basic Law: Human Dignity and Liberty. Although the High Court did not have to rule in this case because the government quickly gave assurances that it would study and reevaluate its policy, it is clear that the petition caused policymakers to realize that, in an era of liberal values and equality, they could not maintain an exclusionary and discriminatory civic service policy. This reevaluation of the right to serve from the perspective of liberal citizenship and equality was the first stage in a more controversial reassessment of the government policy of draft deferments for yeshiva students and exemptions from service that was soon to follow.

A program for youth excused by the IDF was finally instituted in 2001 after the Knesset passed the authorizing legislation. Civic national service would now be an option for hundreds of youth not conscripted to the IDF, giving them the same rights, benefits, and service opportunities as religious girls. It opened up new avenues of service for the physically and mentally impaired, for youth from disadvantaged homes, and those at risk. However, at the IDF's insistence, civic national service remained closed to conscientious objectors, nor were conscripts given a choice between service in the military and civic national service. Because of civic national service and later the establishment of special programs for the disabled to volunteer in the IDF, Israeli society has become more inclusive of youth with special needs and of youth from difficult social backgrounds.

In light of the change in the dominant ethos in the country from republican to liberal, it was inevitable that the fairness of the deferment policy for yeshiva students would be questioned and challenged in the Court. During the republican period, the number of yeshiva student deferments had remained low, limited by a ceiling set by Labor governments. The Haredi parties during this period also had less visibility; their few representatives sat in the opposition. The exclusion of the Haredim from service in a sense served the interests of the republican advocates; it differentiated between the fraternity of those who serve and the secluded Haredi community, who did not. However, after the election upset of 1977, the Haredi Agudat Yisrael party entered the coalition and became partners in the national leadership. Among the conditions it posed was an end to the ceiling on the number of yeshiva students. Subsequently, it used its political clout as the lynchpin of right-wing coalitions to obtain increased funding for yeshivas and yeshiva students and increased subsidies for large families, most of whom were Haredi or Arab. Additionally, a new Sephardic Haredi party, SHAS, entered the national political arena in 1984, gaining four seats in the Knesset and a prominent place in the government coalition. By 1996, the Haredi parties numbered 14 seats and 22 in 1999.

With this increased political power, more funding, and the removal of the deferment ceiling, the number of yeshiva students rose precipitously. It was only a matter of time until it led to an eruption of resentment and anger directed at the Haredim, their special funds, and their deferments. Reservists and others raised the question of equity, asking why they should serve and risk their lives while "others" do not. They demanded that Haredim too "share the burden" in service that should be equal and compulsory for all. Protestors in support of "sharing the burden" filled the streets but failed to change government policy since the government chose to sidestep the issue rather than rock the stability of the coalition.

The favored venue for those seeking equity in conscription policy became the Israel High Court of Justice, an institution that was insulated from the political influence of the Haredi parties. In a landmark decision in 1997, the Court revoked the authority of the defense minister to defer thousands of yeshiva students from service and sent the government to the drawing board to design a more equitable policy. The government established the Tal Committee in response. Significantly, the committee adopted a moderate communitarian approach to service, rejecting the idea of conscripting all yeshiva students by force of statute. It acknowledged the cherished value of Torah study in the Haredi community, but at the same time offered incentives to encourage those who wished to leave their studies to serve in the IDF or in civic national service. It recommended setting up special programs in the IDF and in civic national service appropriate to Haredim. The Tal Law that was passed by the Knesset in 2002 offered civic national service as an alternative to military service, which could be performed within the Haredi's own community. It also offered yeshiva students "a year of decision" to enable them to leave yeshiva studies for a year without foregoing their draft deferments.

As we have shown there were administrative delays in implementing the Tal Law; it had only limited success in increasing the number of Haredim serving in the IDF or in national service. It was however the start of gradual change in the Haredi community and its attitude toward service. The new option of leaving yeshiva studies, serving a short period of time in either military or civic national service, and then being free to go out to work, all at a relatively young age, opened up a vista for change, particularly for those who were unsuited to long-term yeshiva studies. It was the start of change in the Haredi community and, because it was moderate in its range, was reasonably acceptable to Haredi leaders, despite their protests. They too understood that in a democracy the government could not ignore the ruling of the Court.

The High Court however was dissatisfied with the achievements of the law. Only a limited number of Haredim took advantage of the "year of decision" and the numbers of those serving in the IDF and in civic national service were not high. Undeniably the law had gotten off to a slow start. Instead of giving the government more time to implement the law, the High Court struck it down in 2012 as unconstitutional because it had failed to meet the test of equitability. It left the government scrambling to formulate a new law that would meet the high standard of the Court.

In our view, it is unfortunate that the Court revoked the Tal Law without allowing it more time to take effect. A minority of justices had ruled that the law should not be struck down, opining that more time was needed to assess its achievements, particularly in light of the difficult challenges it faced. It saw the harbingers of change in the increasing numbers that did sign up for service and the ripple effect that their service could have in the Haredi community. In 2020, and with the benefit of hindsight, it is clear that the Tal Law had been the best and most politically realistic option for change in service policy.

The next conscription law, Amendment 19, was adopted by the Knesset in 2013 when the Haredim were out of the coalition. It included specific conscription targets and punitive sanctions against yeshiva students if the targets were not met, and it placed the responsibility to meet the targets on the Haredi community itself. This was a clear departure from previous policy. The law threatened to draft all yeshiva students except for a select few (1,800) unless the conscription quotas of Haredim were met. It also included punitive sanctions against yeshiva students who would fail to comply. The Haredim were incensed by the law and held mass protest demonstrations against it. They averred that the law would be revised as the first order of business when the Haredi parties would return to the coalition after the next election. The anger over the law wiped out much of the progress and goodwill toward service that had begun under the Tal Law and set back relations between the secular majority and the Haredim.

When they returned to the government in 2015, the Haredi parties insisted on amending Amendment 19. The Knesset then passed Amendment 21 with the changes they demanded. The age ceiling for conscription of yeshiva students was lowered from 29 to 24, after which time yeshiva students would have a complete exemption from service. This change exempted most Haredim from all service, since most would study in yeshiva anyway until age 24. The law also broadened the definition of Haredi to include all youth who had studied at least two years in a Haredi educational institution between the ages of 14 and 18, a proviso that could apply to those who were no longer Haredim at the time of their conscription. These "former Haredim" could fill the quotas set for yeshiva students, leaving others exempted. The law in effect exempted most Haredim from service, both civic and military, and postponed the implementation of the quotas to a later date. As a result of the law, the number of Haredim serving in civic national service plummeted, since after age 24 they were excused from service anyway.

This third law was challenged in the High Court and unsurprisingly was voided by the Court in September 2017, effective December 2, 2018, for failing to achieve equality in conscription. This move left the country with a law that would soon expire and with relations with the Haredim again in turmoil.

Conclusion

It is not unexpected that the program of civic national service in the Haredi community today can be considered pretty much a failure. Reports of irregularities abound; the number of volunteers has declined precipitously, the administrators of the program demoralized. While under the Tal Law the number of Haredim in civic national service had reached 1,070, under the new law the number dropped to 562, meeting only 28 percent of the target set by the government. The ruling of the High Court left the country without a conscription law, dependent on the Court to issue an extension on the old law if new legislation was not yet completed. At the time of this writing, April 2020, the country had three rounds of elections within a little over a year with the issue of conscription still unresolved. The High Court was forced to extend the deadline for the passage of a new conscription law until after the elections, when the volatile issue of service will become the headache of the new government, with the Haredim inside the government or in the opposition.

The election of April 2019 ended up in a stalemate between the right and left, with Prime Minister Netanyahu having only 60 MKs willing to join the right-wing coalition. One of the stumbling blocks toward forming a coalition was the refusal of former defense minister Avigdor Lieberman of the Yisrael Beiteinu party to join unless he received a hard and fast commitment that the version of the conscription law that he proposed in the previous government would be adopted. This was unacceptable to the Haredi parties who were in an alliance with the Likud. Netanyahu rejected Lieberman's terms, leaving him without a government. The new Kahol Lavan party with 35 seats had announced from the start that it would not join a government led by Netanyahu because he faced charges of bribery and corruption. A government led by the Kahol Lavan party was also not a possibility, since the Haredi parties were unwilling to join it because in that list's formation agreement it promised a rotation in the premiership between party leader Benny Ganz and Yair Lapid, the head of the Yesh Atid faction. Lapid was reviled by the Haredim for his anti-Haredi stance and for his leading role in passing the noxious Amendment 19 of the defense law.

In retrospect, the Tal Law, with all its deficiencies, had held out promise that slow measured change could take place in service policy. The Haredim as a community would have begun to take on citizen obligations as have other Israelis, secular and religious, and after completing service, military or civic, would have entered the workforce. The High Court's failure to recognize that it was counterproductive to apply a liberal egalitarian standard to relations with the Haredi community has resulted in a cycle of political crises, revised laws, new elections and multiple appeals to the Court.

The lifestyle of the Haredim and their commitment to the strictest observance of Jewish law preclude drafting most into the IDF or to national service, nor will they ever integrate fully into Israel's secular society. Their political clout will probably prevent the adoption of a draconian law that would draft the majority of the yeshiva students, whether they are in the government or in opposition. Such a law would also be unnecessary. The IDF has stated on numerous occasions that it does not need to conscript most of the Haredim. If the Court would boldly admit the limits of imposing change via the legal system and policymakers would offer better programs and attractive incentives to encourage Haredim to serve, change will take place and some measured integration achieved.

There is slow change already taking place within the Haredi community. There is an increasing number of Haredim seeking paths to academic study and employment. A recent study suggests that the number of Haredim who define themselves as modern is growing. A small but growing number identify with the state and its institutions.[1] These so-called "moderns" are the ones who are likely to welcome an abbreviated period of service in the military or to serve in civic national service.

Similarly in the Arab sector, major strides have been taken in the last decade to open up civic service to Arab youth and to Druze girls. Arab youth are now offered the same options of civic service as Jewish citizens and the many benefits that accrue to those who serve. Civic service is a path of self-empowerment and an opportunity for personal growth; through service one can gain some of the skills necessary for success in academia or employment. As in the Haredi sector, it is unrealistic to expect most Arab youth to embrace civic service given the complex relations between Arabs and Jews in the country. With the significant exception of Druze girls who sign up in large numbers with the consent and encouragement of their religious leaders, the number of Arab youth volunteering in civic service has been limited. If we look at the total number of youth that are eligible for civic national service and how many actually serve, the percentage is quite low. Nonetheless, one should not underestimate the importance of this development and the potential it holds for the further integration of Israeli Arabs into Israeli society. With almost 5,000 Arabs and Druze serving in civic service and the numbers slowly increasing every year, the Arab sector will move a step closer toward Israel's mainstream.

And these volunteers have family and friends who will be better informed about civic national service and more aware of its important contribution to schools, hospitals, and government offices.

The main obstacle to the expansion of civic national service in the Arab sector is the Arab political leadership, which has been unwavering in its opposition. Arab leaders have asserted that they are not against voluntarism as such and readily admit that the volunteers do make a significant contribution to education and welfare services in the community. However, they continue to oppose service because of what they consider its underlying intent: to create loyal, involved Arab citizens. Arab leaders contend that participation under Israeli government auspices is in effect a sellout to the Palestinian cause, a measure that will weaken the youths' Palestinian identity. For them, being an Arab in Israel is a zero-sum game; one may have an Israeli identity or a Palestinian identity, but not both. For this reason, the leaders say they will accept civic service only if it would be placed under their direct and exclusive control, to set its priorities and determine its content.

Admittedly civic national service under government auspices is intended to inculcate in its participants the essentials of good citizenship and loyalty to the state. And an ideal program aims at achieving greater social integration and bridging social capital between Arabs and Jews, for example, by having the volunteers serve outside their communities with youth different from themselves. The latter, however, is not a sine qua non for service. Service can and should be tailored to a community's needs and values. If a volunteer chooses to serve within his or her community, that choice should be respected and encouraged.

A communitarian approach to citizenship sees society as being composed of communities rather than of individuals. By strengthening communities through voluntary civic national service, the national society will be fortified as well. Volunteers are generally more active citizens after service, both in exercising their right to vote and in their involvement in civic society. A growing number of Israeli Arabs would like to integrate into Israeli society, work in professions, and enjoy a high standard of living while at the same time maintaining an identity as Palestinians. For these Arabs there need not be an insolvable clash between these two identities. Civic national service is an opportunity for them to give service and then to enter academia or employment as all Israelis do, as an equal, although without having to serve in the IDF. By completing civic national service, they have in effect leveled the playing field, in a country that values service. Like their Jewish peers, they too can devote one year or two years to service and contribute to their communities.

It is incumbent upon Israel's leaders to remove the obstacles to service and to encourage more youth in the Arab sector to serve. It is important that their program remain voluntary and that sufficient funds be allocated so that all who wish to serve can do so. The government should continue to reach out to more moderate Arab leaders who would be willing to endorse the program in return for giving them a greater say in the placements and conditions of service. It should also utilize the clout of the Education Ministry to require principals in schools funded by the state (as most schools are) to accept volunteers and to assign them to meaningful jobs. Such a directive issued by the ministry would take off some of the pressure on principals who may want to admit volunteers but are reluctant to take a stand against the Arab leadership, particularly when refusing volunteers has become a measure of their loyalty to the "Palestinian cause."

Admittedly, promoting civic service in the Arab sector is a daunting task in the present polarized political atmosphere in Israel, and particularly, during periods of unrest in the West Bank or Gaza and with the peace process stalled. However, this should not be a reason for the government to put civic service in the Arab community on hold; quite the opposite. It should strengthen efforts by the ANCS to recruit Arab youth to civic national service. "Community volunteering," as it was branded anew in the Civic-National Service Law, 2017, is a win-win endeavor for the state and for the Arab community. It is an opportunity to develop leadership and good citizenship in Arab youth and to raise the status of Arab women, all of which will be a gain for the state, for the Arab community, and for the individual volunteer.

We began this book with a quote from a speech given by Israel's president Reuven Rivlin at the 15th Annual Herzliya Conference in 2015, in which he described Israeli society as being composed of "four tribes, essentially different from each other and growing closer in size . . ." Rivlin challenged Israeli leaders to confront this new reality and to take concrete steps to bring these tribes closer in common citizenship:

> If we truly want to deal with the significance of the "new Israeli order," then we must bravely face the issue, and ask ourselves some tough questions. Are we, the members of the Zionist population, able to accept the fact that two significant groups, a

half of the future population of Israel, do not define themselves as Zionists? They do not watch the torch-lighting ceremony on Mount Herzl on Independence Day. They do not sing the national anthem with eyes glistening. Are we willing to give up military service, as an entry ticket into Israeli society and economy, and settle for civilian or community service? And on the other hand, are the Arab and Haredi publics willing to commit to contributing their share in molding Israeli identity and the Israeli economy, and to participate in civil national and community service, with a sense of responsibility and commitment?

In this study we have concentrated on three of Israel's tribes, the national religious, the Haredim, and the Arabs and their relationship with the fourth tribe, the secular Zionist. We traced the evolution of different ethea of citizenship, republican and liberal, and have suggested that it is time to adopt a new ethos of communitarian citizenship as suggested by Rivlin, which accepts and appreciates the different communities that compose the Israel nation, their beliefs, lifestyles and different attitudes toward the state. A communitarian approach to citizenship could be the adhesive that brings together the tribes into one multicultural nation without forcing upon one the perspective of the other. Rivlin said, "The 'new Israeli order' now requires us to abandon the accepted view of a majority and minorities, and move to a new concept of partnership between the various population sectors in our society." Civic national service is one step toward achieving that partnership.

Notes

Introduction

1. Although the reserve law does not differentiate between men and women, until the mid-1990s women were usually not called to reserve service. After age 41 the law permitted a reservist in a combat unit to decline to serve. In 2008 new age ceilings were adopted: age 40 for soldiers and age 45 for officers. Single women are usually called up to serve in the reserves until age 24, but they can be called up by law until age 38.

2. Yagil Levy, *MiTsava HaAm LeTsava Haperiferiyot* [From a people's army to an army of the peripheries] (Jerusalem: Carmel, 2007).

3. IDF website, www.idf.il/2018.

4. See Maurice Roumani, *From Immigrant to Citizen: The Contribution of the Army to National Integration in Israel* (The Hague: Foundation of Plural Societies, 1979).

5. See Raef Zreik, "Ezrahut, Zekhuyot Vehovot: Al Diyunim BeNose HaSherut HaEzrahi BeYisrael" [Citizenship, rights and obligations: Discussions of civic service in Israel], *Iyunei Mishpat* 37, no. 2 (2015): 289–340.

6. Gilad Malach, Maya Choshen, and Lee Cahaner, *Statistical Report on Ultra-Orthodox Society in Israel, 2016* (Jerusalem: Israel Democracy Institute, 2016).

7. *Haaretz*, June 14, 2016.

Chapter 1. Alternative Ethea of Citizenship: Republican, Liberal, and Communitarian

1. Reuven Gal, Karin Amit, Nicole Fleischer, Nancy Strichman, *Volunteers of National Youth Service in Israel: A Study on Motivation for Service, Social Attitudes and Volunteers' Satisfaction* (St. Louis: Washington University Center for Social Development, Global Service Institute, 2003). See also Huiting Wu, "Social Impact of Volunteerism," Points of Light Institute, 2011, http://www.pointsoflight.org/

sites/default/files/site-content/files/social_impact_of_volunteerism_pdf, accessed July 15, 2018.

2. Wu, "Social Impact."

3. Aristotle, *Politics*, trans. Carnes Lord (Chicago: University of Chicago Press, 1989), 1291a, 7, 27–28, 33–35. See also Andres Rosler, "Civic Virtue: Citizenship, Ostracism and War," in *The Cambridge Companion to Aristotle's Politics*, ed. Marguerite Deslauriers and Pierre Destrée (London: Cambridge University Press, 2013), 144–175.

4. Donald Morrison, "The Common Good," in *The Cambridge Companion to Aristotle's Politics*, ed. Marguerite Deslauriers and Pierre Destrée (London: Cambridge University Press, 2013), 176–198.

5. Aristotle, *Politics III*, 6–7; Morrison, "The Common Good," 179.

6. Aristotle *Politics II*, 21261a, 37. Christoph Horn, "Law, Governance, and Political Obligation," in *The Cambridge Companion to Aristotle's Politics*, ed. Marguerite Deslauriers and Pierre Destrée (London: Cambridge University Press, 2013), 238.

7. Thomas N. Mitchell "Roman Republicanism: The Underrated Legacy," *Proceedings of the American Philosophical Society* 145, no. 2 (June 2001): 127–137.

8. Marcus Tullius Cicero, *On Duties (De Officiis)*, trans. M. T. Griffin and E. M. Atkins (New York: Cambridge University Press, 1991), bk. 1, 33.

9. Niccolò Machiavelli, *The Discourses* (Harmondsworth: Penguin, 1970), vol. 1, 58.

10. Jean-Jacques Rousseau, *The Social Contract* (Harmondsworth: Penguin, 1968), 60.

11. Jean-Jacques Rousseau, *The Social Contract and Other Later Political Writings*, ed. and trans. Victor Gourevitch (London: Cambridge University Press, 1997). See also J. S. Maloy, "The Very Order of Things: Rousseau's Tutorial Republicanism," *Polity* 37, no. 2 (2005): 243–244.

12. Colleen A. Sheehan, "Madison and the French Enlightenment: The Authority of Public Opinion," *The William and Mary Quarterly* 59, no. 4 (2002): 925–956.

13. James Madison, *The Papers of James Madison*, ed. William T. Hutchinson et al. (Charlottesville: University Press of Virginia, 1977), vol. 11, chap. 13, doc. 36.

14. Marshall also lists as an obligation industrial citizenship that includes collective bargaining and agreements by trade unions. See Thomas H. Marshall, *Citizenship and Social Class and Other Essays* (London: Cambridge University Press, 1950), 68–80. For further discussion of Marshall on citizenship, see Morris Janowitz, "Observations on the Sociology of Citizenship: Obligations and Rights," *Social Forces* 59, no. 1 (1980): 7.

15. Marshall, *Citizenship and Social Class*, 41.

16. Janowitz, "Observations on the Sociology of Citizenship," 21.

17. Philip Pettit, *Republicanism: A Theory of Freedom and Government* (London: Oxford University Press, 1997), 41.

18. Richard Dagger, "Republican Citizenship," in *Handbook of Citizenship Studies*, eds. Engin F. Isin and Bryan S. Turner (Thousand Oaks: Sage, 2002), 148.

19. Dagger, "Republican Citizenship," 147.

20. Dagger, "Republican Citizenship," 155. For further discussion, see Paul Weithman, "Political Republicanism and Perfectionist Republicanism," *The Review of Politics* 66, no. 2 (2004): 285–312.

21. Gerald F. Gaus, *Justificatory Liberalism: An Essay on Epistemology and Political Theory* (London: Oxford University Press, 1996), 162–166.

22. John Locke, *Two Treatises of Government: An Essay Concerning the True Original, Extent and End of Civil Government*, 1689, online https://books.google.com/books/download/Two_Treatises_of_Government.pdf?id=K5UIAAAAQAAJ&output=pdf.

23. John Stuart Mill, *On Liberty*, 1859 (Kitchener: Batoche Books, 2001), 13.

24. Immanuel Kant, *Kant Political Writings*, ed. Hans Reiss (London: Cambridge University Press, 1991), 74.

25. Mill, *On Liberty*, 15–16.

26. Mill, *On Liberty*, 18.

27. Mill, *On Liberty*, 8–9.

28. Mill, *On Liberty*, 96–97.

29. Kathleen Knight Abowitz and Jason Harnish, "Contemporary Discourses of Citizenship," *Review of Educational Research* 76, no. 4 (2006): 661.

30. John Rawls, *A Theory of Justice* (Cambridge: Harvard University Press, 1971), 207–221.

31. Rawls, *Theory of Justice*, 217–221.

32. Dagger, "Republican Citizenship," 155.

33. Iris Marion Young, *Justice and the Politics of Difference* (Princeton: Princeton University Press, 1990), 117.

34. This critique is particularly correct in the case of Israel in the post-independence period. It will be discussed extensively in chapters 5 and 6.

35. Michael Sandel, *Liberalism and the Limits of Justice*, second ed. (Cambridge: Cambridge University Press, 2012); Alasdair McIntyre, *After Virtue: A Study in Moral Theory*, third ed. (Notre Dame: University of Notre Dame Press, 2007); and Michael Walzer, *Spheres of Justice: A Defence of Pluralism and Equality* (Oxford: Robertson, 1983). See also Shlomo Avineri and Avner de Shalit, eds., *Communitarianism and Individualism* (London: Oxford University Press, 1992).

36. Michael Sandel, "The Procedural Republic and the Unencumbered Self," *Political Theory* 12, no. 1 (1984): 81–96.

37. Sandel, *Liberalism and the Limits of Justice*, 150.

38. Amitai Etzioni, "The Responsive Community: A Communitarian Perspective," *American Sociological Review* 61, no. 1 (1996): 1–11.

39. Etzioni, "Responsive Community," 5.

40. Avineri and de Shalit, *Communitarianism and Individualism*, 3. Kymlicka maintains that central to the liberal view is that we "understand our selves to be prior to our ends, in the sense that no end or goal is exempt from possible re-examination." That means that there are no predetermined and unchangeable ends that one is bound by (e.g., set by the community) but rather they can be changed or reevaluated by man's capacity for rational thought. He writes, "This doesn't require that I can ever perceive a self totally unencumbered by any ends—the process of ethical reasoning is always one of comparing one 'encumbered' potential self with another 'encumbered' potential self. There must always be some ends given with the self when we engage in such reasoning, but it doesn't follow that any particular ends must always be taken as given with the self." Will Kymlicka, *Liberalism, Community and Culture* (Oxford: Oxford University Press, 1989), 52–53.

41. Charles Taylor, "Atomism," in *Communitarianism and Individualism*, ed. Shlomo Avineri and Avner de Shalit (London: Oxford University Press, 1992), 45–47.

42. Taylor, "Atomism," 49.

43. See Mary Ann Glendon, *Rights Talk: The Impoverishment of Political Discourse* (New York: Free Press, 1991).

44. Avineri and de Shalit, *Communitarianism and Individualism*, 7.

45. Elizabeth Frazer, *The Problems of Communitarian Politics: Unity and Conflict* (London: Oxford University Press, 1999), 22.

46. Henry Tam, *Communitarianism: A New Agenda for Politics and Citizenship* (Basingstoke: Macmillan, 1998), 115.

47. Frazer, *Problems of Communitarian Politics*, 205.

48. Sandel, "The Procedural Republic and the Unencumbered Self," 94.

49. Cited in James Arthur, "Community Involvement and Communitarian Theory," n.d., http://citeseerx.ist.psu.edu/viewdoc/download?doi=10.1.1.522.2930&rep=rep1&type=pdf.

50. Cited in Frazer, *Problems of Communitarian Politics*, 12.

51. See Arthur Schlesinger Jr., *The Disuniting of America* (New York: Norton, 1992), cited in Etzioni, "Responsive Community," 10.

52. See Robert Putnam and Kristin A. Goss, "Introduction," in *Democracies in Flux: The Evolution of Social Capital in Contemporary Society*, ed. Robert Putnam (New York: Oxford University Press, 2002), 3–20.

53. Etzioni, "Responsive Community," 10.

54. Benjamin R. Barber, "A Proposal for Mandatory Citizen Education and Community Service," *Michigan Journal of Community Service Learning* 1, no. 1 (1994): 92.

55. Amitai Etzioni, *The Spirit of Community: The Reinvention of American Society* (New York: Simon and Shuster, 1994), 114.

56. Etzioni, *Spirit of Community*, 114.

57. Etzioni, *Spirit of Community*, 115.

58. Melissa Bass, *The Politics and Civics of National Service: Lessons from the Civilian Conservation Corps, VISTA, and AmeriCorps* (Washington, DC: Brookings Institution Press, 2013), 154; and Harris Wofford, "The Politics of Service: How a Nation Got Behind AmeriCorps," *Brookings Review* 20, no. 4 (2002), https://www.brookings.edu/articles/the-politics-of-service-how-a-nation-got-behind-americorps/. Not all observers applauded the expansion of civic service programs. For a scathing critique of civic service programs in the United States, see Eric B. Gorham, *National Service, Citizenship, and Political Education* (Albany: State University of New York Press, 1992).

59. *New York Times*, August 30, 2014.

60. Fact Sheet: Corporation for National and Community Service, https://voicesforservice.org/wp-content/uploads/2017/05/Backgrounder-on-CNCS-May-2017.pdf.

61. Corporation for National and Community Service FY 2020 Congressional Budget Justification, March 2019, www.nationalservice.gov/sites/default/files/documents/CNCSFY2020CBJ-FinalwupdatedOIG508compliant.pdf.

62. Gershon Shafir and Yoav Peled, *Being Israeli: The Dynamics of Multiple Citizenship* (Port Chester: Cambridge University Press, 2002), 17.

63. See Avi Barali and Nir Keidar, *Mamlakhtiyut Yisraelit* [Israeli republicanism] (Jerusalem: Israel Democracy Institute, 2011).

64. Uri Ben-Eliezer, "The Meaning of Political Participation in a Nonliberal Democracy," *Comparative Politics* 25, no. 4 (1993): 397–412.

65. David Ben-Gurion, "Netsah Yisrael" [The eternity of Israel], in *Hazon VaDerekh* (Tel Aviv: Mapai, 1953), vol. 4, 269.

66. Barali and Keidar, *Mamlakhtiyut Yisraelit*, 32. See also Ben-Gurion, "Netsah Yisrael," 284–287.

67. Ben-Gurion assigned to the army an important role in integrating society. He wrote, "The main purpose of the state of Israel is the ingathering of the exiles; and the IDF has been designated one of the main factors in integrating the exiles. . . . The army must convert this mix of tribes with their various languages into one national unit, teach them Hebrew, and the fundamental values of the state and prepare them for the task of pioneering and making the desert bloom." Ben-Gurion, "Netsah Yisrael," 104.

68. Natan Yanai, "Musag HaEzrachut Betfisato Shel David Ben-Gurion" [The concept of citizenship in the thought of David Ben-Gurion], *Iyunim BeTekumat Yisrael* 4 (1994): 494–504.

69. Israel Defense Service Law, first reading, 1949. The IDF still has the characteristics of a "people's army," with conscripts and reservists strongly

outnumbering long service professionals. Able-bodied boys serve 32 months in compulsory service and then decades in the reserves (according to the current law until age 40 and officers until age 45). Women serve a mandatory two years and can be called to reserve duty as well. Religious women can ask to be excused and the defense minister is authorized to defer service for some, for example, yeshiva students, medical students, and others. Arabs are not called up to serve but are permitted to volunteer.

70. Menachem Begin, "Herzl and Jabotinsky," in *BaMahteret* [In the underground] (Tel Aviv: Hadar, 1978), vol. 1, 57–60.

71. Yagil Levy, "Is There a Motivation Crisis in Military Recruitment in Israel?," *Israel Affairs* 15, no. 2 (2009): 136.

72. Paul Rivlin, *The Israeli Economy from the Foundation of the State through the 21st Century* (Cambridge: Cambridge University Press, 2010), 27.

73. Rivlin, *Israeli Economy*, 43.

74. Rivlin, *Israeli Economy*, 47–48.

75. Ricki Shiv, "Tokhnit Hayitsuv 1985: Kalkala Nekhona o' Ideologia" [Israel's Stabilization Plan 1985—Correct Economics or Ideology], *Iyunim BeTekumat Yisrael* 23 (2013): 326–327.

76. *Globes, Israel Business News*, May 29, 2001.

77. Shafir and Peled, *Being Israeli*, 231. See also Eyal Lewin, *Ethos Clash in Israeli Society* (Lanham: Lexington Books, 2014).

78. Asher Arian, Nir Atmor, and Yael Hadar, *The 2007 Israeli Democracy Index* (Jerusalem: Israel Democracy Institute, 2007).

79. *Davar*, the daily of the Labor party, folded in 1996. *Al Hamishmar*, the newspaper of the Mapam party, closed in 1995 after operating several years with heavy losses.

80. Arian, Atmor, and Hadar, *Israeli Democracy Index*. In the same survey, fewer Israelis (29%) said they were willing to pay higher taxes in order to pay for the increased costs of defense. This was a change from the 48% that had been willing to pay in 1986.

81. Mizrahim (Orientals) is the term used to denote Jews who immigrated to Israel from Middle Eastern countries and North Africa.

82. Levy, "Is There a Motivation Crisis," 138.

83. Levy, "Is There a Motivation Crisis."

84. Levy, "Is There a Motivation Crisis."

85. Etta Bick, "Lip-Service to Service: The Knesset Debates over Civic National Service in Israel, 1953–2005," *Israel Affairs* 22, no. 1 (2016): 126–149.

86. Levy, "Is There a Motivation Crisis," 150.

87. Levy, "Is There a Motivation Crisis," 142.

88. Shafir and Peled, *Being Israeli*, 170.

89. See discussion in Yoav Peled and Horit Herman Peled, *The Religionization of Israeli Society* (London: Routledge, 2018).

Chapter 2. Religious Girls and Civic National Service, 1951–1953: An Initiative That Failed

1. In the first five years after independence (1948–1953) Israel absorbed 740,000 Jewish immigrants from all over the world. The total Jewish population in Israel was only 1,500,000. Ben-Gurion, "Netsah Yisrael," 266.

2. *Divrei HaKnesset* [Knesset proceedings], vol. 2, August 15, 1949 (Jerusalem: Government of Israel), 1336–1341.

3. In the early years, Ben Gurion assigned to the IDF a central role in political socialization. He said in the Knesset, "Only the military can and should serve as the unifying and inspiring force in shaping the new image of the people and the adoption of the new culture and society that we are creating in Israel. This educational role is not just a domestic national need but it is also a necessary requisite for our security. A military of hired soldiers that is not deeply connected to the people's independence and to its vision for the future will not meet the test when it is required to fight, a fight of the few against the many." *Divrei HaKnesset*, Vol. 2, August 15, 1949, 1338.

4. *Divrei HaKnesset*, vol. 2, August 15, 1949, 1338.

5. *Divrei HaKnesset*, vol. 2, September 5, 1949, 1569.

6. The Religious Front was an alignment of four religious parties that had very different worldviews on Zionism and the Jewish state. Both the Mizrachi and the Hapoel Hamizrachi parties were religious and Zionist in ideology. The Mizrachi represented the religious Zionist urban middle class and as such had a capitalist perspective; the Hapoel Hamizrachi represented religious workers and religious collective settlements, kibbutzim, and moshavim, and shared the economic views of the ruling socialist party Mapai and the Histadrut Federation of Labor. Both parties were members of the Zionist movement almost from its inception and were partners with the Revisionist and Socialist Zionist parties in the establishment of the state. They were less insular in their outlook and more open in their attitudes toward academic studies and secular culture than was the ultra-orthodox Agudat Yisrael.

Both the Mizrachi and the Hapoel Hamizrachi parties revered the first chief rabbi in Palestine, Rabbi Avraham Hacohen Kook, and had adopted his eschatological view of the Jewish state as marking the beginning of messianic times. For them, the very establishment of the state was a miracle and had special religious significance. The Chief Rabbinate was recognized and respected as the Halachic authority of the state whose rulings were binding. The ultra-orthodox parties, in contrast, obeyed their own rabbis and did not accept the authority of the "Zionist" chief rabbis.

7. The Agudat Yisrael party was an amalgamated party of Lithuanian and Hassidic ultra-orthodox Jews (Haredim), most of whom had opposed Zionism at the start of the 20th century but later accepted a modus vivendi with the Zionist movement in the aftermath of the Holocaust. Many came to Israel as refugees during and after World War II. Agudat Yisrael, unlike religious Zionists,

did not consider the Jewish state to have any religious significance, nor did it share their readiness to cooperate with the secular Jews in building the state. It had mainly an instrumental attitude toward the state. It would support it and participate minimally in its institutions in order to strengthen and expand the study of Torah. The party's relations with the secular parties were pragmatic. It would enter into a coalition with them in order to gain funding and support for ultra-orthodox institutions, particularly for yeshivas and yeshiva students, and to protect its interests. The Council of Torah Sages was the party's supreme authority and it determined its stand on the issues. It chose the party's representatives in the Knesset and instructed them how to vote.

8. Poalei Agudat Yisrael was a small party representing ultra-orthodox urban workers and agricultural settlements, ultra-orthodox collective moshavim, and kibbutzim. While aligned for many years with Agudat Yisrael, it was somewhat more modern and moderate in its outlook and less insular in its lifestyle.

9. Deuteronomy 22: 5.

10. For a discussion of the rabbinic sources pertaining to women and military service, see Yehezkel Cohen, *Giyus Banot VeSherut Leumi: Iyun BaHalakha* [The conscription of girls and national service: A study in Jewish law] (Jerusalem: Ne'emanei Torah VaAvodah, 1979).

11. *Divrei HaKnesset*, vol. 2, speech by Y. M. Levin, First Reading, Defense Service Law, August 29, 1949, 1446–1447.

12. Shlomo Cohen, ed., *Peer HaDor: Prakim MeMasechet Hayav U'peilato Shel Avraham Yeshayahu Karelitz* [The glory of a generation: Chapters in the life and deeds of Avraham Yeshayahu Karelitz) (Bnei Brak: Netsach, 1974), vol. 5, 18–19.

13. See Zerach Wahrhaftig, *Huka LeYisrael: Dat UMedina* [A constitution for Israel: Religion and the state] (Jerusalem: Mesilot, 1988), 252. See also Moshe Unna, *BeDrakhim Nifradot* [On separate paths] (Alon Shvut: Yad Shapira, 1983), 274.

14. Already in 1947, Ben-Gurion, Yitzhak Greenblum, and Rabbi Yehuda Leib Maimon representing the Jewish Agency came to an understanding with the representatives of the Agudat Yisrael party, later to be known as the "Status Quo Agreement," that assured the ultra-orthodox that in the new state the secular parties would meet the interests of the religious minority on questions of marriage and divorce, the Sabbath (Saturday) as a national day of rest, kosher food in public institutions, and a separate educational stream in public education for religious children. While the agreement was left intentionally vague, it set up the framework for cooperation and even partnership between secular parties and the religious parties in establishing the state and for accommodation, albeit limited, of religious interests in formulating public policy. The commitment to "maintain the status quo" became an essential element of all coalition agreements between religious and secular parties throughout the years. Menachem Friedman, "VeEleh Toldot HaStatus-quo: Dat UMedina BeYisrael" [This is the story of the status quo: Religion and state in Israel], in *Shevet Ahim: Yahase Hilonim-Datiyim: Emdot,*

Hatsaot, Amanot [Brethren dwelling together], ed. Uri Dromi (Jerusalem: Israel Democracy Institute, 2005), 57–89.

15. Unna, *BeDrakhim Nifradot*, 271.
16. *Divrei HaKnesset*, vol. 2, 1570–1571.
17. Zvi Zameret, "Judaism in Israel: Ben-Gurion's Private Beliefs and Public Policy," *Israel Studies* 4, no. 2 (1999): 65. See also Zvi Zameret, "Ben-Gurion BeShnot HaMedina HaRishonot VeYahaso LaTsiyonut HaDatit UlaHaredim," in *Ayin Tova: Du-Siach UPulmus BeTarbut Yisrael*, ed. Nacham Ilan (Tel Aviv: Hakibbutz Hameuchad, 1999), 349–370.
18. Ben-Gurion, "Netsah Yisrael," 279.
19. Zameret, "Judaism in Israel," 82.
20. A public opinion survey conducted in September 1949 indicated that 63 percent of the Yemenite Jews opposed military service for women, compared to 47.5 percent of the general Jewish population. Government of Israel, Hamakhon LeHeker Daat Kahal, Publication #10, 1950, Religious Zionist Archives, Mosad Harav Kook, Jerusalem.
21. Unna, *BeDrakhim Nifradot*, 259.
22. The government educational policy in the immigrant camps was an important concern of the religious parties in 1949–1951. There were reports that officials in the camps run by Mapai had forced Yemenite children to cut off their side locks and attend secular schools against their parents' wishes. The Religious Front's strong reaction forced the government to set up a Government Investigatory Committee (Vaadat Frumkin) to investigate the charges. The committee validated the charges of the religious parties thereby increasing the tension and distrust between Mapai and the religious parties. See Zvi Zameret, "Vaadat Frumkin: Vaadat Hakira Memshaltit BeNose Hinukh Yaldei HaOlim BeShnot HaMedina Harishonot" [The Frumkin Committee: The government committee to investigate the education of immigrant children during the first years of the state], *Iyunim BeTekumat Yisrael* 1, no. 1 (1991): 404–439. See also Eliezer Don-Yehiya, "Mamlakhtiyut, Education and Religion in the Struggle over the Mass Immigration," *Journal of Israeli History* 26, no. 2 (2007): 246.
23. Warhaftig, *Huka LeYisrael*, 247–248. Former MK Moshe Unna claims in his memoirs that in proposing this amendment, which he knew would be totally unacceptable to the orthodox, Ben-Gurion was taking revenge for their vote against the government's education policy. Unna, *BeDrakhim Nifradot*, 279.
24. Unna, *BeDrakhim Nifradot*, 284. The Lamifne faction of the Hapoel Hamizrachi, aligned with the religious kibbutz movement, threatened to run as a separate list if it would join up again with the Haredim.
25. Letter from Prime Minister Ben-Gurion to Transportation Minister D. Pinchas regarding the 1951 Coalition Agreement, December 2, 1951. Ben-Gurion Online Archives.
26. Unna, *BeDrakhim Nifradot*, 284.

27. Cohen, *Peer HaDor*, 40–41.

28. *Digleinu*, cited in Cohen, *Peer HaDor*, 40–41.

29. Letter to Prime Minister Ben-Gurion from the President of the Rabbinical Council of America, September 11, 1952, Ben-Gurion Online Archives.

30. *Shearim* (newspaper of Poalei Agudat Yisrael), December 24, 1952.

31. The Knesset Archives, The National Service Law, 1953, Proposal #178, July 20, 1953.

32. Cohen, *Peer HaDor*, 18–19. See also Warhaftig, *Huka LeYisrael*, 238.

33. *Haaretz*, July 15, 1953.

34. Warhaftig, *Huka LeYisrael*, 250.

35. Zerach Warhaftig and Moshe Shapira (Hapoel Hamizrachi) visited the Hazon Ish at his home in order to discuss national service. They asked the rabbi where it was written in the Code of Jewish Law (the four books of the Shulhan Arukh) that national service was forbidden. The Hazon Ish replied that it was found in the "fifth" book, the one that only the sages "understand." Here he is stating an important principle: the rabbis know what is right or wrong, without requiring a written, explicit Halakhic source. See Binyamin Brown, *HaHazon Ish: Haposek, Hamaamin, UManhig HaMahapekha HaHaredit* [The Hazon Ish: Halakhist, believer, and leader of the Haredi revolution] (Jerusalem: Magnes, 2010), 90–91.

36. Ben-Gurion visited the Hazon Ish at his home at the height of the tensions over the national service law. While there is no evidence that the two discussed the national service law specifically, they did discuss at length whether the orthodox and the secular could ever live together peacefully in the new sovereign state. Ben-Gurion left the meeting feeling very pessimistic about the future. Brown, *HaHazon Ish*, 265–270. After the law was passed, the Hazon Ish wrote a personal letter to Ben-Gurion imploring him not to implement the law, a request that the prime minister refused. Brown, *HaHazon Ish*, 271–272.

37. The newspaper *Yediot Ahronot* (July 6, 1953) reported that 150 sextons from synagogues throughout Jerusalem held a demonstration outside the chief rabbi's residence to pressure him to direct the Mizrachi and Hapoel Hamizrachi parties to oppose the law.

38. Warhaftig, *Huka LeYisrael*, 253.

39. See *Divrei HaKnesset*, MK Eliezer Shostak, August 26, 1953, 2533.

40. Men whose wives refused to accept divorce could be permitted to remarry with the special permission of 100 rabbis.

41. *Divrei HaKnesset*, MK Moshe Sneh, August 26, 1953, 2550. See also Warhaftig, *Huka LeYisrael*, 253.

42. See Eliezer Don-Yehiya, *HaPolitika Shel HaHasdara: Yishuv Sikhsukhim BeNose Dat BeYisrael* [Religion and political accommodation in Israel] (Jerusalem: The Floersheimer Institute for Policy Studies, 1997).

43. *Divrei HaKnesset*, Minister of Labor Golda Meyerson [Meir], August 26, 1953, 2452.

44. Yechiam Weitz, "To Fantasy and Back: David Ben-Gurion's First Resignation," *Israel Affairs* 8, no. 1 (2002): 59–78.

45. Protocol, Knesset Labor Committee, August 5, 1953.

46. Israel State Archives, File #132/54, Letter from Prime Minister Moshe Sharett to Chief Rabbi Yitzhak Herzog, February 14, 1954.

47. Israel State Archives, File #54/2442, #4728/21—gimel, January 15, 1954.

48. Israel State Archives, File #4728/21—gimel, guidelines of national service proposed by the ministry and the critical response of an unnamed official at the Ministry of Religions (undated document).

49. In the 1950s and 1960s and to a lesser extent today, many IDF soldiers give up religious observance while in the army. The religious parties asked that religious soldiers be placed together in one unit if they request. The IDF agreed to establish separate religious Nahal units and later Hesder yeshiva units for this reason.

50. Israel State Archives, File #13/142-11451, March 10, 1954.

51. Israel State Archives, File #13/142, letter from an assistant in the Ministry of Labor to Golda Meyerson, Minister of Labor, March 16, 1954.

52. For further discussion, see Etta Bick, "Equality, Orthodoxy and Politics: The Conflict over National Service in Israel," *Israel Affairs* 19, no. 3 (July 2013): 505–525.

53. Israel State Archives, File #13/142, March 16, 1954.

54. Warhaftig, *Huka LeYisrael*, 260.

55. *Divrei HaKnesset*, MK Meir Porush, July 1979, vol. 23, 15–16.

56. Zeev Drori, *Utopia BeMadim: Trumat Tsahal LeHityashvut, LeKlitat HaAliyah UleHinuch Breshit Yemi HaMedina* [Utopia in uniform: The contribution of the IDF to settlement, immigrant absorption, and education in the early years of the state) (Sde Boker: Ben-Gurion Heritage Center, 2000).

Chapter 3. Republicanism and Volunteerism: Civic National Service for Religious Girls, 1970–2018

1. Israel State Archives, File #13/142. Letter from Brigadier General Yitzhak Alron, Temporary Head of Human Resources in the IDF, to Yosef Almogi, Chairman of the Government Committee on National Service, September 10, 1971.

2. Israel State Archives, File #13/142, September 10, 1971.

3. While there were 27,150 girls eligible for conscription in 1971, 4,200 were excused because of their insufficient level of education, 2,200 because they were married, 1,250 for medical reasons, and 7,500 for religious reasons. Israel State Archives, File #13/142, September 1971.

4. *Maariv*, June 12, 1970.

5. *Hatzofe*, editorial December 11, 1971.

6. Tamar Rappaport, Anat Panso, and Yoni Garav, "'Ze Davar Hashuv BeEretz Yisrael Latet Latsibur': Naarot Tsiyoniot Datiyot Tormot LaLeum" ["It is important to contribute to the public": National religious girls contribute to the nation], *Teoriya UBikoret* 7 (1995): 223–234.

7. The Mizrachi and Hapoel Hamizrachi parties united into one party called the National Religious Party (NRP) in 1956.

8. Interview with Mr. Avraham Hoffman, Jerusalem, August 2010.

9. *Davar*, February 17, 1971.

10. There was already a group of religious girls that had started to volunteer in schools in 1968. Israel State Archives, File #6216/13–gimel, November 1970–November 1972 letter from Yehezkel Cohen, the Division of Torah Culture at the Education Ministry to Ben Zion Dal, in charge of planning and guidance in the Ministry of Welfare (n.d.).

11. Israel State Archives, File #6216/13–gimel. Petition of the Sephardic rabbis, September 6, 1971. For a more recent ruling, see Rabbi Yitzhak Yosef, *Otsar HaDinim LaIsha VelaBat* [A treasure of Jewish law for women and girls] (Jerusalem: Aish Petuhim, 1988), 384. Ultra-orthodox Sephardic girls who follow the rulings of Rav Yosef do not serve in national service even today.

12. Israel State Archives, File #6216/13–gimel. Decision of the Secretariat of the Young Guard of the NRP, November 17, 1971. The decision supported a voluntary program of national service for girls operated by a religious nonprofit. It stated its opposition to girls serving in the IDF and called on the NRP to appeal to the government to reassess its position on obligatory army service for women and replace it with voluntary national service. The statement also condemned the Agudat Yisrael and Poalei Agudat Yisrael parties for their stand against national service, calling them "hypocritical" because they too have organized volunteering in their institutions. The statement called on all religious girls to volunteer.

13. For a wider discussion of the extent of religious observance among religious Zionist youth during this period, see Mordechai Bar-Lev, "Cultural Characteristics and Group Image of Religious Youth," *Youth and Society* 16, no. 2 (1984): 153–170.

14. Israel State Archives, File #6216/13–gimel, October 1971. The suspicion that the government might take over the program and make it mandatory was shared by others as well. Harabanit Rachel Neriyah, who had been involved in setting up the program and had been considered the frontrunner to head the new national service nonprofit agency, withdrew her candidacy when the press falsely reported that she had agreed to stand at the head of a new government agency that would administer national service.

15. Israel State Archives, File #9684/8, May 10, 1971.

16. *Davar*, Y. Spiegel, 1971. Yitzhak Rosenthal, an ultra-orthodox rabbi from Jerusalem, took the unusual step of bringing suit (*din torah*) against Hazani in the Jerusalem Beit Din (religious court), asking for an injunction to stop him from

participating in the ministerial committee. Rosenthal contended that Hazani's participation was in defiance of the rulings of the revered sages Rabbi Pesach Frank, former chief rabbi of Jerusalem, and the Hazon Ish from 1952 who had prohibited national service for girls. The Jerusalem Beit Din rejected the suit for lack of standing, but the Rabbinical High Court accepted it on appeal and ordered Hazani to show cause why he should not resign from the ministerial committee forthwith. *Hazofeh*, October 29, 1971. The ruling caused a crisis of authority between secular and religious authorities. Attorney General Meir Shamgar argued that the Rabbinical High Court lacked judicial authority over government ministers and advised Hazani to ignore the summons. Shamgar then petitioned the Israel High Court of Justice to rule on the jurisdictional question. The High Court issued an *order nisi* requiring the Rabbinical Court to explain its action and to stop all proceedings against Hazani in the meanwhile. The Rabbinical High Court came to the conclusion that not only would it not win its case against Hazani but it was likely to suffer a stinging and humiliating rebuke from the High Court of Justice. Several days later the plaintiff withdrew his suit against Hazani, presumably after pressure from the rabbis. *Maariv*, October 2, 1972. See the discussion in Bick, "Equality, Orthodoxy and Politics."

17. Israel State Archives, File #6216/13–gimel, November 1, 1971. The government decision to establish the national service program. It assigned administration of the program to the Ministries of Education and Culture, Health, and Welfare in consultation with representatives of the national religious sector. The program would begin as a pilot for one year and would report on its progress after six months. The government recommended that a religious woman be appointed to head the program.

18. *Maariv*, February 2, 1971.

19. A survey conducted by *Dahaf* among Jewish Israelis in April 1972 found the public split on the issue of religious women serving in the armed forces and in national service. While a majority agreed that religious women should serve in either the military or in national service, they disagreed as to the preferred program. 43.9 percent thought that religious women should be drafted to mandatory army service provided they could be assured suitable religious conditions; 28.1 percent thought religious women should do voluntary civic national service in hospitals, development towns, and other places in need and 22.5 percent said they were against a draft of religious girls to the military and favored the continuation of the status quo. Only 1.2 percent said that girls from ultra-orthodox homes should be exempted from service but only after a careful background check. The survey also showed that Israelis from a weaker socioeconomic background, an Oriental background (Mizrahim), and those with large families were largely opposed to religious girls serving in the military or in national service; those from a European- or Israeli-born background, with higher education and a higher income were supportive of a more universal draft.

20. Labor Party Platform, 1973, 21, http://www.archavoda.org.il/avodaarch/matza/pdf/knesset8.pdf, and Labor Party Platform, 1977, 40, http://www.archavoda.org.il/avodaarch/matza/pdf/knesset9.pdf.

21. *Maariv*, November 11, 1974.

22. *Maariv*, November 12, 1974.

23. The students' union at Haifa University had already been on record in June 1975 in support of a resolution calling on the university not to accept students who did not serve in the army or in national service.

24. *Davar*, June 30, 1978.

25. *Divrei HaKnesset*, MK Haike Grossman, November 14, 1978.

26. *Davar*, July 7, 1978.

27. The vote tied at 41 to 41 at the first reading. The coalition worked hard to defeat the law; it had even exchanged some of its representatives on the Labor and Welfare Committee in order to prevent the proposal from ever reaching a first reading.

28. *Divrei HaKnesset*, November 14, 1978.

29. See *Divrei HaKnesset*, MK Dov Shilansky (Likud), November 14, 1978.

30. The DASH party voted with the government. Two members of the Likud, MKs Geula Cohen and Moshe Shamir, voted for the law and were punished by the coalition for their stand. *Maariv*, December 14, 1978.

31. Efraim Sidon, *Davar*, December 15, 1978.

32. There were 14 similar private member bills proposed in the Knesset between 1979 and 1994 to enact two years of mandatory civic national service for religious girls. None however had any chance of passing because of the ruling party's coalition agreements with the Haredi parties.

33. *Davar*, March 13, 1979.

34. The catalyst that forced the government to take some kind of action to resolve the issue was the intervention of the High Court of Justice. In September 1978 Yedidya Be'eri petitioned the High Court in the name of his daughters, one who was serving in the military and the other who was soon to enlist, to direct the government to implement the 1953 national service law because its failure to act had created a grossly inequitable service policy. *Davar*, May 20, 1979. The court accepted Be'eri's arguments and gave the government four months to either amend the law or to implement it as written. Determined to keep its coalition with the religious parties intact, the government in July 1979 added an amendment that in fact legalized the government's inaction! It read, "The implementation of the [national service] law will not begin until there is a government decision to do so." *Davar*, July 24, 1979. This revised version of the law remained on the books until a new national civic service law was passed in 2017.

35. *Maariv*, April 15, 1980.

36. *Maariv*, July 13, 1979.

37. *Maariv*, May 13, 1980. Sara Melzer, a member of the presidium of the Emunah religious women's organization, and Tzivya Goren, wife of the chief rabbi, Shlomo Goren, came out in support of two years of national service and proposed that the universities and prospective employers refrain from accepting students/applicants who did not serve in either national service or the army.

38. Interview with Mr. Avraham Hoffman, Ministry of Labor and Welfare, *Maariv*, April 27, 1984.

39. *Haaretz*, July 20, 2001.

40. For example, during the Rabin government in 1992 the NRP was in the opposition. Education Minister Shlomit Aloni from the far-left Meretz party announced a severe reduction in the number of placements available to national service volunteers due to budget cutbacks.

41. The HaBayit HaYehudi party was the successor party to the NRP. It was formed in 2008 as an amalgam of the NRP and the National Union (Tekuma) party.

42. In 1977 the National Social Insurance–1968 was amended to include rights and benefits for religious girls in national service.

43. *Ynet*, December 21, 2015.

44. Orli Loten and Yuval Vargen, *Sherut Banot Datiyot BeTsahal: Temunat Matsav UMedinut Maarekhet HaHinukh* [Service of religious girls in the IDF: A situation report and the education system's policy] (Jerusalem: Knesset Research and Information Center, 2007), 9.

45. Ariel Finkelstein, *HaHinukh HaMamlakhti Dati: Temunat Matsav, Megamot VeHesegim* [State religious education: Situation report, trends, and accomplishments] (Tel Aviv: Ne'emanei Torah VaAvodah, 2013), 40.

46. Ministry of Industry and Trade, *Tokhnit LeMehkar Haarakha VeLivui LeMaarakh Sherut Ezrahi Leumi BeYisrael* [Research, evaluation, and counseling for the National Civic Service Program] (Jerusalem: Ministry of Industry and Trade, 2010).

47. Ahmed Hatib and Ilan Biton, *Hasherut Haezrahi–Leumi BeYisrael: Skira VeNituah* [Civic-national service in Israel: Overview and analysis] (Jerusalem: Knesset Center for Research and Information, 2011). See also report in *Ynet*, January 29, 2014.

48. Ariel Finkelstein, *Maafyanei Benot Hatsiyonut Hadatit Hameshartot Betsava UBeSherut Leumi: Tmunat Matzav UMegamot* [Religious Zionist girls in the IDF and in national service: Situation report and trends] (Tel Aviv: Ne'emanei Torah VaAvodah, 2018), 10.

49. See *Ashdod Ten*, September 8, 2016.

50. The Kibbutz Hadati movement (religious kibbutzim), which from the start had encouraged girls to serve in the IDF rather than in national service, set up an organization called Aluma (1983), which offers support and religious enrichment to religious girls serving in the IDF and provides them with an

address where they can turn if they need any kind of assistance. The founders of Aluma recognized that religious girls who chose to serve in the IDF against the advice of their principals and teachers were often left to fend for themselves by the schools, without their teachers' support and guidance. For many of the girls this was the first time they had to adjust to a totally secular environment and to experience, as a religious person, being in the minority. Aluma provides the girls with information about service in the pre-induction period and then continues to offer them support throughout their service.

51. Finkelstein, *Maafyane Bnot Hatsiyonut Hadatit*, 16–17.

52. Finkelstein, *Maafyane Bnot Hatsiyonut Hadatit*, 19. See discussion in Elisheva Rosman-Stollman, *For God and Country? Religious Student-Soldiers in the Israel Defense Forces* (Austin: University of Texas Press, 2015).

53. Cited in Finkelstein, *Hahinuch HaMamlakhti Dati*, 42.

54. *Hadashot*, September 25, 2017.

55. *Mako*, February 6, 2018.

56. *Srugim News*, July 6, 2017.

Chapter 4. Fighting to Serve: Youth Excused from Service

1. Orna Sasson-Levy, "Constructing Identities at the Margins: Masculinity and Citizenship in the Israeli Army," *The Sociological Quarterly* 43 (2002): 357–383, doi:10.1111/j.1533-8525.2002.tb00053.x. See also Orna Mayseless, "Tsiirim Yisraelim BeMaavar LeBagrut: Hashpaat HaSherut Hatsvai" [Young Israeli men in the transition from adolescence to adulthood: The role of military service], *Iyunim BeHinukh* 5, no. 1 (2001): 159–190.

2. Approximately 1,200 youths participate in the program each year and are given a second chance to complete their high school diploma and to enter regular combat units.

3. See Sammy Shalom Shitrit, *HaMaavak HaMizrahi BeYisrael, 1948–2003* [The Mizrahi struggle in Israel, 1948–2003] (Tel Aviv: Am Oved, 2004), 195–232.

4. Mizrahim (Orientals) are Jews who immigrated to Israel from Middle Eastern countries and North Africa.

5. See Moshe Sherer, "Rehabilitation of Youth in Distress through Army Service: Full, Partial, or Non-Service in the Israel Defense Forces—Problems and Consequences," *Child and Youth Care Forum* 27, no. 1 (1998): 39–58.

6. See Barak Medina, "Hazekhut HaHukatit LeShivyon BePsikat Beit HaMishpat HaElyon: Kvod Haadam, HaIntares Hatsibori, VeTsedek Halukati" [The constitutional right to equality in the rulings of the Israel High Court], *Mishpat UMimshal* 17 (2015): 1–94.

7. According to statistics presented to the Knesset by Deputy Defense Minister Ze'ev Boim on July 2, 2003, 6.1 percent of the recruits in 2002 were rejected by the IDF for medical and psychological reasons, 1.4 percent because of a criminal record, and 2.6 percent had a low socio-profile. Of those conscripts who begin to serve, 11.1 percent fail to complete service because of medical or emotional reasons and 7.3 percent for failure to adjust.

8. The National Insurance benefits to girls performing two years of national service include unemployment benefits for a year after service, job training courses, pre-academic courses, loans for university studies, and housing and income tax credits. See The State Comptroller, *Din VeHeshbon Al Habikoret Al Hasherut HaLeumi* [Review report on national service] (Jerusalem: 1993), 15.

9. *Eyal Daniel v. the Director of National Insurance*, HC9173/96.

10. Reuven Gal, "Tefisat Nose Hazekhuyot VeHahovot Shel Erahei Yisrael HaAravim BeAspaklariyat Raayon HaSherut HaEzrahi" [Rights and obligations as reflected in the idea of civic service], Position Paper No. 13 (Tel Aviv: Tel Aviv University Harold Hartuch School of Government and Policy, 2008), 13–14.

11. Rachel Wurzberger, *Sherut Leumi LeBne Miutim* [National service for minorities] (Jerusalem: Knesset Research and Information Center, 2003).

12. In many European countries civic national service programs were inextricably linked to compulsory military service. Civic national service was an alternative open to conscientious objectors. The required period of service was usually longer than military service (time and a half or time and a third of service). Compulsory military service was canceled in Germany in 2011 along with the compulsory civic national service *Zivildienst*. Twenty-three European countries canceled mandatory military service in 1990–2013, setting up a volunteer army instead. Civic national service was canceled as well, with only a minority of states replacing it with a voluntary program.

13. *Divrei HaKnesset*, February 8, 1994.

14. See Ofra Ben Ishai, "Hasherut HaEzrahi KeHalufa LeSherut Hatsvai: Keitsad Yagiv Hatsava" [Civic service as an alternative to military service: How will the military respond?], in *Sherut Hova o' Hova Lesharet* [Mandatory service or the duty to serve], ed. Yagil Levy (Ra'anana: Open University, 2015), 38–73.

15. The Defense Service Law, 1986, Paragraph 24A, was amended in 1995 to include service in the police. Service in military prisons was added to the law in 2005, and in 2009 legislation was adopted to extend military service to the areas of health, education, and immigrant absorption that were tangentially related to national security. Service Recognized for the Achieving of National and Security Goals (temporary order), 2009.

16. Ben Ishai, "Hasherut HaEzrahi," 51.

17. Layering is a process by which gradual change is achieved by amending existing laws moderately rather than displacing the existing legislation. See James

Mahoney and Kathleen Thelen, "A Theory of Gradual Institutional Change," in *Explaining Institutional Change: Ambiguity, Agency, and Power*, ed. James Mahoney and Kathleen Thelen (Cambridge: Cambridge University Press, 2010), 1–37; and Jacob S. Hacker, "Privatizing Risk without Privatizing the Welfare State: The Hidden Politics of Social Policy Retrenchment in the United States," *American Political Science Review* 98, no. 2 (2004): 243–260. See also Etta Bick, "Institutional Layering, Displacement, and Policy Change: The Evolution of Civic Service in Israel," *Public Policy and Administration* 31, no. 4 (2016): 342–360.

18. Protocol #50, Knesset Labor, Welfare, and Health Committee, September 10, 2003. Seventeen Arabs also served in the program.

19. Protocol #50. In an interview in the Hebrew weekly *Makor Rishon*, the director general of the Authority for National-Civic Service, Sar Shalom Gerbi, said that he takes pride in the fact that during his tenure he convinced the Knesset to give civic service volunteers the same benefits and post-service grants that are given to noncombatant soldiers. *Makor Rishon* (Yoman), August 6, 2018.

20. Yagil Levy, "Ma Yekhola Yisrael Lilmod Min HaSherut HaEzrahi BeGermaniya" [What Israel can learn from civic service in Germany], in *Sherut Hova o' Hova LeSharet* [Mandatory service or the duty to serve], ed. Yagil Levy (Ra'anana: Open University, 2015), 16–37.

21. Committee for the Institutionalization of Civil-National Service (Ivri Committee), "Hamlatsot Benayim" [Interim recommendations], February 2005, http://ncs.gov.il/ncs/Documents/hamlatsot_ivri.pdf.

22. Committee for the Institutionalization of Civil-National Service, "Hamlatsot Benayim."

23. Hillel Schmid, "Din VeHeshbon Shel Havaada Hatsiburit LeBedikat Matsavam Shel Yeladim UBne Noar BeSikun UBeMetsuka" [Report by the public committee to examine the conditions of endangered children and youth under stress], 2006. See also Drorit Levy, "Teur Havayat HaSherut Haezrahi-Leumi Shel Tsiirim BeSikun MeZavit HaReiya Shel HaMeshartim Likrat Siyum HaSherut" [A description of the civic national service experience of youth at risk from the perspective of the volunteers toward the end of their service], *Bitahon Sotsiali* 91 (2013): 128.

24. Ivri Committee, *Hamlatsot Benayim*, 6. The Ivri Committee had a communitarian perspective in regard to minorities, Haredim, and Arabs, recommending that they be given special consideration for their particular needs and sensitivities. For example, recognizing that volunteers from both sectors might be reluctant to serve in a religious or cultural environment that was foreign to their values, it recommended that they be allowed to serve in their own communities and to live at home. Moreover, it concluded that although mandatory service, military or civic, for all citizens was the ideal, under the current political circumstances service by Haredim and Arabs should be voluntary. (For further discussion, see chapters 5 and 6.)

25. Ivri Committee, *Hamlatsot Benayim*, 9–10.

26. For example, Ehud Barak announced after his appointment as commander in chief of the IDF in 1990 that "anything that doesn't shoot or assist directly in shooting will be cut." He also spoke of turning the IDF into a small, professional army.

27. Interview with Sar Shalom Gerbi, the director general of the Authority for National-Civic Service. *Makor Rishon* (Yoman), August 6, 2018.

28. Meshalvim website, http://bat-ami.org.il/social-change/.

29. In the north there is a similar program operated by Kevunim, another NGO.

30. Meshalvim website, http://bat-ami.org.il/social-change/.

31. Moshe Razilov, Knafayim Preparatory Program (Mechina), in conjunction with Bat Ami and Gevanim, Meshalvim website, http://bat-ami.org.il/social-change/, accessed May 2019.

32. Gevanim website, www.gvanim.org.il/he/node/6, accessed May 2019.

33. For information about the Temura program, see https://www.sherut-leumi.co.il/article.aspx?id=51, accessed May 2019.

34. Information about Otzma, www.sherut-leumi.co.il/article.aspx?id=51; for information about Shalhevet, see shlomit.org.il or http://asperger.org.il/Web/?PageType=0&itemid=288324, accessed May, 2019.

35. In 2005 the IDF set up a special volunteer program for youth with disabilities entitled "Special in Uniform," which gave youth with disabilities the opportunity to volunteer in the IDF in assignments suited to their needs and with an accompanying support program provided by Gevanim and the Lend a Hand to the Special Child Association. Three hundred volunteer soldiers served on 15 bases throughout Israel in 2016. Summary of 2016 activities, video: http://special.org.il/en/about/.

36. Protocol #110, Knesset Labor, Welfare, and Health Committee, December 7, 2015. According to information provided by Sar Shalom Gerbi, the director general of the Authority for National-Civic Service, there were 1,029 volunteers with special needs serving in civic national service in 2015.

37. Protocol #110.

38. Protocol #110.

39. Adalya Economic Consulting, "Cost–Benefit Analysis from Operating a National Civic Service Program for Disadvantaged Populations," executive summary, Forum for the Advancement of Civic National Service, October 2011, www.adalya.co.il/en/case-studies/Cost-%E2%80%93-Benefit.

40. Adalya, "Cost–Benefit Analysis."

41. Adalya, "Cost–Benefit Analysis."

42. Barbara Swirski and Kefalea Yosef, *The Employment Situation of Ethiopian Israelis* (Tel Aviv: Adva Center, 2005), 6, adva.org/wp-content/uploads/2014/09/EthiopianIsraelis.pdf. This disparity can also be explained by the ages of the

women. The volunteers in civic national service were younger than the Adva cohorts and that may be a significant difference. Fewer women aged 25–34 were employed since they might be at home with young children.

43. Adalya, "Cost–Benefit Analysis."

44. Levy, "Teur Havayat." The volunteers' main critique of the program was that the remedial courses they had been given had failed to close the gaps they had in education, nor did it prepare them sufficiently for the psychometric university entrance exams.

45. Anat Zeira et al., "Duah Mehkar: Sherut Ezrahi Leumi MeZavit Hareiya Shel Tseirim VeTseirot Besikun" [Research report: National service from the perspective of youth at risk], submitted to the Ministry of Science and Technology, May 2014, 6.

46. Oriana Almasi, *Sherut Leumi-Ezrahi BeYisrael* [National-Civic Service in Israel] (Jerusalem: Knesset, September 30, 2014), 29. See the remarks of Sar Shalom Gerbi, director general of the Administration for National-Civic Service, Protocol #7 Knesset Committee for Public Appeals, May 28, 2013.

47. Protocol #7.

48. Protocol #20, Knesset Committee for Public Appeals, September 4, 2013.

49. "News from National Civic Service," *Makor Rishon*, February 9, 2018.

50. *Arutz 7 News*, July 12, 2017, https://www.inn.co.il/News/News.aspx/350680.

51. Meshalvim, www.ncsforum.org.il/archives/successtory.

Chapter 5. The Haredim: Will a Communitarian Approach Bring Them to Serve?

1. Daniel Maman, Eyal Ben-Ari, and Zeev Rosenhek, *Military, State and Society in Israel: Theoretical and Comparative Perspectives* (New Brunswick: Transaction, 2001), 87.

2. See Gilad Malach and Lee Cahaner, *Statistical Report on Ultra-Orthodox Society in Israel, 2018* (Jerusalem: Israel Democracy Institute, 2018).

3. The exposure of the Haredim to the general media is limited; 37 percent read the ultra-orthodox *Hamodia* and 30 percent read *Yated Neeman*. Only 13 percent read one of the major secular dailies, and 32 percent read no newspapers at all. In a 1995 survey, 56 percent said they do not listen to radio and 25 percent listen to secular radio stations, mostly Israel Radio's Reshet Bet news and current affairs channel. See Yoel Cohen, "On the Beat: Covering Israel's Religion Wars," *Religion in the News* 2, no. 3 (Fall 1999), http://www.trincoll.edu/depts/csrpl/RIN Vol2No3/Israel'sReligionWars.htm.

4. This pattern has changed somewhat in the last decade. The government has made a concerted effort to offer remedial programs for Haredim and schol-

arships to enable them to close the gap in math, English, and the sciences and allow them to continue toward academic degrees. A small but growing number of Haredim have availed themselves of these opportunities. As of 2014, 2.5 percent of Haredi men and 8 percent of Haredi women among those aged 25–35 had an academic degree—as compared with 28 percent of secular men and 43 percent of secular women. Eitan Regev, *Challenges of Haredi Integration in Academic Studies* (Jerusalem: Taub Center for Policy Studies in Israel, December 2016). In 2009–2010 there were 4,537 Haredim studying in colleges and universities; in 2016 the number rose to 11,013, an increase of 143 percent. However, many do not complete their studies. Central Bureau of Statistics, January 2017, reported in *Kikar Hashabat*, January 18, 2017.

5. Gilad *Malach, Lee Cahaner, and Maya Choshen, Statistical Report on Ultra-Orthodox Society in Israel, 2016* (Jerusalem: Israel Democracy Institute, 2016).

6. A public opinion survey conducted by the Gesher organization in 2006 during heightened tensions between secular and religious revealed that 37 percent of Israelis considered the Haredim to be the most hated group in Israel. *Jerusalem Post*, October 31, 2006. The now-defunct secularist Shinui party unflinchingly labeled them "parasites" in their election campaigns, portraying them as greedily taking from the public till without fulfilling their civic obligations.

7. A totally different case that contrasts sharply with the Haredim is that of national religious women, discussed in chapters 2 and 3. See also Reuven Gal, *Din VeHeshbon Al Hasherut Haleumi* [Report on Sherut Leumi] (Jerusalem: Administration for National-Civic Service, 2009).

8. For further discussion, see Etta Bick, "Sherut Ezrahi Hova: HaHashlakhot al Nashim Harediyot Vedatiyot" [Mandatory civic service: The ramifications for ultra-orthodox and religious women], in *Sherut Hova o' Hova LeSharet* (Mandatory service or the duty to serve), ed. Yagil Levy (Ra'anana: Open University, 2015), 95–120.

9. Letter from Y. Chernowitz and Ze'ev Epstein to the Committee of Yeshiva Heads, Order of March 9, 1948, http:// www.archives.gov.il/NR/rdonlyres/5C300#-DA74CI-46E6-B16C-4235B0B85276/0/herzog02.pdf. See Yehezkel Cohen, ed., *Giyus Kahalakha: Al Shihrur Bahure Yeshiva MiGiyus LeTsahal* [Conscription and Jewish law: On exempting yeshiva students from military service] (Jerusalem: Ne'emanei Torah VaAvodah, 1993), 24–29.

10. Menachem Friedman, "Al Giyus Bechurei Yeshivot" [On conscription of yeshiva students], in *Giyus Kahalakha: Al Shihrur Bahure Yeshiva MiGiyus LeTsahal* [Conscription and Jewish law: On exempting yeshiva students from military service], ed. Yehezkel Cohen (Jerusalem: Ne'emanei Torah VaAvodah, 1993), 262–277.

11. Friedman, "Al Giyus Bechurei Yeshivot."

12. Asaf Malchi, "The "People's Army? A Historical Review of Ultra-Orthodox Conscription to the IDF," Israel Democracy Institute, October 16, 2018, en.idi.org.il/articles/24626.

13. Included in the numbers of yeshiva students receiving deferments are several hundred national-religious yeshiva students who will do full army service after completing a year or more of yeshiva study. The forecast for deferments in the future had worried Israel's defense establishment. In 2007, 23 percent of the Jewish children entering first grade in Israel were Haredim. Given the high birthrate of the Haredim and the low birthrate of secular Israelis, it anticipated that 23 percent of those at conscription age in 2019 will be requesting deferments as yeshiva students. This, it cautioned, will impact national security and relations between Haredim and the rest of the Jewish population. Shachar Ilan, *Haaretz*, January 27, 2007.

14. Malach and Cahaner, *Statistical Report, 2018*.

15. This is a term coined by sociologist Menachem Friedman in his study *HaHevra HaHaredit BeYisrael: Mekorot, Megamot VeTahalikhim* [The ultra-orthodox society in Israel: Sources, trends, and developments] (Jerusalem: Jerusalem Institute for the Study of Israel, 1991).

16. Menachem Friedman, "The Family Community Model in Haredi Society," in *Coping with Life and Death: Jewish Families in the Twentieth Century*, ed. Peter Medding (London: Oxford University Press, 1998), 166–177.

17. Ministry of Education, http://edu.gov.il/owlHeb/Tichon/Bechinot Vbagruyot/BechinotAbagrut/Pages/entitlement-data-city-2014.aspx CBS, 2017.

18. Malach and Cahaner, *Statistical Report, 2018*. For statistics of previous years, see Sharon Ouzieli, *Taasukat Haredim BeYisrael: Tmunat Matsav VeHatsaa LeShipur* [Employment of the ultra-orthodox in Israel: Situation report and proposed improvements] (Tel Aviv: Koret Economic Development Fund, Milken Institute, 2007), 29–34.

19. See Kimi Kaplan, "Orthodoxia VeHarediut BeAmerica U'beYisrael: Hebetim Historiim" [Orthodoxy and ultra-orthodoxy in America and in Israel: Historical aspects], in *Am Levadad: Moledet U'Pezura: Hebetim Historiyim-Hashvatiyim* [A nation that dwelleth alone: Homeland and Diaspora: Aspects of comparative histories], ed. Binyamin Lau (Tel Aviv: Yediot Ahronot, 2006), 301–315. See also Kimi Kaplan, "Haredim and Western Culture: A View from Both Sides of the Ocean," in *Middle Eastern Societies and the West: Accommodation or Clash of Civilizations?*, ed. Meir Litvak (Syracuse: Syracuse University Press, 2007), 269–289.

20. Menachem Friedman, "HaIsha Haharedit" [The ultra-orthodox woman], in *Eshnav Lehayehem Shel Nashim BeHevrot Yehudiyot Kovets Mehkarim Ben Tehumiyim* [A look at the lives of women in Jewish societies], ed. Yael Atzmon (Jerusalem: Zalman Shazar Center for the Study of Jewish History, 1995), 273–290.

21. Malach and Cahaner, *Statistical Report, 2018*. For statistics of previous years, see Hagai Leven, *Hamigzar HaHaredi BeYisrael: Haatzama Tokh Shiluv BeTaasuka* [The ultra-orthodox sector in Israel: Empowerment through integration in employment] (Jerusalem: Prime Minister's Office, National Economic Council, 2004).

22. Malach, Cahaner, and Choshen, *Statistical Report on Ultra-Orthodox Society, 2016*.

23. *Haaretz, The Marker*, April 17, 2016.

24. See Friedman, "HaIsha HaHaredit," 283–285.

25. Friedman, "Al Giyus Bechure Yeshivot," 264.

26. Friedman, "Al Giyus Bechure Yeshivot."

27. The Israel Defense Service Law, 1986, https://www.nevo.co.il/law_html/Law01/P199_009.htm.

28. IDF draft policy before the Tal Law required single men ages 18 to 25, married men, and those married with one child to give three years of service. Single men ages 26 to 28 served 18 months, married men 12 months. Single and married men ages 29 to 34 and married men ages 18 to 34 with two to four children were required to served only four months. See Tal Committee, *Din VeHeshbon HaVaada LeGibush HaHesder Haraui BeNose Giyus Bnei Yeshivot* [Report of the committee to determine the proper arrangement on the draft of yeshiva students], vol. 1 (Jerusalem: Government of Israel, April 2000).

29. For an insightful discussion of the effect of the draft law on the decision of Haredim to prolong their studies at the yeshiva until ages 40 and older, see Eli Berman, "Subsidized Sacrifice: State Support of Religion in Israel," *Contemporary Jewry* 20 (1999): 167–200.

30. Ouzieli, *Taasukat Haredim BeYisrael*, 5–6.

31. National Insurance Institute, *Memadei HaOni VeHaPaarim HaHevratiim 2010* [Poverty and social gaps, 2010] (Jerusalem: National Insurance Institute, 2011), 52.

32. Malach and Cahaner, *Statistical Report, 2018*.

33. Statistics from 2018 show a slight decline in the number of children born to Haredi women, from 7.5 in 2003–2005 to 7.1 in 2015–2017. Malach and Cahaner, *Statistical Report, 2018*, 3.

34. See Tal Committee, *Din VeHeshbon HaVaada*, vol. 1, 35–38.

35. *Baker v. Minister of Defense*, 40/70.

36. *Ressler v. Minister of Defense*, 910/86.

37. For example, a private member bill proposed by Raphael Eitan (Tsomet) 1993 would require all citizens to serve in either military service or civic service. There were several private member bills proposed by Labor and Meretz MKs 1996–2000 to extend voluntary national civic service to all sectors. Yossi Beilin and Yona Yahav (Labor) proposed in 1997 that service, civic or military, should be mandatory for all citizens at age 18. All youth would be given the opportunity to choose between civic national service, paramilitary duties in the IDF, or combat service. Also, leader of the opposition Ehud Barak (Labor) announced a "citizen revolution" in 1997 that included extending civic national service to youth from all sectors.

38. See Daphna Barak-Erez, "Giyus Bachurei HaYeshivot: MePeshara LeMachloket" [Conscription of yeshiva students: From compromise to conflict],

in *Tzomtei Hakhraot U'Parshiot Mafteach Be'Yisrael* [Crossroads of decisions in Israel], ed. Devorah Hacohen and Moshe Lissak (Beersheva: Ben-Gurion Institute of Research, 2010), 20–22.

39. Yisrael Ahat (One Israel party) was established in 1999 as a joint list between the Labor, Meimad, and Gesher parties. In 2000 Gesher withdrew and the party was renamed Labor-Meimad, an alliance that continued until 2009.

40. Testimony of IDF Major-General Yehuda Segev, Head of Personnel, Tal Committee, *Din VeHeshbon HaVaada*, vol. 1, 48–50.

41. Tal Committee, *Din VeHeshbon HaVaada*, vol. 1, 50.

42. These young men created a problem for the community itself since they did not really study in yeshiva, but because they had not served in the army, they could not legally work or learn a trade. In effect they just "bummed around." Shachar Ilan, *HaHaredim B'Am: Hataktsivim, HaHistamtut Veremisat HaHok* [Ultra-orthodox incorporated: Funds, avoiding the draft, and law violation] (Jerusalem: Keter, 2000), 175. Ilan cites a letter written by Haredi educators to the leading Torah scholars decrying the situation of the "dropouts." They wrote, "We are not discussing a few dozen youths, or even a few hundred—but rather thousands of former yeshiva students who have crossed the line, leaving the yeshiva to wander the streets, movie theaters, city squares, and everywhere that a yeshiva boy should not be. . . . We are not speaking about the marginal types; rather, even those from the best homes, the most promising students."

43. The Nahal Haredi program was not the first program for Haredim in the history of the IDF. There had been a Nahal Haredi program in the first decades of the state that had combined service and agricultural work on kibbutzim of Poalei Aguda Yisrael. It was terminated in 1974 because of insufficient registration.

44. Yeshiva students under the age of 25 and without children who deferred service will serve 16 months in military service. Those 26 and over or those married with children will be referred to civic national service. Letter from the Office of the Commander in Chief, Secretariat of the High Command, December 13, 2006.

45. See the testimony of Reuven Gal in Tal Committee, *Din VeHeshbon HaVaada*, vol. 1, 103–104.

46. See the testimony of Shachar Ilan in Tal Committee, *Din VeHeshbon HaVaada*, vol. 1, 110.

47. Rabbi Asher Tannenbaum, chairman of the Yeshiva Council, an umbrella organization representing the Haredi yeshivas, had sat on the Tal Committee throughout the deliberations but had resigned at the summation stage in protest against the proposed "year of decision" and did not sign the final committee report. Rabbi Mordechai Karelitz, mayor of Bnei Brak, who was the other Haredi on the committee, did sign and was assailed by the rabbis for having agreed to the "year of decision."

48. See Joel Rebibo, "The Road Back from Utopia," *Azure* 11 (2001): 158–159.

49. The government in 2003 at the request of Finance Minister Benjamin

Netanyahu amended the Tal Law to permit full-time yeshiva students to work after study hours if they had already completed four years in a yeshiva. This revision was intended to compensate yeshiva students whose stipends had been reduced by the government's "economic emergency plan." In effect it undermined an important aspect of the Tal Law that had prohibited yeshiva students from working (legally) until after they had fulfilled their military or civic service obligation.

    50. Shachar Ilan, *Haaretz*, January 27, 2007. Also, interview with Malkiel Dahan, head of the division for civic service for Haredim at the Administration for National-Civic Service (ANCS), Jerusalem, February 19, 2009.

    51. Naomi Mei-Ami, *Giyus Talmidei Yeshivot LeTsahal VeHok Dehiyat Sherut LeTalmidi Yeshivot SheToratam Omanutam—Hok Tal* [Conscription of yeshiva students to the IDF and the law postponing service for yeshiva dtudents for whom the Torah is their trade—the Tal Law] (Jerusalem: Knesset Center of Research and Information, 2007), 40–43.

    52. Mei-Ami, *Giyus Talmidei Yeshivot*, 31.

    53. In May 2006 the Israel High Court of Justice upheld the legality of the Tal Law, rejecting the petitions of the Movement for Quality Government, of Meretz and Shinui, two secularist political parties, and of Yehuda Ressler, an attorney who had challenged the deferment policy several times in the past. *Jerusalem Post*, May 11, 2006.

    54. The Haredi unit had proven its mettle in its first assignment in the Jordan Valley and had earned the respect of the High Command. It was reassigned to more challenging operations and was expanded to a battalion in 2009. In 2009, 70 percent of the soldiers were Haredim; 30 percent were from national religious backgrounds that chose to do their service in a more restrictive religious framework. Interview with the former commander of the Netzach Yehuda unit, and with the IDF officer responsible for the integration of Haredim, Ariel, June 2009.

    55. Courses were given by Joint Distribution Committee—Brookdale Institute and at the "Haredi College." The Haredi College was established by Adina Bar Shalom, the daughter of Rabbi Ovadia Yosef, spiritual leader of the Shas party in 2001, and was the first of its kind in Israel. It offered academic programs for Haredim in a variety of disciplines, with separate classes for men and women in a totally Haredi environment. The college closed in 2016 for lack of sufficient enrollment and budget deficits. *Jerusalem Post*, November 3, 2016.

    56. The "Shachar" programs are also open to national religious soldiers who deferred service for four years while studying in yeshivas.

    57. Shachar Ilan, *Haaretz*, July 31, 2008.

    58. IDF spokesman press release, March 4, 2009.

    59. *The Marker*, February 14, 2013.

    60. Interview with Channel Ten News religion correspondent Avishai Ben Haim, Israel Democracy Institute, March 18, 2018, https://www.ranlevi.com/2018/03/18/osim_politiqa_giyus_haredim_mst/.

61. *Mako News*, September 25, 2017.

62. In order to encourage service agencies to accept Haredi volunteers, the government had earmarked special funds to subsidize the placement of Haredim in civic service. An agency that accepted a Haredi volunteer paid only 400 shekels for his stipend and the government paid the rest (about 2,000 shekels). A national religious girl doing the same service would cost the agency 1,800 shekels per month. In order to prevent a situation where agencies would prefer Haredi volunteers to national religious girls, agencies were given a ceiling as to how many Haredim they could accept. Interview with Mr. Malkiel Dahan, director of Haredi service Administration for National-Civic Service, Jerusalem, February 19, 2009.

63. Interview with Malkiel Dahan, February 19, 2009.

64. Etta Bick, "The Tal Law: A Missed Opportunity for 'Bridging Social Capital,'" *Journal of Church and State* 52, no. 2 (2010): 298–322.

65. Interview with Malkiel Dahan, February 19, 2009.

66. Interview with Mr. Nahum Benedict, advisor on Haredim, the Administration for National-Civic Service, Jerusalem, February 19, 2009.

67. See Etta Bick, "Tal Law," 298–322. In order to mitigate the problem of the Haredim serving only their own communities, the ANCS stipulated that Haredi nonprofits who want volunteers would have to serve all citizens (e.g., in soup kitchens or the distribution of food packages). Haredim also served in Magen David Adom (emergency ambulance service) and in government offices, but these placements were usually in Haredi municipalities (Beitar-Elite, Elad, and Modiin Elite) or in Haredi neighborhoods in the big cities, and the work environment conformed to strict religious law.

68. The number of Haredim completing national service and employed after service was 48.6 percent compared to only 23.2 percent employed before service and compared to Haredi males in general (41.5%). Office of the Director General, Prime Minister's Office, *Idud Taasuka VeKidum: HaSherut Hatsvai VeHaezrahi BaMigzar HaHaredi* [Encouraging employment and advancement: Military and civic service in the ultra-orthodox sector] (Jerusalem: Government of Israel, 2011).

69. *Haaretz*, August 20, 2013. Minister of the Treasury Yair Lapid announced cuts in child allowances as advocated by Yesh Atid during the election campaign.

70. Yeshiva students would be required to study at least 40 hours a week (45 hours for unmarried students) and to submit a declaration to the Defense Ministry attesting to the fact that they attended and studied as required. The rabbis were also required to sign a document attesting to their students' attendance.

71. The law also included special inducements to encourage young Haredim to join the military. If 1,000 Haredim under the age of 20 would sign up as combat soldiers in any one year, two combat soldiers would be counted as three for the purposes of the enlistment targets, thus freeing more of the older yeshiva students (ages 22–26) from service. The military preferred conscripting younger recruits who were single since their living allowances were far less costly.

72. *BeHedre Haredim*, March 12, 2014, http://www.bhol.co.il/65903/.
73. *Jerusalem Post*, March 29, 2017.
74. *Ynet*, April 14, 2013.
75. *Times of Israel*, March 2, 2014.
76. *Jerusalem Post*, May 14, 2017.
77. *Jerusalem Post*, March 25, 2016.
78. *Jerusalem Post*, July 16, 2015.
79. Hiddush for Religious Freedom and Equality, http://hiddush.org/article-23219-0-Masquerade Ball_Dont_comply_with_the_Haredi_parties_demands.aspx.
80. Statistics released by the IDF indicate that among the 3,070 Haredim serving in the IDF in 2017, 2,478 served in separate Haredi combat units or in the Shachar programs, and 592 served in regular units, an indication that they were probably no longer Haredi yet still included in the Haredi statistics. Oriana Almasi, *Sherut Tsvai Shel Haredim VeHaredim LeSheavar* [Military service of ultra-orthodox and of those formerly ultra-orthodox] (Jerusalem: Knesset Research and Information Center, 2018), 14.
81. The law specifies the following areas of service: welfare, education, health, immigrant absorption, environmental protection, elderly assistance, traffic safety, public safety, employment, citizen rights information, national archives, and civil defense.
82. The law was provisional until June 2020, when the Knesset would be required to evaluate its results.
83. *Jerusalem Post*, March 11, 2015.
84. *Haaretz, Calcalist*, March 19, 2018.
85. State Comptroller, *Report of the State Comptroller* (Jerusalem: March 2018), 67–74. The state comptroller criticized the Ministry of Defense and the IDF for failing to meet the quotas set by the government. There was an 11 percent gap between the number of expected recruits from the Haredi community in 2016 and the number that was actually conscripted (2,850 rather than the expected 3,200). The comptroller determined that the Ministry of Defense had failed to implement the recruitment programs decided upon by an inter-ministry committee of ministry directors general in 2016 and the government had failed to even discuss the plan to increase recruitment in the Haredi sector submitted to it by the minister of defense in February 2017.
86. *The Movement for Quality Government in Israel and Others v. the Knesset and Others*, Israel High Court 1877/14, issued in September 2017.
87. *The Movement for Quality Government in Israel and Others v. the Knesset and Others*. Justice Noam Solberg in the single dissenting minority opinion argued that while the law had indeed failed to create an adequate mechanism to ensure that the enlistment targets would be met, it was still too early to determine that it was a failure and, as such, unconstitutional. He proposed court intervention only after the second adjustment period when it would become clear whether the enlistment targets were being met.

88. Protocol, Shaked Committee, November 24, 2014.

89. Interview with Mr. Avinoam Meir, Authority for National-Civic Service, Jerusalem, June 15, 2017. Conversation with Mr. Malkiel Dahan, at the Authority on the same day.

90. Interview with Mr. Avinoam Meir, Authority for National-Civic Service, Jerusalem, June 15, 2017. When asked why those in civic service continue to serve despite the new law's exemptions and the lower stipend in social services, Meir replied that performing good deeds was an integral part of being ultra-orthodox. Some volunteers were already volunteering in the community and were happy to continue in the framework of civic service and gain credit for doing so. Others wanted to have completion of service written in their résumé when they went to look for a job and preferred to serve in social services, since it was less demanding than service in the military and with far less discipline. Others wished to continue yeshiva studies while serving. Some chose service in the police, firefighting, or emergency health services tracks in order to continue to work in these agencies after service.

91. "Kombinat HaSherut HaEzrachi: HaTachkir HaMale" [Shady deals in civic service: The full inquiry], *Yediot Ahronot*, March 11, 2018.

92. "Kombinat HaSherut HaEzrachi." The Authority for National-Civic Service conceded there was a problem with some of the Haredi volunteers who served in Haredi organizations but said in its defense that they could not effectively supervise the placements since the Treasury allocated funds for only two supervisors in the Haredi sector. The lack of personnel prevented them from doing regular supervisory checks.

93. *Kikar Shabbat*, June 16, 2018. Also reported in *Times of Israel*, January 16, 2018.

94. All told the number of Haredim serving in civic national service in 2018 was 1,425, a number that includes volunteers in their second and third years of part-time service. Information supplied by Noam Amran, legal counsel at the Authority for National-Civic Service.

Chapter 6. From National Service to Community Volunteering: Israel's Arab Citizens and the Controversy over Civic National Service

1. The term "Israeli Arab" includes both Israeli Palestinians and Druze. During the first decades Israeli Arabs identified as Arabs and only in the last decades did many Muslims and Christians define themselves as Palestinians. This term has not been adopted by all Israeli Arabs or by the overwhelming majority of Druze. In this book the broader term "Arab" is used as in official Israeli

government statistics, with no intent implied to deny Israeli Arabs their right to identify as Palestinians or with the Palestinians' national struggle.

2. Israel Central Bureau of Statistics, 2016.

3. See Elie Rekhess, "Initial Israeli Policy Guidelines toward the Arab Minority," in *New Perspectives on Israeli History: The Early Years of the State*, ed. Lawrence J. Silberstein (New York: New York University Press, 1991), 157–174.

4. Ronald R. Krebs, *Fighting for Rights: Military Service and the Politics of Citizenship* (Ithaca: Cornell University Press, 2006), 56–58.

5. Quoted in Krebs, *Fighting for Rights*, 57. See also Jacob M. Landau, *The Arabs in Israel: A Political Study* (London: Oxford University Press, 1969), 108–155.

6. See Gadi Hitman, *Israel and Its Arab Minority, 1948–2008* (Lanham: Lexington Books, 2016), 49–76.

7. Yair Bauml, *Tsel Kahol VeLavan: Mediniyut HaMimsad HaYisraeli UPeulotav BeKerev HaAravim HaYisraelim, 1958–1968* (A Blue and White Shadow: Israeli Establishment, Policy and Actions among Its Arab Citizens, 1958–1968, (Haifa: Pardes, 2007), p. 90.

8. Geremy Forman and Alexandre Kedar, "From Arab Land to 'Israel Lands': The Legal Dispossession of the Palestinians Displaced by Israel in the Wake of 1948," *Environment and Planning D: Society and Space* 22 (2004): 809–830. Yifat Holzman-Gazit, *Land Expropriation in Israel: Law, Culture and Society* (London: Routledge, 2016), 101–118.

9. Eyal Kafkafi, "Segregation or Integration of the Israeli Arabs: Two Concepts in Mapai," *International Journal of Middle East Studies* 30 (1998): 353. Ben-Gurion considered the 1949 armistice borders temporary and the Arab population remaining in Israel transient. He anticipated that hostilities would break out anew and, when it did, the Arabs that had remained in Israel would flee to the surrounding Arab states.

10. Hillel Cohen, *Good Arabs: The Israeli Security Agencies and the Israeli Arabs, 1948–1967* (Berkeley: University of California Press, 2010).

11. Cohen, *Good Arabs*.

12. Bauml, *Tsel Kahol VeLavan*, 80–83.

13. Bauml, *Tsel Kahol VeLavan*.

14. Kafkafi, "Segregation or Integration," 357. See also Bauml, *Tsel Kahol VeLavan*, 81.

15. Ra'anan Cohen, *Zarim BeVetam: Aravim, Yehudim, Medina* [Strangers in their homeland: Arabs, Jews and the State of Israel] (Tel Aviv: Tel Aviv University, Diyunon, 2006).

16. Quoted in Bauml, *Tsel Kahol VeLavan*, 83.

17. See Kais M. Firro, *The Druzes in the Jewish State: A Brief History* (Leiden: Brill, 1999). Krebs argues that Israeli policymakers in the 1950s missed an opportunity to forge a relationship with Israeli Muslims and Christians similar

to that which they developed with the Druze. The loyalty question of the Druze during that period was still unclear and not so different from other Arabs. Many Druze, particularly in the northern region of Israel, had joined the Arab opposition in the War of Independence and had participated in the hostilities and yet the government decided to incorporate them into the Israeli body politic. Krebs, *Fighting for Rights*, 48.

18. Firro, *Druzes in the Jewish State*, 158–159. Mandatory conscription for Druze began in 1956, a policy that split the Druze community. Some religious leaders supported the draft and others did not. Later research suggests that there had been strong opposition by many Druze to mandatory conscription in 1956. The police intervened to enforce the draft. See also Hillel Cohen, *Aravim Tovim: HaModiin HaYisraeli VeHaAravim BeYisrael* [Good Arabs: The Israeli security services and the Israeli Arabs] (Jerusalem: Keter and Ivrit, 2006), 187–191, and Hillel Frisch, "The Druze Minority in the Israeli Military: Traditionalizing an Ethnic Policing Role," *Armed Forces and Society* 20 (1993): 51–67. It is common in Israel to refer to the "covenant of blood" with the Druze since they have served with Jewish Israelis in the IDF in all of Israel's wars and have also suffered serious losses.

19. Liav Orgad, "Hamiut HaAravi BeYisrael VeHovat Sherut Bitahon" [The Arab minority in Israel and the obligation to serve in the defense forces], *HaMishpat* 11 (2007): 395.

20. Ian Lustick, *Arabs in the Jewish State: Israel's Control of a National Minority* (Austin: University of Texas Press, 1980), 98.

21. See Orgad, "Hamiut HaAravi," 385. See also Menachem Hofnung, "Ethnicity, Religion and Politics in Applying Israel's Conscription Law," *Law and Policy* 17, no. 3 (1995): 311–340; Jacob Landau, *The Arab Minority in Israel, 1967–1991: Political Aspects* (New York: Oxford University Press, 1993); and Uzi Benziman and Attala Mansour, *Dayare Mishneh: Arviye Yisrael: Maamadam VeHamediniyut Kelapehem* [Subtenants: Israeli Arabs: Their status and the policy toward them] (Jerusalem: Keter, 1992).

22. Israel State Archives, 13/142 Memorandum from the Secretary of the Cabinet to the Minister of Justice, April 15, 1969.

23. Hitman, *Israel and Its Arab Minority*, 140. There was also a discussion of civic national service for Arabs on Arabic state television on July 27, 1977.

24. *Davar*, December 26, 1978.

25. Benziman and Mansour, *Dayare Mishneh*, 86.

26. Interview with Alexander Bligh, Prime Minister Yitzhak Shamir's advisor on Arab affairs, Ariel, May 6, 2013.

27. Bick, "Lip-Service to service."

28. Knesset Archives, Private Member Legislation, 1984.

29. Knesset Archives, Private Member Legislation, 123/507, 1985.

30. Israel State Archives, File #7/2366 391809, Letter from Yaakov Elkin to Moshe Katsav, Minister of Labor and Welfare, September 9, 1985.

Notes to Chapter 6

31. The legislation was proposed by MK Raphael Eitan (Tsomet); Geula Cohen (Tehiya); Rehavam Zeevi (Moledet); Eliezer Zandberg, Pini Badash, and Haim Dayan (Tsomet); and Avigdor Lieberman (Yisrael Beiteinu). Bick, "Lip-Service to Service," 137.

32. Israel's Basic Laws are the constitutional laws of the country. Israel did not write a formal written constitution after attaining independence. Instead, it decided to adopt a gradual process, which empowered the Knesset to legislate fundamental laws that would be incorporated into one formal constitution at a later date. It is important to note that no special majority is necessary for passing a Basic Law.

33. *Divrei HaKnesset*, January 25, 1993.

34. See the response of Justice Minister David Libai speaking for the government, *Divrei HaKnesset*, January 25, 1993.

35. *Davar*, December 4, 1986.

36. Bick, "Lip-Service to Service," 139.

37. For example, paragraph 17 of the Shinui party platform (1988) (one of the parties that comprise Meretz) supported national service for Israel's Arabs.

38. For example, former minister of education Amnon Rubenstein (Meretz) proposed in 1997 the establishment of a *voluntary* program open to all youth excused from service, Arab and Jew. *Divrei HaKnesset*, May 19, 1997.

39. *Divrei HaKnesset*, December 17, 1997.

40. *Divrei HaKnesset*, December 17, 1997.

41. Levy, *MiTsava HaAm*. See also Gal Levy and Orna Sasson-Levy, "Militarized Socialization, Military Service and Class Reproduction: The Experiences of Israeli Soldiers," *Sociological Perspectives* 51, no. 2 (2008): 349–374.

42. *Divrei HaKnesset*, July 9, 1996.

43. The election in 1999 was one of three in which the prime minister was elected directly by popular vote, 1996, 1999, and 2001. The law that authorized direct election of the prime minister was repealed in 2001.

44. Bick, "Lip-Service to Service," 140.

45. Orgad, "Hamiut HaAravi," 403–404.

46. Orgad, "Hamiut HaAravi." The petitioner, Dr. Shmuel Saadia, asked the court to rule on the legality of not conscripting Arabs.

47. Cited in Reuven Gal, "Tefisat Nose Hazekhuyot," 13–14.

48. Saadia petitioned the High Court again in 2000. The government responded that the sensitive security situation after the October Events precluded introducing any form of national service for Arabs at this time. The Court rejected his petition, advising the petitioner to return when there would be peace. Orgad, "Hamiut HaAravi," 403–404.

49. Bick, "Institutional Layering."

50. *Divrei HaKnesset*, MK Nawaf Masalha, April 12, 1989.

51. Interview with Alexander Bligh, Ariel, May 6, 2013. In June 1991, the government proposed a program to encourage Christians to volunteer to the army,

but the Arab Higher Monitoring Committee rejected the proposal out of hand, contending that all of the non-Jewish minorities belong to one Arab nation and could not be separated. Hitman, *Israel and Its Arab Minority*, 170.

52. Cohen, *Zarim BeVetam*, 236.
53. *Divrei HaKnesset*, MK Salah Saleem, Hadash-Balad, January 31, 1996.
54. See discussions in *Divrei HaKnesset*, 1996–2005.
55. Interview with Amir Abu Issa, the national coordinator of minority volunteers at the Authority for National-Civic Service, January 12, 2017.
56. Sar Shalom Gerbi, director general of the Administration for National-Civic Service (ANCS), pressed the government on numerous occasions to transfer the authority to pay civic service volunteers their postservice grants to the ANCS so that it could pay the volunteers directly. This change would have defused the Arab charge that civic service is but a covert extension of the military. See the testimony of Sar Shalom Gerbi, Shaked Committee, Protocol #27, December 16, 2013.
57. Still today many Arabs see civic national service as a program sponsored by the Defense Ministry. In a recent conversation with Gadir Hani, a social activist in the Bedouin town of Hura, she expressed support for volunteering and encouraged Arab youth to volunteer but was strongly opposed to civic service because she said "it is run by the Defense Ministry." July 10, 2019.
58. Orgad, "Hamiut HaAravi," 401. Hassan Jabareen, director general of Adalah—The Legal Center for Arab Minority Rights in Israel, has said that the Arab refusal to serve is an expression of their wish to preserve their national unity, identity, and culture. *Haaretz*, September 2, 2011.
59. See Arik Rodnisky, *Hamiut Haaravi B'yisrael Vehasiach al Medina Yehudit* [The Arab minority in Israel and the Jewish state narrative] (Jerusalem: Israel Democracy Institute, 2015).
60. Raef Zreik suggests that the government in 2007 exploited the neoliberal catchphrase "a state of all of its citizens," which was promoted by the Balad party as part of its demands for national minority rights, to extend the obligation of national civic service to the Arab sector. Instead of granting the Arabs rights as a national minority, the government extended the obligations. Zreik, "Ezrahut, Zekhuyot Vehovo," 298.
61. Letter from Directors General Amnon Beeri-Sulitzeanu and Mohammad Darawshe of Keren Avraham to Prime Minister Benjamin Netanyahu regarding civic service in the Arab sector, Abraham Fund Initiatives, July 5, 2012.
62. The following is an excerpt from the summary section of the Orr Commission report:

> The events of October 2000 shook the earth. The riots in the Arab sector inside the State of Israel in early October were unprecedented. The events were extremely unusual from several perspectives. Thousands participated, at many locations, at the same time. The intensity

of the violence and aggression expressed in the events was extremely powerful. Against security forces, and even against civilians, use was made of a variety of means of attack, including a small number of live fire incidents, Molotov cocktails, ball bearings in slingshots, various methods of stone throwing and the rolling of burning tires. Jews were attacked on the roads for being Jewish and their property was destroyed. In a number of incidences, they were just inches from death at the hands of an unrestrained mob.

In a number of instances, attempts were made to enter Jewish towns in order to attack them. Major traffic arteries were blocked and traffic to various Jewish towns was seriously disrupted, sometimes even severed, for long periods of time. In a large number of instances, the aggression and violence was characterized by great determination and continued for long periods. The police acted to restore order and used a variety of means to disperse the crowd. As a result of the use of some of these means, which included firing rubber bullets and a few instances of live fire, Arab citizens were killed and many more injured. In the second wave of events, some places saw retaliatory Jewish riots against Arabs.

National Commission of Inquiry (Vaadat Or), *Din VeHeshbon LeBerur Hitnagshuyot Ben Kohot HaBitahon Leven Ezrahim Yisraelim BeHodesh October, 2000* [Report on the clashes between the security forces and Israeli citizens in October 2000] (Jerusalem: Government of Israel, 2003), http://uri.mitkadem.co.il/vaadat-or/.

63. National Commission of Inquiry, *Din VeHeshbon LeBerur.*
64. National Commission of Inquiry, *Din VeHeshbon LeBerur.*
65. Ministerial Committee Regarding the Recommendations of the Or Committee (Vaadat Lapid), *Din VeHeshbon VeHamlatsaot Vaadat HaSarim LeInyan Hamlatsot Vaadat Or* [Report and recommendations of the ministerial committee regarding the findings of the Or Committee] (Jerusalem: Government of Israel, 2004).
66. Ministerial Committee, *Din VeHeshbon VeHamlatsaot,* 13.
67. *Divrei HaKnesset,* June 9, 2004.
68. *Haaretz,* December 18, 2005.
69. David Ivri had been the deputy commander in chief of the IDF and the commander of the air force. He also served as Israel's ambassador to Washington and as head of the National Security Council.
70. The Committee for the Institutionalization of Civil-National Service: Interim Recommendations (Ivri Committee), February 2005, http://ncs.gov.il/ncs/Documents/hamlatsot_ivri.pdf (Hebrew).
71. Committee for the Institutionalization of Civil-National Service, Recommendation #25.
72. Government of Israel, Decision #2295, August 19, 2007.

73. Protocol #376, Knesset Education, Culture, and Sports Committee, January 24, 2008.

74. Protocol #376, Knesset Education, Culture, and Sports Committee, January 24, 2008.

75. The Higher Arab Monitoring Committee is an independent political organization that coordinates the political activities of Israeli Arabs. It is comprised of Arab MKs, local council heads, and representatives of different groups in the Arab sector.

76. Odeh went on to head the Joint Arab List and in 2015 he was elected to the Knesset, representing the Hadash faction.

77. Protocol #376, Knesset Education, Culture, and Sports Committee, January 24, 2008.

78. Protocol #376, Knesset Education, Culture, and Sports Committee, January 24, 2008.

79. Protocol #376, Knesset Education, Culture, and Sports Committee, January 24, 2008.

80. Protocol #271, Knesset Labor, Welfare, and Health Committee, June 21, 2016.

81. Protocol #424, Knesset Education, Culture, and Sport Committee, June 6, 2011.

82. *Jerusalem Post*, June 7, 2011.

83. *Ynet*, October 27, 2007.

84. *Haaretz*, June 9, 2013.

85. "Wanted: An Arab Who Has Lost His Memory," *Ynet*, July 11, 2007, www.ynet.co.il/articles/0,7340,L-3468710,00.html. See also Rhoda Ann Kanaaneh and Isis Nusair, eds., *Displaced at Home: Ethnicity and Gender among Palestinians in Israel* (Albany: State University of New York Press, 2010).

86. "Israel's Arabs Debate National Service," *The Media Line*, July 25, 2011, www.themedialine.org/news/news_detail.asp?NewsID=32801.

87. Sawsan Khalife, "Knesset Moves to Force National Service on Palestinians in Israel," *The Electronic Intifada*, April 7, 2012, https://electronicintifada.net/content/knesset-moves-force-national-service-palestinians-israel/11458.

88. *NRG*, October 27, 2007.

89. *NRG*, October 27, 2007.

90. *Channel Two News*, June 26, 2010, www.mako.co.il/news-israel/local/Article-88875cec3957921004.htm&Partner=flash_embedplayer.

91. *NRG*, July 28, 2013.

92. Statistics provided to the author by the Authority for National-Civic Service, 2018.

93. Sammy Smooha and Zohar Lechtman, *Civic Service of Arabs in Israel: Research Findings 2007–2011* (Haifa: Jewish-Arab Center, University of Haifa, 2012).

Notes to Chapter 6

94. The targets set were 2,300 in 2011–2012, 2,830 in 2012–2013, and 3,280 in 2013–2014. The real enlistment numbers were slightly higher, 2,711, 3,238, and 3,689, respectively.

95. Ministry of Finance and the Administration for National-Civic Service, *Din VeHeshbon Shel HaTsevet LeHarhavat Maarakh HaMitnadvim MeHamiutim UMehaHaredim* [Report of the taskforce for the expansion of minority and Haredi volunteers] (Jerusalem: Ministry of Finance, 2011).

96. Ministry of Finance and the Administration for National-Civic Service, *Din VeHeshbon*, 22.

97. Yohanan Plesner, *Din VeHeshbon Shel Yohanan Plesner, Yoshev Rosh HaVaada LeKidum HaShiluv BeSherut VehaShivyon BaNetel* [Report of MK Yohanan Plesner, chairman of the Committee to Advance Integration in Service and Sharing the Burden], July 2012, 4, https://www.makorrishon.co.il/nrg/images/news1/plesner.pdf.

98. Sammy Smooha, *The Lost Decade of Arab-Jewish Relations in Israel: Survey of the Index 2003–2009, Findings and Conclusions* (Haifa: University of Haifa, 2010).

99. Since the mid-1990s, the Arab political leadership has been divided into four separate parties, Hadash, Balad, Taal, and the United List (Raam). In 2015 these four parties united into one list HaRishima HaMishutefet (the Joint List) because the Knesset in 2014 raised the electoral threshold to 3.25 percent.

100. Sammy Smooha, *Lo Shovrim Et HaKelim: Madad Yachase Aravim-Yehudim BeYisrael* [Still playing by the rules: Index of Arab-Jewish relations in Israel, 2012] (Jerusalem: Israel Democracy Institute and Haifa University, 2013), 105–106.

101. Smooha, *Lo Shovrim*, 108.

102. Smooha and Lechtman, *Civic Service of Arabs in Israel*.

103. Smooha and Lechtman, *Civic Service of Arabs in Israel*.

104. Smooha and Lechtman, *Civic Service of Arabs in Israel*.

105. Sammy Smooha and Zohar Lechtman, "Hatsayat Kav Adom: Hatalat Hovat Sherut Ezrahi Al Tseirim Aravim BeYisrael" [Crossing a red line: Requiring civic service from Arab youth in Israel], in *Sherut Hova o' Hova LeSharet* [Mandatory service or the duty to serve], ed. Yagil Levy (Ra'anana: Open University, 2015), 121–152. Another opinion survey conducted among Israeli Arabs by Shibley Telhami of the University of Maryland found comparable findings. In 2009, 51 percent and in 2010 47 percent of the respondents said they were against mandatory civic national service for Arabs "under all circumstances." In 2009 and 2010, 38 percent said they would support civic service if Arabs were granted equal rights to Jews, and a small minority said they would support civic service only after the establishment of a Palestinian state (7% in 2009 and 11% in 2010). Shibley Telhami, Principal Investigator, University of Maryland with Zogby International, Israeli Arab/Palestinian Public Opinion Survey, www.brookings.edu/wp-content/uploads/2016/06/israeli_arab_powerpoint.pdf.

106. Data courtesy of the Guttman Center for Public Opinion and Policy Research at the Israel Democracy Institute.

107. Information supplied by the Authority for National-Civic Service, March 2018.

108. Protocol #27, Testimony of Sar Shalom Gerbi, director general of the ANCS, Shaked Committee, December 16, 2013.

109. See Galit Yanay-Ventura and Moshe Sharabi, "The Civic Service of Young Arabs in Israel: A Narrative Understanding," unpublished paper presented at the ninth Conference of the European Research Network on Philanthropy, July 4–5, 2019, Basil, Switzerland.

110. *NRG*, May 30, 2016.

111. Interview with Amir Abu Issa, the national coordinator of minority volunteers Authority for National-Civic Service, Jerusalem, October 28, 2018.

112. Interview with Amir Abu Issa, October 28, 2018.

113. Interview with Zenav Abu Said, deputy coordinator of civic national service in the Arab sector, Authority for National-Civic Service, Jerusalem, June 15, 2017.

114. Interview with Zenav Abu Said, June 15, 2017. Druze girls beginning national service in 2013 numbered 618, more than 50 percent of their age group.

115. *Ynet*, October 22, 2017.

116. Interview with Amir Abu Issa, October 28, 2018. The response among the Bedouin has been notably mixed. While many Bedouins in the north welcomed the opportunity to participate in civic national service, Bedouins in the south are less inclined to serve.

117. Interview with Zenav Abu Said, June 15, 2017.

118. In 2013 the total number of Bedouin men serving in the IDF was 1,404, 320 were inducted that year. This is a very small percentage of the Bedouin population, which numbers about 300,000. The Shaked Committee, Protocol #27, December 16, 2013. In 2000 the number of volunteers was almost the same, 330. *Haaretz*, June 14, 2001. There were some years when the numbers declined significantly, influenced by political events.

119. Interview with Amir Abu Issa, October 28, 2018.

120. Interview with Amir Abu Issa, October 28, 2018. See also Protocol #110 of the Knesset Labor, Welfare, and Health Committee, December 7, 2015, remarks by Amnon Bari-Soliziyano, director of Keren Avraham Initiatives.

121. They issued this statement in response to the preliminary recommendations issued by the short-lived Plesner Committee discussed earlier.

122. *Haaretz*, June 24, 2012.

123. Interview with Amir Abu Issa, January 12, 2017.

124. See National Committee for the Heads of the Arab Local Authorities in Israel, "The Future Vision of the Palestinian Arabs in Israel," 2006, Adalah, www.adalah.org/uploads/oldfiles/newsletter/eng/dec06/tasawor-mostaqbali.pdf.

125. Interview with Amir Abu Issa, October 28, 2018. MKs from the Joint Arab List addressed a conference in March 2017 sponsored by the Abraham Fund and AJEEC, two NGOs that run voluntary service programs in the Arab sector. While they expressed opposition to civic service run by the government, they for the first time sounded a positive note in support of volunteering under other auspices. Ayman Odeh, head of the Joint Arab List, said: "Volunteering is a value but we are against the politicization of civic volunteering. . . . Linking obligations to rights is politicization, linking civic volunteering to the Defense Ministry is politicization. In addition, there is a real danger that programs operated by volunteers will cause a rise in unemployment. All alternative projects . . . are welcome; when there is a local need it must be met." MK Massood Ghanaim added that "funding should be given to local governments so they can develop programs according to community needs, and MK Jamal Zahalka called for setting up a framework for volunteering that will strengthen the Arab identity of the youth. *Maariv*, March 3, 2017.

126. Head of the Joint Arab List MK Ayman Odeh attended the second session of the Labor, Welfare, and Health Committee on civic service in 2015 and expressed interest in taking part in a meaningful discussion devoid of political bashing and one-upmanship. However, he conditioned his participation on discontinuing the committee's deliberations while the discussions were being held. The chairman of the committee, Eli Alaluf, while welcoming Odeh's willingness to engage in a dialogue, refused to suspend the work of the committee and offered to engage in a separate dialogue with Odeh concurrent with the committee deliberations. This Odeh found unacceptable and he stormed out of the committee in anger. Protocol #120, Knesset Labor, Welfare, and Health Committee, December 21, 2015.

127. Protocol #427, Knesset Labor, Welfare, and Health Committee, January 18, 2017.

128. Interview with Zenav Abu Said, June 15, 2017. See also Protocol #120, Knesset Labor, Welfare, and Health Committee, December 21, 2015.

129. Government of Israel, Decision #1889, August 11, 2016.

130. Statistics provided to this author by the Authority for National-Civic Service, January 2019.

131. Interview with Amir Abu Issa, October 28, 2018.

132. On January 18, 2017, the government, buttressed with a court order, sent a demolition squad accompanied by a police unit to demolish houses in the unrecognized Bedouin village of Umm al Hiran in the Negev. In the course of protests, village resident Yacoub Abu Al-Qia'an was shot by police who suspected him of being an armed terrorist. His car then careened into a group of policemen, killing First Sergeant Erez Levi. Abu Al-Qia'an was then killed by police. The demolition order was part of a government plan to remove the residents of Umm al Hiran from the lands they occupy and to resettle them in the nearby Bedouin township of Hura. The government planned to build a large Jewish town

in its stead. Residents of Umm al Hiran had challenged the demolition plan in the High Court but their petition had been turned down. *Ynet*, January 18, 2017.

133. In 2018 there was a substantial increase in the number of Bedouins serving in the IDF, 420, while only 300 in 2016. This rise is due in part to improved benefits offered to Bedouins and new training courses that will improve their chances of finding employment after service. *Maariv*, January 16, 2018.

134. Interview with Amir Abu Issa, October 28, 2018.

135. Government of Israel, Decision #638, paragraph 41c, July 28, 2013.

136. The reasons given by the government not to carry out the decision are essentially procedural: the administrative change would be costly, it would entail setting up a separate disbursement division within the ANCS, and would require more personnel. Interview with Amir Abu Issa, October 28, 2018.

Conclusion. Four Tribes: Is a Communitarian Model the Answer?

1. A recent study by Lee Cahaner found that 11 percent of the Haredi consider themselves "modern" and 29 percent "partly modern." Of the "modern" Haredim, 67 percent were employed (compared to 34% among those who define themselves as "classic and conservative"), and 59 percent said they will encourage their children to engage in academic studies in addition to Torah studies. Almost half of the modern Haredim said they identify with the state and support greater integration into Israeli society, while only 10 percent of the conservative Haredim identify as such. *Calcalist*, April 4, 2019.

Bibliography

Abowitz, Kathleen Knight, and Jason Harnish. "Contemporary Discourses of Citizenship." *Review of Educational Research* 76, no. 4 (2006): 653–690.

Adalya Economic Consulting. "Cost–Benefit Analysis from Operating a National Civic Service Program for Disadvantaged Populations." Executive Summary. Forum for the Advancement of Civic National Service, October 2011.

Almasi, Oriana. *Hasherut Haleumi-Ezrahi BeYisrael* [National-civic service in Israel]. Jerusalem: Knesset Center for Research and Information, 2014.

———. *Sherut Tsvai Shel Haredim VeHaredim LeSheavar* [Military service of Haredim and the formerly Haredim]. Jerusalem: Knesset Research and Information Center, 2018.

Arian, Asher, Nir Atmor, and Yael Hadar. *The 2007 Israeli Democracy Index*. Jerusalem: Israel Democracy Institute, 2007.

Aristotle. *Politics*. Translated by Carnes Lord. Chicago: University of Chicago Press, 1989.

Arthur, James. "Community Involvement and Communitarian Theory." n.d., January 12, 2018. citeseerx.ist.psu.edu/viewdoc/summary?doi=10.1.1.522.2930.

Avineri, Shlomo, and Avner de Shalit, eds. *Communitarianism and Individualism*. London: Oxford University Press, 1992.

Barak-Erez, Daphna. "Giyus Bakhurei Hayeshivot: MePeshara LeMahloket" [Conscription of yeshiva students: From compromise to dispute]. In *Tsomte Hakhraot U'Parshiot Mafteakh BeYisrael* [Crossroads of decisions in Israel], edited by Devorah Hacohen and Moshe Lissak, 20–22. Beersheva: Machon Ben-Gurion LeCheker Yisrael, 2010.

Barali, Avi, and Nir Keidar. *Mamlakhtiyut Yisraelit* [Israeli republicanism]. Jerusalem: Israel Democracy Institute, 2011.

Barber, Benjamin R. "A Proposal for Mandatory Citizen Education and Community Service." *Michigan Journal of Community Service Learning* 1, no. 1 (1994): 86–93.

Bar-Lev, Mordechai. "Cultural Characteristics and Group Image of Religious Youth." *Youth and Society* 16, no. 2 (1984): 153–170.

Bass, Melissa. *The Politics and Civics of National Service: Lessons from the Civilian Conservation Corps, VISTA, and AmeriCorps*. Washington, DC: Brookings Institution Press, 2013.

Bauml, Yair. *Tsel Kahol VeLavan: Mediniyut HaMimsad HaYisraeli UPeulotav BeKerev HaAravim HaYisraelim, 1958-1968* [A blue and white shadow: Israeli establishment, policy, and actions among its Arab citizens, 1958-1968]. Haifa: Pardes, 2007.

Begin, Menachem. *BaMahteret* [In the underground]. Tel Aviv: Hadar, 1978.

Ben Ami, Naomi. *Giyus Talmidei Yeshivot LeTsahal VeHok Dehiyat Sherut LeTalmidei Yeshivot SheToratam Omanutam—Hok Tal* [Conscription of yeshiva students to the IDF and the law postponing service for yeshiva students for whom the Torah is their trade—The Tal Law]. Jerusalem: Knesset Center of Research and Information, 2007.

Ben-Eliezer, Uri. "The Meaning of Political Participation in a Nonliberal Democracy: The Israeli Experience." *Comparative Politics* 25, no. 4 (1993): 397-412.

Ben Yishai, Ofra. "Hasherut HaEzrahi KeHalufa LeSherut Hatsvai: Keitsad Yagiv Hatsava" [Civic service as an alternative to military service: How will the military respond?]. In *Sherut Hova o' Hova LeSharet* [Mandatory service or the duty to serve], edited by Yagil Levy, 38-73. Ra'anana: Open University, 2015.

Ben-Gurion, David. *Hazon VaDerekh* [The vision and the way], vol. 4. Tel Aviv: Mapai, 1953.

———. "Netsah Yisrael." In *Hazon VaDerekh*, vol. 4. Tel Aviv: Mapai, 1953.

Benziman, Uzi, and Attala Mansour. *Dayare Mishneh: Arviye Yisrael: Maamadam VeHamediniyut Kelapehem* [Subtenants: Israeli Arabs: Their status and the policy toward them]. Jerusalem: Keter, 1992.

Berman, Eli. "Subsidized Sacrifice: State Support of Religion in Israel." *Contemporary Jewry* 20 (1999): 167-200.

Bick, Etta. "Equality, Orthodoxy and Politics: The Conflict over National Service in Israel." *Israel Affairs* 19, no. 3 (July 2013): 505-525.

———. "Institutional Layering, Displacement, and Policy Change: The Evolution of Civic Service in Israel." *Public Policy and Administration* 31, no. 4 (2016): 342-360.

———. "Lip-Service to Service: The Knesset Debates over Civic National Service in Israel, 1953-2005." *Israel Affairs* 22, no. 1 (2016): 126-149.

———. "Sherut Ezrahi Hova: HaHashlakhot al Nashim Haredyiot Vedatiyot" [Mandatory civic service: The ramifications for ultra-orthodox and religious women]. In *Sherut Hova o' Hova LeSharet* [Mandatory service or the duty to serve], edited by Yagil Levy, 95-120. Ra'anana: Open University, 2015.

———. "The Tal Law: A Missed Opportunity for 'Bridging Social Capital.'" *Journal of Church and State* 52, no. 2 (2010): 298-322.

Brown, Binyamin. *HaHazon Ish: Haposek, Hamaamin, UManhig HaMahapekha HaHaredit* [The Hazon Ish: Halakhist, believer, and leader of the Haredi revolution]. Jerusalem: Magnes, 2010.

Cahaner, Lee. "The Ultra-Orthodox Community on the Conservatism-Modernism Spectrum." May 2019. Israel Democracy Institute. https://en.idi.org.il/articles/26911.

Chetrit, Sami Shalom. *The Mizrahi Struggle in Israel: Between Oppression and Liberation, Identification and Alternative, 1948–2003*. Tel Aviv: Am Oved, 2004. Hebrew.

Cicero, Marcus Tullius. *On Duties (De Officiis)*. Translated by M. T. Griffin and E. M. Atkins. New York: Cambridge University Press, 1991.

Cohen, Hillel. *Aravim Tovim: HaModiin HaYisraeli VeHaAravim BeYisrael* [Good Arabs: The Israeli security services and the Israeli Arabs]. Jerusalem: Keter and Ivrit, 2006.

———. *Good Arabs: The Israeli Security Services and the Israeli Arabs, 1948–1967*. Berkeley: University of California Press, 2010.

Cohen, Ra'anan. *Zarim BeVetam: Aravim, Yehudim, Medina* [Strangers in their homeland: Arabs, Jews, and the State of Israel]. Tel Aviv: Tel Aviv University, Diyunon, 2006.

Cohen, Shlomo, ed. *Peer HaDor: Prakim MeMasechet Hayav U'pielato Shel Avraham Yeshayahu Karelitz* [The glory of a generation: Chapters in the life and deeds of Avraham Yeshayahu Karelitz], vol. 5. Bnei Brak: Netzach, 1974.

Cohen, Yehezkel. *Giyus Banot VeSherut Leumi: Iyun BeHalakha* [The conscription of girls and national service: A study in Jewish law]. Jerusalem: Ne'emanei Torah VaAvodah, 1979.

———, ed. *Giyus Kahalakha: Al Shihrur Bahure Yeshiva MiGiyus LeTsahal* [Conscription and Jewish law: On exempting yeshiva students from military service]. Jerusalem: Ne'emanei Torah VaAvodah, 1993.

Cohen, Yoel. "On the Beat: Covering Israel's Religion Wars." *Religion in the News* 2, no. 3 (Fall 1999). http://www.trincoll.edu/depts/csrpl/RINVol2No3/Israel's ReligionWars.htm.

Committee for the Institutionalization of Civil-National Service (Ivri Committee). "Hamlatsot Benayim" [Interim recommendations]. February 2005. http://ncs.gov.il/ncs/Documents/hamlatsot_ivri.pdf.

Dagger, Richard. "Republican Citizenship." In *Handbook of Citizenship Studies*, edited by Engin F. Isin and Bryan S. Turner, 145–157. Thousand Oaks: Sage, 2002.

Don-Yehiya, Eliezer. *HaPolitika Shel HaHasdara: Yishuv Sikhsukhim BeNose Dat BeYisrael* [Religion and political accommodation in Israel]. Jerusalem: Floersheimer Institute for Policy Studies, 1997.

———. "Mamlakhtiyut, Education and Religion in the Struggle over the Mass Immigration." *Journal of Israeli History* 26, no. 2 (2007): 229–250.

Drori, Zeev. *Utopia BeMadim: Trumat Tsahal LeHityashvut, LeKlitat HaAliyah UleHinuch Breshit Yemi HaMedina* (Utopia in uniform: The contribution of the IDF to settlement, immigrant absorption, and education in the early years of the state]. Sde Boker: Ben-Gurion Heritage Center, 2000.

Etzioni, Amitai. "The Responsive Community: A Communitarian Perspective." *American Sociological Review* 61, no. 1 (1996): 1–11.

———. *The Spirit of Community: The Reinvention of American Society*. New York: Touchstone Books, 1993.

Finkelstein, Ariel. *HaHinukh HaMamlakhti Dati: Temunat Matsav, Megamot VeHesegim* [State religious education: Situation report, trends, and accomplishments]. Tel Aviv: Ne'emanei Torah VaAvodah, 2013.

———. *Maafyanei Benot Hatsiyonut Hadatit Hameshartot Betsava UBeSherut Leumi: Tmunat Matzav UMegamot* [Religious Zionist girls in the IDF and in national service: Situation report and trends]. Tel Aviv: Ne'emanei Torah VaAvodah, 2018.

Firro, Kais M. *The Druzes in the Jewish State: A Brief History*. Leiden: Brill, 1999.

Forman, Geremy, and Alexandre Kedar. "From Arab Land to 'Israel Lands': The Legal Dispossession of the Palestinians Displaced by Israel in the Wake of 1948." *Environment and Planning D Society and Space* 22 (2004): 809–830.

Frazer, Elizabeth. *The Problems of Communitarian Politics: Unity and Conflict*. London: Oxford University Press, 1999.

Friedman, Menachem. "Al Giyus Bechurei Yeshivot" [On conscription of yeshiva students]. In *Giyus Kahalakha: Al Shihrur Bahure Yeshiva MiGiyus LeTsahal* [Conscription and Jewish Law: On Exempting Yeshiva Students From Military Service], edited by Yehezkel Cohen, 262–277. Tel Aviv: Ne'emanei Torah VaAvodah, Hakibbutz Hadati, 1993.

———. "The Family Community Model in Haredi Society." In *Coping with Life and Death: Jewish Families in the Twentieth Century*, edited by Peter Medding, 166–177. London: Oxford University Press, 1998.

———. *Hachevra HacHaredit B'Yisrael: Mekorot, Megamot VeTahalichim* [The ultra-orthodox society in Israel: Sources, trends and developments]. Jerusalem: Jerusalem Institute for the Study of Israel, 1991.

———. "HaIsha Haharedit" [The ultra-orthodox woman]. In *Eshnav Lehayehem Shel Nashim BeHevrot Yehudiyot Kovetz Mehkarim Ben Tehumiyim* [A look at the lives of women in Jewish societies], edited by Yael Atzmon, 273–290. Jerusalem: Zalman Shazar Center for the Study of Jewish History, 1995.

———. "VeEleh Toldot HaStatus-quo: Dat UMedina BeYisrael" [This is the story of the status quo: Religion and state in Israel]. In *Shevet Ahim: Yahase Hilonim-Datiyim: Emdot, Hatsaot, Amanot* [Brethren dwelling together], edited by Uri Dromi, 57–89. Jerusalem: Israel Democracy Institute, 2005.

Frisch, Hillel. "The Druze Minority in the Israeli Military: Traditionalizing an Ethnic Policing Role." *Armed Forces and Society* 20 (1993): 51–67.

Gal, Reuven. *Din VeHeshbon Al Hasherut Haleumi* [Report on Sherut Leumi]. Jerusalem: National Civic Service Administration, 2009.

———. "Tefisat Nose Hazekhuyot VeHahovot Shel Erahei Yisrael HaAravim BeAspaklariyat Raayon HaSherut HaEzrahi" [Rights and obligations as reflected in the idea of civic service]. Position Paper No. 13. Tel Aviv: Tel Aviv University, Harold Hartuch School of Government and Policy, 2008.

Gal, Reuven, Karin Amit, Nicole Fleischer, and Nancy Strichman. *Volunteers of National Youth Service in Israel: A Study on Motivation for Service, Social Attitudes and Volunteers' Satisfaction*. St. Louis: Washington University, Center for Social Development, Global Service Institute, 2003.

Gaus, Gerald F. *Justificatory Liberalism: An Essay on Epistemology and Political Theory*. London: Oxford University Press, 1996.

Glendon, Mary Ann. *Rights Talk: The Impoverishment of Political Discourse*. New York: Simon and Schuster, 2008.

Gorham, Eric B. *National Service, Citizenship, and Political Education*. Albany: State University of New York Press, 1992.

Hacker, Jacob S. "Privatizing Risk without Privatizing the Welfare State: The Hidden Politics of Social Policy Retrenchment in the United States." *American Political Science Review* 98, no. 2 (2004): 243–260.

Hatib, Ahmed, and Ilan Biton. *Hasherut Haezrahi–Leumi BeYisrael: Skira VeNituah* [Civic-national service in Israel: Overview and analysis]. Jerusalem: Knesset Center for Research and Information, 2011.

Hitman, Gadi. *Israel and Its Arab Minority, 1948–2008*. Lanham: Lexington Books, 2016.

Hofnung, Menachem. "Ethnicity, Religion and Politics in Applying Israel's Conscription Law." *Law and Policy* 17, no. 3 (1995): 311–340.

Holzman-Gazit, Yifat. *Land Expropriation in Israel: Law, Culture and Society*. London: Routledge, 2016.

Horn, Christoph. "Law Governance and Political Obligation." In *The Cambridge Companion to Aristotle's Politics*, edited by Marguerite Deslauriers and Pierre Destrée, 223–246. London: Cambridge University Press, 2013.

Ilan, Shachar. *HaHaredim B'Am: Hataktsivim, HaHistamtut Veremisat HaHok* [Ultra-orthodox incorporated: Funds, avoiding the draft, and law violation]. Jerusalem: Keter, 2000.

Janowitz, Morris. "Observations on the Sociology of Citizenship: Obligations and Rights." *Social Forces* 59, no. 1 (1980): 1–24.

Kafkafi, Eyal. "Segregation or Integration of the Israeli Arabs: Two Concepts in Mapai." *International Journal of Middle East Studies* 30 (1998): 347–367.

Kanaaneh, Rhoda Ann, and Isis Nusair. *Displaced at Home: Ethnicity and Gender among Palestinians in Israel*. Albany: State University of New York Press, 2010.

Kant, Immanuel. *Kant: Political Writings*. Edited by Hans Reiss. London: Cambridge University Press, 1991.
Kaplan, Kimi. "Haredim and Western Culture: A View from Both Sides of the Ocean." In *Middle Eastern Societies and the West: Accommodation or Clash of Civilizations*, edited by Meir Litvak, 269–289. Syracuse: Syracuse University Press, 2007.
———. "Orthodoxia VeHarediut BeAmerica U'beYisrael: Hebetim Historiim" [Orthodoxy and ultra-orthodoxy in America and in Israel: Historical aspects]. In *Am Levadad: Moledet U'Pezura: Hebetim Historiyim-Hashvatiyim* [A nation that dwelleth alone: Homeland and diaspora: Aspects of comparative histories], edited by Binyamin Lau, 301–315. Tel Aviv: Yediot Ahronot, 2006.
Knesset. *Divrei HaKnesset*. Jerusalem: Government of Israel, n.d.
Krebs, Ronald R. *Fighting for Rights: Military Service and the Politics of Citizenship*. Ithaca: Cornell University Press, 2006.
Kymlicka, Will. *Liberalism, Community and Culture*. Oxford: Oxford University Press, 1989.
Landau, Jacob. *The Arab Minority in Israel, 1967–1991: Political Aspects*. New York: Oxford University Press, 1993.
———. *The Arabs in Israel: A Political Study*. London: Oxford University Press, 1969.
Leven, Hagai. *Hamigzar HaHaredi BeYisrael: Haatzama Tokh Shiluv BeTaasuka* [The ultra-orthodox sector in Israel: Empowerment through integration in employment]. Jerusalem: Prime Minister's Office, National Economic Council, 2004.
Levy, Drorit. "Teur Havayat HaSherut Haezrahi-Leumi Shel Tsiirim BeSikun MeZavit HaReiya Shel HaMeshartim Likrat Siyum HaSherut" [A description of the civic national service experience of youth at risk from the perspective of the volunteers toward the end of their service]. *Bitahon Sotsiali* 91 (2013): 125–155.
Levy, Gal, and Orna Sasson-Levy. "Militarized Socialization, Military Service and Class Reproduction: The Experiences of Israeli Soldiers." *Sociological Perspectives* 51, no. 2 (2008): 349–374.
Levy, Yagil. "Is There a Motivation Crisis in Military Recruitment in Israel?" *Israel Affairs* 15, no. 2 (2009): 135–158.
———. "Ma Yekhola Yisrael Lilmod Min HaSherut HaEzrahi BeGermaniya" [What Israel can learn from civic service in Germany]. In *Sherut Hova o' Hova LeSharet* [Mandatory service or the duty to serve], edited by Yagil Levy, 16–37. Ra'anana: Open University, 2015.
———. *MiTsava HaAm LeTsava Haperiferiyot* [From a people's army to an army of the perpheries]. Jerusalem: Carmel, 2007.
Lewin, Eyal. *Ethos Clash in Israeli Society*. Lanham: Lexington Books, 2014.
Locke, John. *Two Treatises on Government: An Essay Concerning the True Original Extent and End of Civil Government*. 1689. https://books.google.com/books/

download/Two_Treatises_of_Government.pdf?id=K5UIAAAAQAAJ&output=pdf. Accessed January 2019.

Loten, Orli, and Yuval Vargen. *Sherut Banot Datiyot BeTsahal: Temunat Matsav UMedinut Maarekhet HaHinukh* [Service of religious girls in the IDF: A situation report and the education system's policy]. Jerusalem: Knesset Research and Information Center, 2007.

Lustick, Ian. *Arabs in the Jewish State: Israel's Control of a National Minority.* Austin: University of Texas Press, 1980.

Machiavelli, Niccolò. *The Discourses.* Harmondsworth: Penguin, 1970.

Madison, James. *The Papers of James Madison*, vol. 11. Edited by William T. Hutchinson et al. Charlottesville: University Press of Virginia, 1977.

Mahoney, James, and Kathleen Thelen. "A Theory of Gradual Institutional Change." In *Explaining Institutional Change: Ambiguity, Agency, and Power*, edited by James Mahoney and Kathleen Thelen, 1–37. Cambridge: Cambridge University Press, 2010.

Malach, Gilad, Lee Cahaner, and Maya Choshen. *Statistical Report on Ultra-Orthodox Society in Israel, 2016.* Jerusalem: Israel Democracy Institute, 2016.

Malach, Gilad, and Lee Cahaner. *Statistical Report on Ultra-Orthodox Society in Israel, 2018.* Jerusalem: Israel Democracy Institute, 2018.

Malach, Gilad, Maya Choshen, and Lee Cahaner. *Statistical Report on Ultra-Orthodox Society in Israel, 2015.* Jerusalem: Israel Democracy Institute, 2016.

Malchi, Asaf. "The People's Army? A Historical Review of Ultra-Orthodox Conscription to the IDF." Israel Democracy Institute. October 16, 2018. https://en.idi.org.il/articles/24626.

Maloy, J. S. "The Very Order of Things: Rousseau's Tutorial Republicanism." *Polity* 37, no. 2 (2005): 235–261.

Maman, Daniel, Eyal Ben-Ari, and Zeev Rosenhek. *Military, State and Society in Israel: Theoretical and Comparative Perspectives.* New Brunswick: Transaction, 2001.

Marshall, Thomas H. *Citizenship and Social Class and Other Essays.* London: Cambridge University Press, 1950.

Mayseless, Orna. "Tsiirim Yisraelim BeMaavar LeBagrut: Hashpaat HaSherut Hatsvai" [Young Israeli men in the transition from adolescence to adulthood: The role of military service]. *Iyunim BeHinukh* 5, no. 1 (2001): 159–190.

McIntyre, Alasdair. *After Virtue: A Study in Moral Theory.* Third ed. Notre Dame: University of Notre Dame Press, 2007.

Medina, Barak. "Hazekhut HaHukatit LeShivyon BePsikat Beit HaMishpat HaElyon: Kvod Haadam, HaIntares Hatsibori, VeTsedek Halukati" [The constitutional right to equality in the rulings of the Israel High Court]. *Mishpat UMimshal* 17 (2015): 1–94.

Mill, John Stuart. *On Liberty, 1859.* Kitchener: Batoche Books, 2001.

Ministerial Committee Regarding the Or Committee (Vaadat Lapid). *Din VeHeshbon VeHamlatsaot Vaadat HaSarim LeInyan Hamlatsot Vaadat Or* [Report and recommendations of the ministerial committee regarding the findings of the Or Committee]. Jerusalem: Government of Israel, 2004.

Ministry of Finance and the National Civil Service Authority. *Din VeHeshbon Shel HaTsevet LeHarhavat Maarakh HaMitnadvim MeHamiutim UMehaHaredim* [Report of the taskforce for the expansion of minority and Haredi volunteers]. Jerusalem: Ministry of Finance, 2011.

Ministry of Industry and Trade. *Tokhnit LeMehkar Haarakha VeLivui LeMaarakh Sherut Ezrahi Leumi BeYisrael* [Research, evaluation, and counseling for the national civic service program]. Jerusalem: Ministry of Industry and Trade, 2010.

Mitchell, Thomas N. "Roman Republicanism: The Underrated Legacy." *Proceedings of the American Philosophical Society* 145, no. 2 (June 2001): 127–137.

Morrison, Donald. "The Common Good." In *The Cambridge Companion to Aristotle's Politics*, edited by Marguerite Deslauriers and Pierre Destrée, 176–198. London: Cambridge University Press, 2013.

National Commission of Inquiry (Vaadat Or). *Din VeHeshbon LeBerur Hitnagshuyot Ben Kohot HaBitahon Leven Ezrahim Yisraelim BeHodesh October, 2000* [Report on the clashes between the security forces and Israeli citizens in October 2000]. Jerusalem: Government of Israel, 2003. uri.mitkadem.co.il/vaadat-or/.

National Committee of the Heads of the Arab Local Authorities in Israel. "The Future Vision of the Palestinian Arabs in Israel." 2006. Adalah. https://www.adalah.org/uploads/oldfiles/newsletter/eng/dec06/tasawor-mostaqbali.pdf.

National Insurance Institute. *Memadei HaOni VeHaPaarim HaHevratiim 2010* [Poverty and social gaps, 2010]. Jerusalem: National Insurance Institute, 2011.

Office of the Director General, Prime Minister's Office. *Idud Taasuka VeKidum: HaSherut Hatsvai VeHaezrahi BaMigzar HaHaredi* [Encouraging employment and advancement: Military and civic service in the ultra-orthodox sector]. Jerusalem: Government of Israel, 2011.

Orgad, Liav. "Hamiut HaAravi BeYisrael VeHovat Sherut Bitahon" [The Arab minority in Israel and the obligation to serve in the Defense Forces]. *HaMishpat* 11 (2007): 381–407.

Ouzieli, Sharon. *Taasukat Haredim BeYisrael: Tmunat Matsav VeHatsaa LeShipur* [Employment of the ultra-orthodox in Israel: Situation report and proposed improvements]. Tel Aviv: Koret Economic Development Fund, Milken Institute, 2007.

Peled, Yoav, and Horit Herman Peled. *The Religionization of Israeli Society*. London: Routledge, 2018.

Pettit, Philip. *Republicanism: A Theory of Freedom and Government*. London: Oxford University Press, 1997.

Plessner, Yohanan. *Din VeHeshbon Shel Yohanan Plesner, Yoshev Rosh HaVaada LeKidum HaShiluv BeSherut VehaShivyon BaNetel* [Report of MK Yochanan Plesner, chairman of the Committee to Advance Integration in Service and Sharing the Burden]. Jerusalem: Knesset, 2011.

Putnam, Robert, and Kristin A. Goss. "Introduction." In *Democracies in Flux: The Evolution of Social Capital in Contemporary Society*, edited by Robert Putnam, 3–20. New York: Oxford University Press, 2002.

Rappaport, Tamar, Anat Panso, and Yoni Garav. " 'Ze Davar Hashuv BeEretz Yisrael Latet Latsibur': Naarot Tsiyoniot Datiyot Tormot LaLeum" ["It is important to contribute to the public": National religious girls contribute to the nation]. *Teoriya UBikoret* 7 (1995): 223–234.

Rawls, John. *A Theory of Justice*. Cambridge: Harvard University Press, 1971.

Rebibo, Joel. "The Road Back from Utopia." *Azure* 11 (2001): 131–167.

Regev, Eitan. *Challenges of Haredi Integration in Academic Studies*. Jerusalem: Taub Center for Policy Studies in Israel, 2016.

Rekhess, Elie. "Initial Israeli Policy Guidelines toward the Arab Minority." In *New Perspectives on Israeli History: The Early Years of the State*, edited by Lawrence J. Silberstein, 157–174. New York: New York University Press, 1991.

Rivlin, Paul. *The Israeli Economy from the Foundation of the State through the 21st Century*. Cambridge: Cambridge University Press, 2010.

Rodnisky, Arik. *Hamiut Haaravi B'yisrael Vehasiach al Medina Yehudit* [The Arab minority in Israel and the Jewish state narrative]. Jerusalem: Israel Democracy Institute, 2015.

Rosler, Andres. "Civic Virtue: Citizenship, Ostracism and War." In *The Cambridge Companion to Aristotle's Politics*, edited by Marguerite Deslauriers and Pierre Destrée, 144–175. London: Cambridge University Press, 2013.

Rosman-Stollman, Elisheva. *For God and Country? Religious Student-Soldiers in the Israel Defense Forces*. Austin: University of Texas Press, 2015.

Roumani, Maurice. *From Immigrant to Citizen: The Contribution of the Army to National Integration in Israel*. The Hague: Foundation of Plural Societies, 1979.

Rousseau, Jean-Jacques. *The Social Contract*. Harmondsworth: Penguin, 1968.

———. *The Social Contract and Other Later Political Writings*. Edited and translated by Victor Gourevitch. London: Cambridge University Press, 1997.

Sandel, Michael. *Liberalism and the Limits of Justice*. Second ed. Cambridge: Cambridge University Press, 2012.

———. "The Procedural Republic and the Unecumbered Self." *Political Theory* 12, no. 1 (1984): 81–96.

Sasson-Levy, Orna. "Constructing Identities at the Margins: Masculinity and Citizenship in the Israeli Army." *The Sociological Quarterly* 43 (2002): 357–383.

Schlesinger, Arthur, Jr. *The Disuniting of America*. New York: Norton, 1992.

Schmid, Hillel. "Din VeHeshbon Shel Havaada Hatsiburit LeBedikat Matsavam Shel Yeladim UBne Noar BeSikun UBeMetsuka" [Report by the Public

Committee to Examine the Conditions of Endangered Children and Youth under Stress]. 2006.

Shafir, Gershon, and Yoav Peled. *Being Israeli: The Dynamics of Multiple Citizenship*. Port Chester: Cambridge University Press, 2002.

Sheehan, Colleen A. "Madison and the French Enlightenment: The Authority of Public Opinion." *The William and Mary Quarterly* 59, no. 4 (2002): 925–956.

Sherer, Moshe. "Rehabilitation of Youth in Distress through Army Service: Full, Partial, or Non-Service in the Israel Defense Forces—Problems and Consequences." *Child and Youth Care Forum* 27, no. 1 (1998): 39–58.

Shitrit, Sammy Shalom. *HaMaavak HaMizrahi BeYisrael, 1948–2003* [The Mizrahi struggle in Israel, 1948–2003]. Tel Aviv: Am Oved, 2004.

Shiv, Ricki. "Tokhnit Hayitsuv 1985: Kalkala Nekhona o' Ideologia" [Israel's stabilization plan 1985: Correct economics or ideology]. *Iyunim BeTekumat Yisrael* 23 (2013): 315–349.

Smooha, Sammy. *Lo Shovrim Et HaKelim: Madad Yachase Aravim-Yehudim BeYisrael* [Still playing by the rules: Index of Arab-Jewish relations in Israel, 2012]. Jerusalem: Israel Democracy Institute and Haifa University, 2013.

———. "Madad Yachasei Aravim-yehudim B'Yisrael." Haifa: IDI and Haifa University, 2013. 105–106.

———. *The Lost Decade of Arab-Jewish Relations in Israel: Survey of the Index 2003–2009, Findings and Conclusions*. Haifa: Haifa University, 2010.

Smooha, Sammy, and Zohar Lechtman. *Civic Service of Arabs in Israel: Research Findings 2007–2011*. Haifa: Jewish-Arab Center, University of Haifa, 2012.

———. "Hatsayat Kav Adom: Hatalat Hovat Sherut Ezrahi Al Tseirim Aravim BeYisrael" [Crossing a red line: Requiring civic service from Arab youth in Israel]. In *Sherut Hova o' Hova LeSharet* [Mandatory service or the duty to serve], edited by Yagil Levy, 121–152. Ra'anana: Open University, 2015.

Spragens, Thomas, Jr. "Communitarianism: Epitaph for a Monument to a Successful Reminder." *The Responsive Community* 14, no. 2/3 (Spring/Summer 2004).

State Comptroller. *Din VeHeshbon Al Habikoret Al Hasherut HaLeumi* [Review report on national service]. Jerusalem: Government of Israel, 1993.

———. *Report of the State Comptroller*. Jerusalem: Government of Israel, 2018.

Swirski, Barbara, and Kefalea Yosef. *The Employment Situation of Ethiopian Israelis*. Tel Aviv: Adva Center, 2005. adva.org/wp-content/uploads/2014/09/EthiopianIsraelis.pdf.

Tal Committee. *Din VeHeshbon HaVaada LeGibush HaHesder Haraui BeNose Giyus Bnei Yeshivot* [Report of the committee to determine the proper arrangement on the draft of yeshiva students]. Jerusalem: Government of Israel, 2000.

Tam, Henry. *Communitarianism: A New Agenda for Politics and Citizenship*. Basingstoke: Macmillian, 1998.

Taylor, Charles. "Atomism." In *Communitarianism and Individualism*, edited by Shlomo Avineri and Avner de Shalit, 45–47. London: Oxford University Press, 1992.

Teixiera, Ruy A. *The Disappearing American Voter*. Washington, DC: Brookings Institution Press, 2011.
Unna, Moshe. *BeDrakhim Nifradot* [On separate paths]. Alon Shvut: Yad Shapira, 1983.
Wahrhaftig, Zerach. *Huka LeYisrael: Dat UMedina* [A constitution for Israel: Religion and the state]. Jerusalem: Mesilot, 1988.
Walzer, Michael. *Spheres of Justice: A Defence of Pluralism and Equality*. Oxford: Robertson, 1983.
Weithman, Paul. "Political Republicanism and Perfectionist Republicanism." *The Review of Politics* 66, no. 2 (2004): 285–312.
Weitz, Yechiam. "To Fantasy and Back: David Ben-Gurion's First Resignation." *Israel Affairs* 8, no. 1 (2002): 59–78.
Wofford, Harris. "The Politics of Service: How a Nation Got Behind AmeriCorps." September 1, 2002. *Brookings Review*. https://www.brookings.edu/articles/the-politics-of-service-how-a-nation-got-behind-americorps/. Accessed June 21, 2016.
Wu, Huiting. "Social Impact of Volunteerism." 2011. Points of Light Institute. www.pointsoflight.org/sites/default/files/site-content/files/social_impact_of_volunteerism_pdf.pdf. Accessed July 18, 2018.
Wurzberger, Rachel. *Sherut Leumi LeBne Miutim* [National service for minorities]. Jerusalem: Knesset Research and Information Center, 2003.
Yanai, Natan. "Musag Haezrachut Betfisato Shel David Ben-Gurion" [The concept of citizenship in the thought of David Ben-Gurion]. *Iyunim Betekumat Yisrael* 4 (1994): 494–504.
Yanay-Ventura, Galit, and Moshe Sharabi. "The Civic Service of Young Arabs in Israel: A Narrative Understanding." Unpublished paper presented at the ninth Conference of the European Research Network on Philanthropy, July 4–5, 2019, Basil, Switzerland.Yosef, Yitzhak. *Otzar HaDinim LaIsha VelaBat*. Jerusalem: Aish Petuchim, 1988.
Young, Iris Marion. *Justice and the Politics of Difference*. Princeton: Princeton University Press, 2011.
Zameret, Zvi. "Ben-Gurion BeShnot HaMedinah HaRishonot VeYachaso LaTsyonut HaDatit UlaHaredim." In *Ayin Tovah: Du-Siach UPulmus BeTarbut Yisrael*, edited by Nacham Ilan, 349–370. Tel Aviv: Hakibbutz Hameuchad, 1999.
———. "Judaism in Israel: Ben-Gurion's Private Beliefs and Public Policy." *Israel Studies* 4, no. 2 (1999): 65.
———. "Vaadat Frumkin: Vaadat Hakira Memshaltit BeNose Hinukh Yaldei HaOlim BeShnot HaMedina Harishonot" [Frumkin Committee: The government committee to investigate the education of immigrant children during the first years of the state]. *Iyunim BeTekumat Yisrael* 1, no. 1 (1991): 404–439.
Zreik, Raef. "Ezrahut, Zekhuyot Vehovot: Al Diyunim BeNose HaSherut HaEzrahi BeYisrael" [Citizenship, rights, and obligations: The discussions of civic service in Israel]. *Iyunei Mishpat* 37, no. 2 (2015): 289–340.

Zeira, Anat, et al. "Duah Mehkar: Sherut Ezrahi Leumi MeZavit Hareiya Shel Tseirim VeTseirot Besikun" [Research report: National service from the perspective of youth at risk]. May 2014.

Index

Administration for National-Civic Service (ANCS)
 establishment, 104, 115, 138–39.
 See Ivri Committee
 recruitment strategy
  Arab sector, 142, 151
  Haredim, 105–06
Agudat Yisrael, 39, 43–44, 52, 59, 61, 70, 92
Amendment 19. See National Defense Law, 2014
Amendment 21. See National Defense Law, 2015
Americorps, 24
Arab civic national service
 campaign against, 139–42
 leadership, 148–50
 number of volunteers, 146
Arabs, Israeli policy, 1948–1966
 conscription, 124–25
 "divide and rule," 125
 loyalty, 121–24
 military rule, 121, 123–24, 126
Arabs, Israel
 public opinion, 144–46, 207
Aristotle, 12–13, 15
Auerbach, Rabbi Shmuel
 protests, 110–11, 114
Authority for Civic National Service
 disbursement authority, 154–55
 establishment, 66
 program supervision, 115–16

Baharan, Rabbi Avraham, 56–57
Baladna, 140–41, 151
Bar Ilan University Student Council, 63
Barak, Ehud
 appointment of Tal Committee, 99
 Arab national service, 131–33
Barber, Benjamin, 23
Basic Law
 Human Dignity and Liberty, 31, 75, 107, 114, 162–63
 Israel as the Nation State of the Jewish people, 152–53
Bedouin
 civic national service, 146–49, 152–54
 military service, 125–26, 154
 proficiency in Hebrew, 149
Begin, Menachem
 coalition with Haredim, 61, 92
 republican ideal, 27
Beilin-Yahav proposal
 national service, 129–30
Ben-Gurion, David
 attitude toward religious parties, 41
 conscription of Arabs, 121–25
 conscription of women, 39–41

223

Index

Ben-Gurion, David *(continued)*
   deferments, yeshiva students, 41, 91–92
   mamlachtiiyut, 25–26
   military service, 26, 38
   National Defense Law, 1949, 38–43
   National Service Law, 43–49, 70
   republican ethos, 25–27, 122
Ben-Shalom Committee, 76–77, 131–32

citizen-pioneer, 27–28
"common good," 12–15, 17, 19, 21
communitarian model
   citizenship, 5–8, 19–23
   civic national service, 23–24
   Israeli policy, 109, 118–19, 143, 156–58, 169–71
   Tal Law, 103, 118, 165
"community volunteering," 151, 157, 170
conscription
   Druze, 125, 152
   Haredim, 91, 96, 107–15, 166
   in the West, 11
   Israeli Arabs, 124–25, 142
   National Defense Law, 1949, 38–43
   reform, 98–105, 107–10, 112–14
   religious girls, 40–42, 55–56
   statistics, 3, 55–56, 78–79, 113
   women, 39–41, 47
   youth with physical or mental limitations, 4, 6, 73, 81, 86, 163
conscription, avoiding, 33–34
Council of Arab Mayors, 150
Council of Torah Sages, 43–46, 180

Dagger, Richard, 18
deferments, yeshiva students, 5, 33, 41, 61, 90–93, 96–117, 164
disabled youth
   IDF policy, 163–64

civic national service, 81, 83–86
   High Court of Justice, 31, 76, 87
Discharged Soldiers Fund, 135, 142, 154–55
Druze
   Basic Law Israel as the Nation-State, 196–97
   conscription, 121, 125, 134, 141, 146, 196
   women, 96, 148, 152

Economy, Israel
   neo-liberal, 29–32
   socialist, 28–29
education
   civic national service, 43–45, 53, 66
   dropouts, 74, 196
   Haredi, 93–97, 125
   in IDF, 2, 26–27, 38, 77 80
   shortage of teachers, 53, 55, 58–60
Eitan, Raphael
   civic national service proposal, 128
   "Raful's boys," 74
Emergency Stabilization Plan, 30
employment after service, 3, 84, 104, 112, 115, 155, 157
Emunah Women's Organization, 58, 187
Etzioni, Amitai, 23
exemption from military service
   Haredim, 109–13, 166
   others, 33, 40–42, 46
   religious women, 51, 52, 55–57, 61–64, 68–69

Frank, Rabbi Pesach, 40, 185
Friedman, Menachem, 93–94, 100

Gal, Reuven, 138
Gerbi, Sar Shalom, 85, 148, 154, 190, 204

Index

Gevanim, 81–82
Ginat, Yosef, 127
Glendon, Mary Ann, 21
Grossman, Chaike, 62–63
Gush Emunim, 34

Halakha
  women in armed forces, 39–40, 52
  women in national service, 45–48, 57–59, 70
Hapoel Hamizrachi party, 179
  Army service, 41–42
  National service law, 42–52, 57
  See also religious front
Haredi community
  conscription, 91, 96, 107–15, 166
  education, 93–97, 125
  employment in Israel, 97
  employment in the United States, 96, 101
  family size, 97
  lifestyle, 93–97
  role of women, 94–95
Haredim, modern, 168, 210
Hassidim, Gerer, 116
Hazani, Michael, 59–60, 184–85
Hazon Ish, (Rabbi Avraham Yeshayau Karelitz), 40, 46–48, 91, 182, 185
Herzliya Conference, 5, 170
Herzog, Rabbi Isaac, 47, 50
High Court of Justice, 4, 6–8
  Amendment 19. See National Defense Law, 2014
  Amendment 21. See National Defense Law, 2015
  Arab national service, 132, 203
  disabled youth, 31, 76, 87
  The Tal Law. See Tal Law
  yeshiva students. See deferments, yeshiva students

Higher Arab Monitoring Committee
  Arab civic national service, 139, 206
Histadrut (Israel Federation of Labor), 28–30, 179
Hoffman, Avraham, 56
Holocaust, 38, 41, 91, 102

immigrants, new
  Ethiopian, 81, 84–85
  Israel Defense Force (IDF), 2–3, 27–28, 32–34, 38–41, 74, 77
Islamic Movement, 141, 147, 154–55
Israel Defense Force (IDF)
  conscription. See conscription
  Nahal Hadati, 42, 52, 58, 64, 183
  Nahal Haredi, 100, 104, 196
  programs for
    disabled youth, 163–64
    disadvantaged youth, 74, 163
    Haredim, 104–05, 115
    religious women, 67
Ivri committee
  recommendations, 78–80, 103–04, 135, 138

Jabotinsky, Ze'ev, 25, 27
Janowitz, Morris, 15
Jews in the Diaspora, 26, 41, 44, 46, 50, 83, 96, 122

Kant, Immanuel, 17
Kibbutz Hadati, 57–58, 187
Knesset, private member proposals
  civic national service, Arabs, 127–30
  civic national service, Haredim, 128–30
Kol Moshe, 58, 61
Koor Industries, 30

Labor, government, 62, 92, 126, 164
Lapid committee, 137–38
Lapid, Yair, 108, 167
  Yesh Atid, 108, 112–13, 167
Lavon, Pinchas, 45, 53, 124–25
Levy, Yagil, 28, 32–33
liberalism
  ethos in Israel, 4, 29–34, 73–79, 86–87, 98, 130–32, 162–64
  theory, 16–19, 21
Likud, 61–62, 74, 92, 117, 162
Locke, John, 16

Machiavelli, Niccolo, 13
Madison, James, 14
mamlachtiyut, 7, 25–26, 60
Mapai, 25–28, 42–45, 48–52, 59, 70, 162
Mapam party, 49, 52
Marshall, Thomas H., 15, 174
Meir (Meyerson) Golda, 45, 50–51, 60–63
Meshalvim, 81
Mill, John Stuart, 16–17
Ministry of Education, Religious Division, 66
Mintz, Binyamin, 45–46, 53, 60, 161
Mizrachi Party, 39–40, 43, 46–48, 52, 56, 179
Mizrachim, 74

Naamat Women's Organization, 61, 63
Nahal Hadati
  See Israel Defense Forces
National Civic Service Law, 1953, 45–53, 186
National Civic Service Law, 2014, 112, 151
National Civic Service Law, 2017, 85, 87, 151, 170
National Defense Law, 1949, 3, 38–43

National Defense Law, 2014
  Amendment 19, 109–15, 118–19
National Defense Law, 2015
  Amendment 21, 113–15, 118
National Religious Party(NRP), 34, 56–66, 161–62
  young guard, 58
National Security Council recommendations
  Arab national service, 132–33
Netanyahu, Benjamin, 108, 110, 112–13, 117, 131, 143, 167

Obama, Barack, 24
October 2000 events, 133, 136–37, 204–05
Odeh, Ayman, 139, 209
Orr Commission, 133, 136–37, 204–05

Palestinians
  identification with, 132–35, 141, 145, 151, 156–58
  Intifada, 133
Peres, Shimon, 30
pioneer citizen, 27–28
pioneer-soldier, 38–39, 42, 52, 177
Plesner Committee, 144
Poalei Agudat Yisrael, 39, 44–45, 180
public opinion surveys
  Haredim, self definition, 210
  Israel Arabs. *See* Israel Arabs public opinion
  self interest or interest of country, 31

Rabbinical Courts Law (Marriage and Divorce), 43, 47–49, 53
Rabin, Yitzchak, 61
  national service, Arabs, 129

Rawls, John, 17–19
Religious Front, 39, 41–43, 179
religious girls
  civic national service, 56–70
  exemption from service. *See* National Defense Law, 1949
  military service, 40–42, 55–56
  National Service Law, 1953, 42–53
  service statistics, 66–69
  state religious schools, 3, 57, 62, 66, 70
  ulpanot, 56–57, 66–70
republican citizenship
  criticism, 5, 18–19
  theory, 12–16
republican ethos in Israel, 3–4, 25–29, 45–47, 75, 79–87, 151, 160–62
  decline of republican ethos, 4, 31–34, 98, 131, 162–64
  Haredim, 95, 105
  religious Zionists, 45–47, 56–58, 65–70, 161–62
Resler v. Knesset, HCJ 6298/07, 107
reserves (IDF), 2, 33, 63, 173, 178
Rivlin, Reuven, 5–6, 120, 170–71
Rousseau, Jean Jacque, 14
Rubinstein v. the Minister of Defense 3267/97, 98–99

Salah, Ra'ad, 141
Sandel, Michael, 19, 21
Sarsur, Ibrahim, 141–42
secularization, 2
  Haredim, 90, 94, 96, 102
  religious girls, 51, 56, 66–68
Sephardic rabbis
  national service, 46, 57, 59
Shachar programs (IDF), 104–05
Shafir committee report, 77, 80
Sharett, Moshe, 50–51, 70, 124, 161
Sharon, Ariel, 103, 137
Sharon, Moshe, 126–27
"Sherut Shaveh," 63–64
Shlomit organization, 75–78, 82, 87, 130, 163
Sidon, Efraim, 63
Smooha, Sammy, 144–46
social capital, bridging, 12, 23, 89, 106, 169
socialism, 25, 28–30, 44, 162
"society of scholars," 93–94, 100
Solodar, Edna, 127–28

Tal Committee, 99–102, 132
  civic national service, 102
  year of decision, 101–03
The Tal Law, 99, 109, 115, 118–19
  cancellation, High Court of Justice, 107–08, 165–66
  implementation, 99, 103–06, 165–66
  legislation, 99, 102–03
Taylor, Charles, 20
"Third Way," 22
Trump, Donald, 24
"Two Principles of Justice," 18

Umm al Hiran, 153–54, 209–10
Unna, Moshe, 41–42, 181

"veil of ignorance," 18
Voluntary National Service Law (Boys), 2001, 78
volunteering
  benefits, 147, 155, 209
  civic importance, 11–12

Wanted: An Arab who has Lost his Memory, 140–41

Warhaftig, Zerach, 43, 52

Yesh Atid, 108, 112–13, 167
yeshiva students, 41, 61, 90–99
   deferments. *See* deferments, yeshiva students
   numbers, 90, 93–94, 106
   See also Tal Committee
Yom Kippur War, 29, 60
Yosef, Rabbi Ovadia, 57, 59

youth, excused from IDF service
   at risk, 79–87
   disadvantaged, 74, 79, 81, 85–87
   physically unfit, 81–86, 163–64
   psychological difficulties, 79, 161, 189
   special needs, 79–83, 85–87, 164

Zahalka, Jamal MK, 139–40
Zivildienst in Germany, 133, 189

www.ingramcontent.com/pod-product-compliance
Ingram Content Group UK Ltd.
Pitfield, Milton Keynes, MK11 3LW, UK
UKHW041918140426
5217IPUK00013B/206